Sacred Therapies

Other Titles by David Shannahoff-Khalsa

Kundalini Yoga Meditation for Complex Psychiatric Disorders:
Techniques Specific for Treating the Psychoses, Personality,
and Pervasive Developmental Disorders

Kundalini Yoga Meditation: Techniques Specific for Psychiatric Disorders,
Couples Therapy, and Personal Growth

Psychophysiological States: The Ultradian Dynamics of Mind-Body Interactions

Sacred Therapies
The Kundalini Yoga Meditation Handbook
for Mental Health

David Shannahoff-Khalsa

W. W. Norton & Company
New York • London

The techniques and protocols taught in this book are not meant to be a substitute for medical care and advice. You are advised to consult with your health care professional with regard to matters relating to your health, including matters that may require diagnosis or medical attention. In particular, if you have been diagnosed with anxiety disorders, panic disorder, phobias, obsessive-compulsive disorder, depression, bipolar disorders, an addictive disorder, impulse control disorder, eating disorder, insomnia or any other sleep disorder, chronic fatigue syndrome, attention deficit hyperactivity disorder, attention deficit disorder, dyslexia or any other learning disorder, post traumatic stress disorder, a personality disorder, schizophrenia, autism or Asperger's Disorder, or any related disorder, or if you are taking or have been advised to take any medication, you should consult regularly with your physician regarding any changes in medication use.

Photos by Suzanne Pitts and Beatrice Ring

For reader comments or to order a video mentioned in the book, please visit the author's web site at *www.theinternetyogi.com* (to order videos), or email him at dsk@ucsd.edu (for reader comments).

For information about permission to reproduce selections from this book, write to Permissions, W. W. Norton & Company, Inc., 500 Fifth Avenue, New York, NY 10110

Manufacturing by LSC Harrisonburg
Production Manager: Leeann Graham

Library of Congress Cataloging-in-Publication Data

Shannahoff-Khalsa, David.
  Sacred Therapies: The Kundalini yoga meditation handbook for mental health / David Shannahoff-Khalsa.
    p. cm.
  Includes bibliographical references and index.
  ISBN: 978-0-393-70702-1
  1. Psychotherapy. 2. Kundalini—Therapeutic use. I. Title.

ISBN: 978-0-393-70702-1

W. W. Norton & Company, Inc., 500 Fifth Avenue, New York, N.Y. 10110
www.wwnorton.com

W. W. Norton & Company Ltd., 15 Carlisle Street, London W1D 3BS

3 4 5 6 7 8 9 0

This book is dedicated to
Raj Yog Guru Ram Das, my Guru in the Divine;

Raj Yog Yogi Bhajan, Master of Kundalini Yoga, my Spiritual Teacher in the Divine;

David and Sarah Shannahoff, my parents in the Divine, for their lifelong loving support;

Pierre Henri Lallouette (in the Divine) and Monique Lallouette, for making my life so much more pleasant with their perpetual care and love;

And to My Great Golden Sons,

Bubba, Patrick, and JJ, for their endless love, devotion, and playful affection.

Contents

Acknowledgments		ix
Preface		xiii
CHAPTER 1	A Brief Introduction to Kundalini Yoga Meditation	1
CHAPTER 2	Treating Anxiety and Generalized Anxiety Disorder	5
CHAPTER 3	Treating Obsessive–Compulsive Disorder and Obsessive Compulsive Spectrum Disorders (Trichotillomania and Body Dysmorphic Disorder)	19
CHAPTER 4	Treating Phobias	36
CHAPTER 5	Treating Panic Attacks and Panic Disorders	45
CHAPTER 6	Treating Acute Stress Disorder	57
CHAPTER 7	Treating Posttraumatic Stress Disorder	65
CHAPTER 8	Treating the Abused and Battered Psyche	80
CHAPTER 9	Treating the Major Depressive Disorders	95
CHAPTER 10	Treating Grief	105
CHAPTER 11	Treating the Bipolar Disorders	109
CHAPTER 12	Treating the Addictive, Impulse Control, and Eating Disorders	126
CHAPTER 13	Treating Insomnia and Other Sleep Disorders	150

CONTENTS

CHAPTER 14   **Treating Chronic Fatigue Syndrome**   162

CHAPTER 15   **Treating Attention-Deficit/Hyperactivity Disorder and Comorbid Disorders (Conduct Disorder and Oppositional Defiant Disorder)**   171

CHAPTER 16   **Treating Dyslexia and the Other Learning Disorders**   188

CHAPTER 17   **Treating Schizophrenia and Other Psychotic Disorders**   196

CHAPTER 18   **Treating the Personality Disorders (Paranoid, Schizoid, Schizotypal, Antisocial, Borderline, Histrionic Narcissistic, Avoidant, Dependent, and Obsessive–Compulsive Personality Disorders)**   234

CHAPTER 19   **Treating Autism and Asperger's Disorder**   297

References   321

Index   325

Acknowledgments

First and foremost, I want to thank Guru Ram Das for his guidance and blessings, for many of the insights that have helped to construct some of the multipart protocols in this book, and for several of the individual techniques for treating psychiatric disorders. I am deeply indebted to Yogi Bhajan, my spiritual teacher, for his spiritual guidance, for most of the techniques in this book, and for the other teachings that have made my scientific work and this book possible. I want to thank Floyd E. Bloom, MD, for his efforts as my first scientific collaborator on yogic research, when we were both at The Salk Institute, and for helping to launch this work and make it a respectable and important scientific endeavor that has now led to new and important insights for treating and preventing psychiatric disorders. His active participation inspired many others to collaborate in the early phases of my career. I am truly grateful for the many years of his support and guidance that have followed. He gave me the idea of establishing a nonprofit foundation to help fund this work, and he committed to serve as the first vice president on the board of directors and first scientific advisor in the early years of The Khalsa Foundation for Medical Science. I am also grateful to Drs. David Schubert, Tony Hunter, and Walter Eckhart, who gave me many years of institutional support at The Salk to help establish my scientific career. I am indebted to Sheldon S. Hendler, MD, PhD, for his role as my first scientific mentor and for facilitating my initial engagement at The Salk, his role as a vice president of The Khalsa Foundation for Medical Science, and his sage advice over the last 42 years.

Many others have been instrumental in the scientific and clinical work that have now made this book possible. They include Michael G. Ziegler, MD, for nearly 20 years of collaboration on pioneering physiological studies in his laboratory and at the General Clinical

Research Center at the University of California, San Diego (UCSD). F. Eugene Yates, MD, University of California, Los Angeles (UCLA) made critical contributions to studies on multivariate physiology that have led to new insights for defining psychophysiological states. The late J. Christian Gillin, MD, Department of Psychiatry, UCSD, made substantial collaborative efforts toward novel insights for sleep medicine and psychophysiological states. Liana Beckett, MA, MFCC, Department of Psychiatry, UCSD, invited me to collaborate using Kundalini yoga meditation techniques for my first clinical trial in treating obsessive compulsive disorder (OCD). Saul Levine, MD, Departments of Psychiatry, UCSD and Children's Hospital, San Diego, was instrumental in helping to obtain and conduct a study funded by the National Institutes of Health for our first randomized and controlled clinical trial for treating OCD.

I want to acknowledge Christopher C. Gallen, MD, PhD, for his collaboration on the second OCD trial, for study design and professional guidance throughout, for his invitation to employ magnetoencephalography (MEG) for studying patients with OCD and healthy controls, and the study of the OCD breath technique when he directed the MEG lab at The Scripps Research Institute. I am grateful to Leslie Ellen Ray, MA, MFCC, for running the control group in the second OCD clinical trial, and to Barry J. Schwartz, PhD, when at Scripps, and John Sidorowich, PhD, UCSD, for collaboration on the second OCD trial. In addition, I am grateful to Henry D. I. Abarbanel, PhD, formerly director of the Institute for Nonlinear Science (INLS), UCSD, for providing institutional support and a most wonderful, open, rigorous, creative, and productive atmosphere in which to conduct much of this scientific work. I want to thank my other colleagues in the BioCircuits Institute (formally INLS), UCSD, Drs. Jon A. Wright, Roy Schult, Evgeny Novikov, Barry J. Schwartz, and Matthew B. Kennel for collaboration on pioneering MEG studies. I thank Drs. Luigi Fortuna, Maide Bucolo, Manuela La Rosa, Mattia Frasca, Francesca Sapuppo, and Federica Di Grazia at the University of Catania in Sicily, Dipartimento di Ingegneria Elettrica Elettronica e dei Sistemi, Catania, Sicily, for their enduring and creatively collaborative efforts on MEG signal processing for the study of yogic meditation techniques, normals, and patients with OCD. I am grateful to Stuart W. Jamieson, MB, Head of the Division of Cardiothoracic Surgery, UCSD, and B. Bo Sramek, PhD, Czech Technical University Prague, Department of Mechanical Engineering, for collaboration on yogic techniques for altering the cardiovascular system and for novel work on defining hemodynamic states. I thank Brian Fallon, MD, Columbia University, Department of Psychiatry, and New York State Psychiatric Institute, for inviting me to present at a 2003 symposium on OCD at the Annual American Psychiatric Association (APA) Conference. This event led to my teaching APA full-day courses on Kundalini yoga meditation techniques specific for treating some of the psychiatric disorders that are now included in this book. There are many other scientific collaborators and support staff who have helped to make this work possible over the last 34 years, and I am grateful to all of them for their key roles.

I especially want to acknowledge, with deepest gratitude, Dr. Mona Baumgartel and Mr. John DeBeer for providing financial support to The Khalsa Foundation for Medical Science every year since its inception in 1984. Their generosity has made the continuation of much of this work possible. I also acknowledge Dr. David Schubert and Susan Frazar for their generous contributions that have helped to support my presentations for the APA meetings. In addition, I want to thank the Fetzer Institute, the Waletzky Charitable Lead Trust, Earl Bakken, and the National Institutes of Health for funding some of the scientific studies that have helped lead to the successes in my career.

And last but not least, I am very grateful and indebted to my editors at W. W. Norton & Company. I want to especially thank Deborah Malmud, vice president and director of Norton Professional Books, for her continued interests and creative insights that have led to this new handbook format. I am also very thankful to Vani Kannan, Associate Managing Editor, to Libby Burton, Assistant Editor, and to Ben Yarling, Editorial Assistant, for helping to make this book a reality.

Preface

The intent of this book is to simplify the presentation and combine the protocols from my first two books published by Norton on the use of Kundalini yoga meditation techniques that are specific for the treatment of psychiatric disorders. This handbook now combines all of the previously published disorder-specific multipart protocols along with some updates for a few disorders so that they are also now more accessible to the public. This convenient handbook includes protocols that cover all of the major and common psychiatric disorders as they are recognized today. In addition, the critical definitions, diagnostic criteria, diagnostic features, and associated features and disorders are included to give a clearer and more in-depth perspective on each disorder for the public and the nonmedical professional. We reproduce here the formal descriptions for these criteria with the express permission of the American Psychiatric Association (APA). These definitions, criteria, features, and lists of the commonly associated disorders are the result of the intense work over many decades by the esteemed members of the psychiatric community. This critical information has been previously published in the key APA text known as the *Diagnostic and Statistical Manual of Mental Disorders, Fourth Edition, Text-Revised* (DSM-IV-TR; (APA, 2000). Although a fifth edition (DSM-V) is expected to be published in May 2013, most of the disorders covered in this handbook are likely to remain intact in the DSM-V, with some minor changes for diagnostic criteria and perhaps some changes in coding and group associations. At this time the DSM-V is still a work in progress. The psychiatric experts tasked with this update are considering additional ways to help clinicians identify the symptoms and severity of mental illnesses, such as using dimensional assessments, that can help to better evaluate patients on the full range of symptoms they may be experiencing. This is expected to be the biggest and most important change for the DSM-V. These dimensional assessments will help clinicians rate both the presence and severity of the symptoms, such as "very severe," "severe," "moderate, or "mild," and this new information can also aid in tracking the patients' progress in treatment. The dimensional ratings will also provide a more comprehensive view of the patient than giving only a primary diagnosis. These new changes to the DSM-V will not conflict or interfere with the yogic approaches to treatment presented in this handbook. In fact, my second Norton book, *Kundalini Yoga Meditation for Complex Psychiatric Disorders: Techniques Specific for Treating the Psychoses, Personality, and Pervasive Developmental Disorders*, includes considerable information for treating the complexities and multimorbidities that are often common with psychiatric patients and those with mental health problems.

The DSM-IV-TR provides the following important cautionary statement that certainly deserves coverage here for the nonprofessional reader (American Psychiatric Association, 2000):

> The specified diagnostic criteria for each mental disorder are offered as guidelines for making diagnoses, because it has been demonstrated that the use of such criteria enhances agreement among clinicians and investigators. The proper use of these criteria requires specialized clinical training that provides both a body of knowledge and clinical skills. These diagnostic criteria and the DSM-IV classification of mental disorders reflect a consensus of current formulations of evolving knowledge in our field. They do not encompass, however, all the conditions for which people may be treated or that may be appropriate topics for research efforts.

> The purpose of DSM-IV is to provide clear descriptions of diagnostic categories in order to enable clinicians and investigators to diagnose, communicate about, study, and treat people with various mental disorders. It is to be understood that inclusion here, for clinical and research purposes, of a diagnostic category such as Pathological Gambling or Pedophilia does not imply that the condition meets legal or other nonmedical criteria for what constitutes mental disease, mental disorder, or mental disability. The clinical and scientific considerations involved in categorization of these conditions as mental disorders may not be wholly relevant to legal judgments, for example, that take into account such issues as individual responsibility, disability determination, and competency.

Although the yogic knowledge in this book goes back many thousands of years, the more recent origins of the teachings in this book come from Guru Ram Das and Yogi Bhajan. I am deeply indebted to Guru Ram Das for his sharing, guidance, and tutlege regarding the treatment of many mental health disorders, and to Yogi Bhajan for his help with some of these disorders and for most of the individual techniques that are included in this book.

Sacred Therapies

ONE

A Brief Introduction to Kundalini Yoga Meditation

The meditation techniques and other yogic practices in this book are commonly referred to as "Kundalini yoga as taught by Yogi Bhajan." This descriptor helps to differentiate these techniques and this system of teachings from other schools and systems of yoga and meditation, whether they are currently taught in India or in the West, including any other system that might be called *Kundalini yoga*. Yogi Bhajan openly taught these techniques to the public during his life in the West from 1969 to 2004. Prior to his efforts, these techniques had been kept secret for approximately the last three millenia, and during this time they were taught only by a master to selected diciples. These masters were few in number, but they remained as the guardians of these once secret and sacred ancient techniques. The reason for the secrecy during the last 3,000 years resulted initially from a nomadic invasion in India that forced the teachings underground. The invaders knew that these powerful techniques would make it much more difficult to control and exploit the masses if they were empowered by their practice. Consequently, the invaders forbade the practice of these techniques (Shannahoff-Khalsa, 2012). During this long era of secrecy, others were left mostly with only remnants of the original integrated parent science of yoga and meditation, what we refer to here as "Kundalini yoga as taught by Yogi Bhajan." Before this suppression, this highly integrated, evolved, and comprehensive science was practiced openly by both the dedicated yogis and the common householder. Thanks to Yogi Bhajan's efforts, it is now again possible to bring these teachings to humanity at large. He recognized the extraordinary societal need along with the newly emergent spiritual hunger to become awakened and to better understand the nature of the human psyche and consciousness itself. Why these techniques did not reemerge in society once India again became a sovereign country remains a matter of speculation.

The exact historical origins of these ancient yogic meditation techniques also remain unclear. However, the evolution of this ancient science far predates the advent of the formal religions that we know about today. This suggests that the initial experimental studies that led to this vast body of teachings may go back to at least 7000 B.C.E., and perhaps much before that. The people who participated in this ancient process of discovery, called the *rishis* (people of power), are thought to have lived in the region of the Indus river valley (Shannahoff-Khalsa, 2012). This ancient society is now known as the Indus-Sarasvati civilization, which is believed to be the first civilization in the Indian subcontinent.

During the 35 years that Yogi Bhajan taught in the West, he transmitted approximately 5,000 different meditation techniques and hundreds of different sequence-specific yoga exercise sets that also have different and unique benefits and effects. Frequently, he would teach an exercise set followed by a meditation technique. This coupling of exercise and meditation remains the practice today for most standard Kundalini yoga classes taught in this system. However, each yoga exercise set or meditation technique can also be practiced independently. During each class Yogi Bhajan usually taught a different meditation technique in an effort to help transmit this vast knowledge. His tireless teachings on the nature of the human psyche and healthy living remain critical to our lives and to our understanding of the modern world. He called this knowledge *humanology*. These additional topics, however, go far beyond the scope of this book. Here, the focus is to introduce a subset of the techniques in this system for improving mental health, treating psychiatric disorders, and as strategies for the prevention of mental health problems. In addition, although most of these techniques and protocols are designated for the treatment of specific disorders and conditions, they can also help the individual attain a profoundly elevated state of mental excellence that provides a new and firm footing in the mental realm. Many of these techniques were used in the ancient times in the making of saints, sages, seers, healers, and other masters of the mental realms who had what many may consider to be supernatural powers and abilities. Many have rightly argued that consciousness is the last, most complex, and most important scientific frontier. All true growth in the mental and spiritual realms begins from a place of great clarity and mental stability. After the achievement of that clarity and stability, the higher realms of consciousness become a new arena for play, exploration, and the development and refinement of skills. However, a clear and stable foundation for the psyche is always a must. These teachings can help lay that foundation toward this development and awakening of the higher and otherwise dormant human potential. Yogi Bhajan also called Kundalini yoga the "yoga of awareness." We are indebted to the countless generations of yogic experimentalists that have already provided us with an enormous technology of the mind that is a common heritage for all of humanity.

While some of what Yogi Bhajan learned and taught came through living teachers during his first 39 years while living in India, prior to his emigration to the West, he was also granted constant access to the cosmic storehouse under the safeguard of his "Guru in the Divine," Guru Ram Das. Yogi Bhajan often refered to these teachings as the gifts from "The House of Guru Ram Das." When there has been a relevant need, I have also had the privilege to gain access to small amounts of this knowledge from the same source. The three techniques specific for treating bipolar disorders (the phase- independent and the two phase-dependent techniques), the multipart protocol specific for chronic fatigue syndrome, the approach and symbols for treating the 10 personality disorders, the exercise set for the psychoses, and the approach for treating autism and Asperger's disorder are the gifts to me from Guru Ram Das. The eight-part protocol specific for posttraumatic stress disorder and the one specific for psycho-oncology patients and caregivers (Shannahoff-Khalsa, 2005) were transmitted to me from Yogi Bhajan in late October 2004. I created the remaining multipart protocols by the grace of Guru Ram Das and Yogi Bhajan.

In the system of Kundalini yoga as taught by Yogi Bhajan there is a mantra that is always chanted prior to the practice of any of these techniques; we call this process *tuning in*. This procedure helps to induce a protected meditative state of mind and to keep the practitioner both balanced and safe on an auric level during practice. This specific mantra is a unique and exclusive feature for this yogic system. One of the guiding principles and laws of practice for this system is to never alter any of the techniques or to reorganize any of the sequences of the multipart exercise sets or protocols. Doing so can only lessen and weaken their efficacy and possibly lead to an imbalance. There are many wives tales that circulate about Kundalini yoga, propogated by those without the direct knowledge and experience with this protected and safe system. Often, these tales are spread by individuals who do not want to see this system emerge again for whatever personal reasons or misunderstandings that they may have. These techniques, as taught, are perfectly safe and often lead, very quickly, to symptomatic relief, and with time to long-term therapeutic cures and personal transformation.

The advanced nature of this system and its complexity are best described by noting the variety, uniqueness, and often the disorder-specific nature of many of these techniques. The psychiatric disorders, as we know them today, are not unique to modern times. They were all also recognized by the rishis and yogis in ancient times. While approximately 5,000 different meditation techniques were taught by Yogi Bhajan, it is likely that many more remain in the "storehouse" under the safeguard of Guru Ram Das, who was recognized by his contemporary yogis, gurus, swamis, siddhas, and spiritual masters as the Raj (royal) Yogi of his day for his extraordinary compassion, undying selflessness, and tireless service to humanity. (He was also known as the Lord of Miracles.) This honored recognition was the reason that he became the chosen guardian of this sacred trust, which is truly a heritage that belongs to all humanity. During Yogi Bhajan's lifetime, he was recognized as the "first servant" of The House of Guru Ram Das with the unique privilege to share openly this sacred trust. Yogi Bhajan became the living embodiment of Guru Ram Das and equally manifested all of the same attributes of human and spiritual achievement that came by the grace of his lord and personal guru, Guru Ram Das.

Sacred Therapies includes a selected and limited collection of 100 different meditation techniques from this system. I started practicing Kundalini yoga as taught by Yogi Bhajan in 1974. In 1976 I started my scientific efforts to help bring credibility and awareness to this sacred, powerful, and once-secret knowledge. This book is also an attempt to bring these formulas forward in a very practical way in this modern age, where they can be practiced most efficiently and effectively for treatment. This brief introduction to Kundalini yoga meditation is, at best, a minimal and inadequate introduction to this vast science and technology of the human mind. The only way to truly appreciate this science is through the personal practice of these techniques and by a thorough exploration of the many very different techniques discovered by the ancient rishis over many thousands of years.

TWO

Treating Anxiety and Generalized Anxiety Disorder

Although this chapter includes the descriptions and specific protocols for treating only Anxiety Disorder Not Otherwise Specified and the common Generalized Anxiety Disorder (GAD), the American Psychiatric Association's (2000) *Diagnostic and Statistical Manual of Mental Disorders*, Fourth Edition—Text Revised (DSM IV-TR) also includes other disorders in the anxiety category. These include Panic Disorder With or Without Agoraphobia, Agoraphobia Without History of Panic Disorder, Specific Phobia, Social Phobia, Obsessive Compulsive Disorder (OCD), Posttraumatic Stress Disorder (PTSD), Acute Stress Disorder (ASD), Anxiety Disorder Due to a General Medical Condition, and Substance-Induced Anxiety Disorder (APA, 2000). There is also the condition called Separation Anxiety Disorder that results from the separation of a parental figure and that almost always develops in childhood; the American Psychiatric Association includes this disorder in the section for "Disorders Usually First Diagnosed in Infancy, Childhood, or Adolescence." Finally, there is the condition called *Sexual Aversion Disorder*, which addresses aversion to genital sexual contact with a sexual partner and is included in the section on "Sexual and Gender Identity Disorders." However, only the disorders of panic attacks, phobias, OCD, PTSD, and ASD are covered in *Sacred Therapies*, in their respective chapters, each with a disorder-specific protocol for treatment. The following descriptions of the diagnostic criteria, additional diagnostic features, and associated features and disorders are reproduced here from the DSM-IV-TR (with permission from the American Psychiatric Association).

DSM DISORDERS

Diagnostic Criteria for 300.00 Anxiety Disorder Not Otherwise Specified (American Psychiatric Association, 2000)

This category includes disorders with prominent anxiety or phobic avoidance that do not meet criteria for any specific Anxiety Disorder, Adjustment Disorder With Anxiety, or Adjustment Disorder With Mixed Anxiety and Depressed Mood. Examples include

1. Mixed anxiety-depressive disorder: clinically significant symptoms of anxiety and depression, but the criteria are not met for either a specific Mood Disorder or a specific Anxiety Disorder
2. Clinically significant social phobic symptoms that are related to the social impact of having a general medical condition or mental disorder (e.g., Parkinson's disease, dermatological conditions, Stuttering, Anorexia Nervosa, Body Dysmorphic Disorder)
3. Situations in which the disturbance is severe enough to warrant a diagnosis of an Anxiety Disorder but the individual fails to report enough symptoms for the full criteria for any specific Anxiety Disorder to have been met; for example, an individual who reports all of the features of Panic Disorder Without Agoraphobia except that the Panic Attacks are all limited-symptom attacks
4. Situations in which the clinician has concluded that an Anxiety Disorder is present but is unable to determine whether it is primary, due to a general medical condition, or substance induced

Reprinted with permission from the *Diagnostic and Statistical Manual of Mental Disorders, Fourth Edition, Text Revision.* Copyright 2000 American Psychiatric Association.

The disorders of Anorexia Nervosa and Body Dysmorphic Disorder, listed in item 2 above, are included in other chapters. Anorexia Nervosa is described along with a treatment protocol in Chapter 12 (Treating the Addictive, Impulse Control, and Eating Disorders), and Body Dysmorphic Disorder is included in Chapter 3 (Treating Obsessive Compulsive Disorder and Obsessive Compulsive Spectrum Disorders).

Diagnostic Criteria for 300.02 Generalized Anxiety Disorder

A. Excessive anxiety and worry (apprehensive expectation), occurring more days than not for at least 6 months, about a number of events or activities (such as work or school performance).

B. The person finds it difficult to control the worry.

C. The anxiety and worry are associated with three (or more) of the following six symptoms (with at least some symptoms present for more days than not for the past 6 months). **Note:** Only one item is required in children.

1. restlessness or feeling keyed up or on edge
2. being easily fatigued
3. difficulty concentrating or mind going blank
4. irritability
5. muscle tension
6. sleep disturbance (difficulty falling or staying asleep, or restless unsatisfying sleep)

D. The focus of the anxiety and worry is not confined to features of an Axis I disorder, e.g., the anxiety or worry is not about having a Panic Attack (as in Panic Disorder), being embarrassed in public (as in Social Phobia), being contaminated (as in Obsessive-Compulsive Disorder), being away from home or close relatives (as in Separation Anxiety Disorder), gaining weight (as in Anorexia Nervosa), having multiple physical complaints (as in Somatization Disorder), or having a serious illness (as in Hypochondriasis), and the anxiety and worry do not occur exclusively during Posttraumatic Stress Disorder.

E. The anxiety, worry, or physical symptoms cause clinically significant distress or impairment in social, occupational, or other important areas of functioning.

F. The disturbance is not due to the direct physiological effects of a substance (e.g., a drug of abuse, a medication) or a general medical condition (e.g., hyperthyroidism) and does not occur exclusively during a Mood Disorder, a Psychotic Disorder, or a Pervasive Developmental Disorder.

Additional Diagnostic Features for 300.02 Generalized Anxiety Disorder (APA, 2000)

The intensity, duration, or frequency of the anxiety and worry is far out of proportion to the actual likelihood or impact of the feared event. The person finds it difficult to keep worrisome thoughts from interfering with attention to tasks at hand and has difficulty stopping the worry. Adults with Generalized Anxiety Disorder often worry about everyday, routine life circumstances such as possible job responsibilities, finances, the health of family members, misfortune to their children, or minor matters (such as household chores, car repairs, or being late for appointments). Children with Generalized Anxiety Disorder tend to worry excessively about their competence or the quality of their performance. During the course of the disorder, the focus of worry may shift from one concern to another.

Associated Features and Disorders for 300.02 Generalized Anxiety Disorder (APA, 2000)

Associated with muscle tension, there may be trembling, twitching, feeling shaky, and muscle aches or soreness. Many individuals with Generalized Anxiety Disorder also experience somatic symptoms (e.g., sweating, nausea, or diarrhea) and an exaggerated startle response. Symptoms of autonomic hyperarousal (e.g., accelerated heart rate, shortness of breath, dizziness) are less prominent in Generalized Anxiety Disorder than in other Anxiety Disorders, such as Panic Disorder and Posttraumatic Stress Disorder. Depressive symptoms are also common.

Generalized Anxiety Disorder very frequently co-occurs with Mood Disorders (e.g., Major Depressive Disorder or Dysthymic Disorder), with other Anxiety Disorders (e.g., Panic Disorder, Social Phobia, Specific Phobia), and with Substance-Related Disorders (e.g., Alcohol or Sedative, Hypnotic, or Anxiolytic Dependence or Abuse). Other conditions that may be associated with stress (e.g., irritable bowel syndrome, headaches) frequently accompany Generalized Anxiety Disorder.

THE SEVEN-PART KUNDALINI YOGA PROTOCOL FOR TREATING 300.00 ANXIETY DISORDER NOT OTHERWISE SPECIFIED OR 300.02 GENERALIZED ANXIETY DISORDER*

1. Technique to Induce a Meditative State: "Tuning In"

Sit with a straight spine and with the feet flat on the floor if sitting in a chair (see Figure 2.1). Put the hands together at the chest in "prayer pose"—the palms are pressed together with 10–15 pounds of pressure (a mild to medium pressure, nothing too intense). The area where the sides of the thumbs touch rests on the sternum with the thumbs pointing up (along the sternum), and the fingers are together and point up and out at a 60-degree angle to the ground. The eyes are closed and focused on the third eye (imagine a sun rising on the horizon, or the equivalent of the point between the eyebrows at the origin of the nose). This mantra is chanted out loud in a 1½-breath cycle:

"Ong Namo Guru Dev Namo"

Inhale first through the nose and chant "Ong Namo" with an equal emphasis on the *Ong* and the *Namo*. Then immediately follow with a half-breath inhalation through the mouth and chant "Guru Dev Namo" with approximately equal emphasis on each word. (The *o* in *Ong* and *Namo* is a long-*o* sound; *Dev* sounds like *Dave*, with a long-*a* sound.)

- *Ong Namo* means I bow with reverence to that infinite energy that is the basis of all creation.
- *Guru* means teacher or wisdom.
- *Dev* means divine or of God.

In all it means, "I bow to the infinite creative energy, and I bow to the divine wisdom as it is awakened within me."

*Copyright © David Shannahoff-Khalsa, 2010. No portion of this protocol may be reproduced without the express written permission of the author.

Figure 2.1.
Technique to Induce a Meditative State: Tuning In

The practitioner should focus on the experience of the vibrations these sounds create on the upper palate and throughout the cranium, while letting the mind be carried by the sounds into a new and pleasant mental space. This mantra should be repeated a minimum of three times. However, this mantra can also be practiced up to 10–12 times or more. This technique helps to create a meditative state of mind and is *always* used as a precursor to the other techniques.

2. Spine-Flexing Technique for Vitality

This technique can be practiced while sitting either in a chair or on the floor in a cross-legged position. If you are in a chair, hold the knees with both hands for support and leverage. If you are sitting cross-legged, grasp the ankles in front with both hands. Begin by pulling the chest up and slightly forward, inhaling deeply through the nose at the same time. Then exhale as you relax the spine down into a slouching position. Keep the head up straight, as if you were looking forward, without allowing it to move much while flexing the spine. This position will help prevent a whip effect in the cervical vertebrae. Breathe only through the nose for both the inhalation and exhalation. The eyes are closed, as if you were looking at a central point on the horizon, the third eye. Your mental focus is kept on the sound of the breath while listening to the fluid movement of the inhalation and exhalation. Begin the technique slowly while loosening up the spine. Eventually, a very rapid movement can be achieved with practice, reaching a rate of one to two times per second for the entire movement. A few minutes are adequate in the beginning. Later, there is no upper time limit. Food should be avoided just prior to this exercise. Be careful to flex the spine *slowly* in the beginning. Relax for 1 minute when finished.

3. Shoulder-Shrug Technique for Vitality

While keeping the spine straight, rest the hands on the knees if sitting in a cross-legged position or with hands on the thighs if sitting in a chair. Inhale and raise the shoulders toward the ears, then exhale, relaxing them down. Again, breathe only through the nose. Keep eyes closed and focused on the third eye. Mentally focus on the sound of the inhalation and exhalation. Continue this action rapidly, building to three times per second for a *maximum* of 2 minutes. *Note*: This technique should not be practiced by individuals who are hyperactive.

4. Ganesha Meditation for Focus and Clarity

Sit with a straight spine, the eyes closed (see Figure 2.2). The left thumb and little finger are sticking out from the hand. The other fingers are curled into a fist with fingertips on the moon mound (the root of the thumb area that extends down to the wrist). The left hand and elbow are parallel to the floor, with the pad of the tip of the left thumb pressing on the curved notch of the nose between the eyes. The little finger is sticking out. With right hand

Figure 2.2.
Ganesha Meditation

and elbow parallel to the floor, grasp the left little finger with the right hand and close the right hand into a fist around it, so that both hands now extend straight out from your head. Push the notch with the tip of the left thumb to the extent that you feel some soreness as you breathe long and deep. (This soreness lessens with continued practice.) Do this for no longer than 3 minutes. To finish, inhale as you maintain the posture with eyes closed. Push a little more and pull the naval point in by tightening the abdominal muscles for 10 seconds, then exhale. Repeat one more time.

5. *Gan Puttee Kriya: Eliminating Negativity from the Past, the Present, and the Future*

Gan Puttee Kriya has also been called the "Kriya to Make the Impossible Possible." Yogi Bhajan originally taught this meditation technique on November 2, 1988 (Bhajan, 1998). Yogis disovered this technique as a tool for eliminating the blocks that form in the subconscious mind and stifle growth, frequently leading to destructive, neurotic, and self-defeating patterns of mental activity.

Sit with a straight spine, either on the floor or in a chair. The backs of your hands are resting on your knees with the palms facing upward. The eyes are nine-tenths closed (one-tenth open, but looking straight ahead into the darkness, not the light below), focused on the third eye. Chant from your heart in a natural, relaxed manner, or chant in a steady, relaxed monotone:

"Sa Ta Na Ma Ra Ma Da Sa Sa Say So Hung"

More specifically:

Chant out loud the sound "Sa" (the *a* sounds like *ah*), and touch your thumb tips and index fingertips together quickly and simultaneously with about 2 pounds of pressure.
Chant "Ta" and touch the thumb tips to the middle fingertips.
Chant "Na" and touch the thumb tips to the ring fingertips.
Chant "Ma" and touch the thumb tips to the little fingertips.
Chant "Ra" and touch your thumb tips and index fingertips.
Chant "Ma" and touch the thumb tips to the middle fingertips.
Chant "Da" and touch the thumb tips to the ring fingertips.
Chant "Sa" and touch the thumb tips to the little fingertips.
Chant "Sa" and touch your thumb tips and index fingertips.
Chant "Say" (sounds like the word *say* with a long-*a*) and touch the thumb tips to the middle fingertips.
Chant "So" and touch the thumb tips to the ring fingertips.
Chant "Hung" and touch the thumb tips to the little fingertips.

Chant at a rate of one sound per second. The thumb tip and fingertips touch with a very light (2–3 pounds) pressure with each connection. This light touch helps to consolidate the circuit created by each thumb–finger link. Start with 11 minutes and slowly work up to 31 minutes of practice. To finish, remain in the sitting posture and inhale, holding the breath for 20–30 seconds while you shake and move every part of your body from the waist up with a special emphasis on letting the fingers shake wildly. Exhale and repeat this shaking motion two more times to circulate the energy and to break the pattern of tapping the thumb and fingertips, which affects the brain. Then immediately proceed without rest to Technique 6, "When You Do Not Know What to Do."

Each sound used in this meditation is unique, and they all have a powerful effect on both the conscious and subconscious minds:

"Sa" gives the mind the ability to expand to the infinite.
"Ta" gives the mind the ability to experience the totality of life.
"Na" gives the mind the ability to conquer death.
"Ma" gives the mind the ability to resurrect.
"Ra" gives the mind the ability to expand in radiance (this sound purifies and energizes).
"Da" gives the mind the ability to establish security on the earth plane, providing a ground for action.
"Say" gives the totality of experience.
"So" is the personal sense of identity.
"Hung" is the infinite as a vibrating and real force. Together, *So Hung* means "I am Thou."

The unique qualities of this 12-syllable mantra help cleanse and restructure the subconscious mind and help heal the conscious mind to ultimately experience the *super*conscious mind. All the blocks that result from traumatic or troubling events are eliminated over time with the practice of Gan Puttee Kriya. When doing the whole protocol, 11 minutes for this technique is often adequate; however, 31 minutes is even better, and the maximum time: *Do not go beyond 31 minutes*. When finished proceed immediately to technique 6.

6. *When You Do Not Know What to Do*

Sit straight and rest the back of one hand in the palm of the other, with the thumbs crossing each other in one palm (see Figure 2.3). If the right hand rests in the palm of the left hand, the left thumb rests in the right palm and the right thumb then crosses over the back of the left thumb. Either this hand orientation is acceptable or the reverse, with the left hand resting in the palm of the right hand, and then the right thumb is in the left palm and covered by the left thumb.

The hands are placed at heart-center level, about 2 inches *in front of* the chest (the hands *do not* touch the chest), and the elbows are resting against the ribs. The eyes are open

Figure 2.3.
When You Do Not Know What to Do

but focused on the tip of the nose (which you cannot actually see). The breathing pattern has four parts that repeat in sequence:

1. Inhale and exhale slowly through the nose only.
2. Inhale through the mouth slowly with the lips puckered as if to kiss or make a whistle. After the inhalation, relax the lips and exhale through the mouth slowly.
3. Inhale through the nose and exhale through the mouth slowly.
4. Inhale through the puckered lips and exhale through the nose. Breathe slowly and deeply.

Continue this cycle for 8 minutes and then take a 2- to 3-minute rest. The maximum time allowed for this technique is 31 minutes. This technique can treat any anxiety-related disorder by helping the person induce a very quiet, still, peaceful, clear, and stable mind. This excellent technique can also be used for prevention or simply to reduce daily mental and emotional stress and strain. Practicing this breathing technique on a regular basis will help a person learn what it means to have a very quiet, clear, peaceful, and stable mind, a mind with very little chatter. The more a person engages this state, the more he or she realizes that this peaceful and clear state only improves with practice. A mind without chatter is a very useful and enjoyable mind.

7. Technique for Fighting Brain Fatigue

This technique was originally taught by Yogi Bhajan on March 27, 1995 (Bhajan, 2000), and was later published in the scientific literature (Shannahoff-Khalsa, 2004). This technique has been used to help prevent depression as well as to treat it, and it is especially beneficial if any form of anxiety is accompanied by depression or fatigue.

■ *Part I.* Sit with a straight spine either in a chair or on the floor with your elbows bent and your upper arms near your rib cage (see Figure 2.4). Your forearms point straight out in front of your body, parallel to the floor. The right palm faces downward and the left palm faces upward. Breathing through your nose, inhale and exhale in eight equal parts. On each part or stroke of the breath, alternate moving either hand up and down, one hand moving up as the other moves down. The movement of the hands is approximately 6–8 inches, as if you were bouncing a ball. Breathe powerfully. Continue for 3 minutes and then change the hand position so that the left palm faces downward and the right palm faces upward. Continue for another 3 minutes and then change the hand position again, so that the right palm faces downward and the left palm faces upward for the last 3 minutes. (The total time is 9 minutes.) The eyes can be either open or closed in Part I.

■ *Part II.* Begin slow and deep breathing (again, only through the nose), ceasing the movement and relaxing the hands in the lap. Close your eyes and visually focus them on the center point of the chin. This requires pulling the eyes downward. Keep the body perfectly still and set the intention that the body should heal itself. Keep the mind quiet, stilling all thoughts. (The total time for this part is 5½ minutes.) To finish:

Figure 2.4.
Technique for Fighting Brain Fatigue

- Inhale deeply and hold your breath, making your hands into fists and pressing the fists strongly against the chest for 15 seconds. Exhale.
- Inhale deeply again and hold your breath, this time pressing both fists against the navel point for 15 seconds. Exhale.
- Inhale again then hold the breath. Bend your elbows and bring your fists in front of you, and press your upper arms strongly against your rib cage for 15 seconds as if you are using the upper arms to crush the chest. Then exhale.

Now relax. "This exercise balances the diaphragm and fights brain fatigue. It renews the blood supply to the brain and moves the serum in the spine. It also benefits the liver, navel point, spleen, and lymphatic system" (Bhajan, 2000).

The Short Form: Vic-tor-y Breath

It should be noted that a person with anxiety may not always have the option or time to sit down and practice this seven-part protocol. When that is the case, the simplest approach to treating or minimizing symptoms of any of the anxiety disorders when the earliest symptoms emerge is to use a technique that can be used "on the run." Here is where the technique called the *Vic-tor-y Breath* can be of use, and it is frequently the technique of choice employed successfully by my patients with OCD and other anxiety disorders when the time or circmstances does not permit the use of the full protocol.

The Vic-tor-y Breath technique is described in detail in Chapter 3 (Technique 9, p. 34) as part of the OCD protocol. This technique was originally taught by Yogi Bhajan for "facing mental challenges." It seems too simple to be effective, but just a few breaths using this technique can sometimes be all that is required, and 3–5 minutes of proper use can yield a perfect result. It can be practiced anywhere and at anytime, and once a person has experience with it, he or she can employ it without anyone else noticing.

Its use does not require a slow deep breath, but can be employed by taking a short breath, filling the lungs about half full. The eyes can remain open or closed. All of the techniques described in this book, *with the exception* of the Vic-tor-y Breath, should be practiced *only after* tuning in, using the mantra "Ong Namo Guru Dev Namo" described above (see Technique 1 in this chapter).

THREE

Treating Obsessive–Compulsive Disorder and Obsessive Compulsive Spectrum Disorders

(Trichotillomania and Body Dysmorphic Disorder)

The American Psychiatric Association definition for Obsessive–Compulsive Disorder (OCD) lists the following diagnostic criteria, and further below are additional diagnostic features and associated features and disorders.

DSM DISORDERS

Diagnostic Criteria for 300.3 Obsessive–Compulsive Disorder (APA, 2000)

A. Either obsessions or compulsions:

Obsessions as defined by (1), (2), (3), and (4):
(1) recurrent and persistent thoughts, impulses, or images that are experienced, at some time during the disturbance, as intrusive and inappropriate and that cause marked anxiety or distress
(2) the thoughts, impulses, or images are not simply excessive worries about real-life problems
(3) the person attempts to ignore or suppress such thoughts, impulses, or images, or to neutralize them with some other thought or action

(4) the person recognizes that the obsessional thoughts, impulses, or images are a product of his or her own mind (not imposed from without as in thought insertion)

Compulsions as defined by (1) and (2):
(1) repetitive behaviors (e.g., hand washing, ordering, checking) or mental acts (e.g., praying, counting, repeating words silently) that the person feels driven to perform in response to an obsession, or according to rules that must be applied rigidly
(2) the behaviors or mental acts are aimed at preventing or reducing distress or preventing some dreaded event or situation; however, these behaviors or mental acts either are not connected in a realistic way with what they are designed to neutralize or prevent or are clearly excessive

B. At some point during the course of the disorder, the person has recognized that the obsessions or compulsions are excessive or unreasonable. **Note:** This does not apply to children.
C. The obsessions or compulsions cause marked distress, are time consuming (take more than 1 hour a day), or significantly interfere with the person's normal routine, occupational (or academic) functioning, or usual social activities or relationships.
D. If another Axis I disorder is present, the content of the obsessions or compulsions is not restricted to it (e.g., preoccupation with food in the presence of an Eating Disorders; hair pulling in the presence of Trichotillomania; concern with appearance in the presence of Body Dysmorphic Disorder; preoccupation with drugs in the presence of a Substance Use Disorder; preoccupation with having a serious illness in the presence of Hypochondriasis; preoccupation with sexual urges or fantasies in the presence of a Paraphilia; or guilty ruminations in the presence of Major Depressive Disorder).
E. The disturbance is not due to the direct physiological effects of a substance (e.g., a drug of abuse, a medication) or a general medical condition.

Specify if: **With Poor Insight:** if, for most of the time during the current episode, the person does not recognize that the obsessions and compulsions are excessive or unreasonable

Additional Diagnostic Features (APA, 2000)

The most common *obsessions* are repeated thoughts about contamination (e.g., becoming contaminated by shaking hands), repeated doubts (e.g., wondering whether one has performed some act such as having hurt someone in a traffic accident or having left a door unlocked), a need to have things in a particular order (e.g., intense distress when objects are disordered or asymmetrical), aggressive or horrific impulses (e.g., to hurt one's child or to shout an obscenity in church), and sexual imagery (e.g., a recurrent pornographic image). The thoughts, impulses, or images are not simply excessive worries about real-life problems (e.g., concerns about current ongoing difficulties in life, such as financial, work, or school problems) and are unlikely to be related to a real-life problem.

The individual with obsessions usually attempts to ignore or suppress such thoughts or impulses or to neutralize them with some other thought or action (i.e., a compulsion). For example, an individual plagued by doubts about having turned off the stove attempts to neutralize them by repeatedly checking to ensure that it is off.

Compulsions are repetitive behaviors (e.g., hand washing, ordering, checking) or mental acts (e.g., praying, counting, repeating words silently) the goal of which is to prevent or reduce anxiety or distress, not to provide pleasure or gratification. In most cases, the person feels driven to perform the compulsion to reduce the distress that accompanies an obsession or to prevent some dreaded event or situation. For example, individuals with obsessions about being contaminated may reduce their mental distress by washing their hands until their skin is raw; individuals distressed by obsessions about having left a door unlocked may be driven to check the lock every few minutes; individuals distressed by unwanted blasphemous thoughts may find relief in counting to 10 backward and forward 100 times for each thought. In some cases, individuals perform rigid or stereotyped acts according to idiosyncratically elaborated rules without being able to indicate why they are doing them. By definition, compulsions are either clearly excessive or are not connected in a realistic way with what they are designed to neutralize or prevent. The most common compulsions involve washing and cleaning, counting, checking, requesting or demanding assurances, repeating actions, and ordering.

By definition, adults with Obsessive–Compulsive Disorder have at some point recognized that the obsessions or compulsions are excessive or unreasonable. This requirement does not apply to children because they may lack sufficient cognitive awareness to make this judgment. However, even in adults there is a broad range of insight into the reasonableness of the obsessions or compulsions. Some individuals are uncertain about the reasonableness of their obsessions or compulsions, and any given individual's insight may vary across times and situations. For example, the person may recognize a contamination compulsion as unreasonable when discussing it in a "safe situation" (e.g., in the therapist's office), but not when forced to handle money. At those times when the individual recognizes that the obsessions and compulsions are unreasonable, he or she may desire or attempt to resist them. When attempting to resist a compulsion, the individual may have a sense of mounting anxiety or tension that is often relieved by yielding to the compulsion. In the course of the disorder, after repeated failure to resist the obsessions or compulsions, the individual may give in to them, no longer experience a desire to resist them, and may incorporate the compulsions into his or her daily routines.

Associated Features and Disorders (APA, 2000)

Frequently there is avoidance of situations that involve the content of the obsessions, such as dirt or contamination. For example, a person with obsessions about dirt may avoid public restrooms or shaking hands with strangers. Hypochondriacal concerns are common, with repeated visits to physicians to seek reassurance. Guilt, a pathological sense of responsibility, and sleep disturbances may be present. There may be excessive use of alcohol or of sedative, hypnotic, or anxiolytic medications. Performing compulsions may become a major life activity, leading to serious marital, occupational, or social disability. Pervasive avoidance may leave an individual housebound.

In adults, Obsessive–Compulsive Disorder may be associated with Major Depressive Disorder, some other Anxiety Disorders (i.e., Specific Phobia, Social Phobia, Panic Disorder, Generalized Anxiety Disorder), Eating Disorders, and some Personality Disorders (i.e., Obsessive–Compulsive Personality Disorder, Avoidant Personality Disorder, Dependent Personality Disorder). In children, it may also be associated with Learning Disorders and Disruptive Behavior Disorders. There is a high incidence of Obsessive–Compulsive Disorder in children and adults with Tourette's Disorder, with estimates ranging from approximately 35% to 50%. The incidence of Tourette's Disorder in Obsessive–Compulsive Disorder is lower, with estimates ranging between 5% and 7%. Between 20% and 30% of individuals with Obsessive–Compulsive Disorder have reported current or past tics.

Diagnostic Criteria for 312.39 Trichotillomania (APA, 2000)

A. Recurrent pulling out of one's hair resulting in noticeable hair loss.
B. An increasing sense of tension immediately before pulling out the hair or when attempting to resist the behavior.
C. Pleasure, gratification, or relief when pulling out the hair.
D. The disturbance is not better accounted for by another mental disorder and is not due to a general medical condition (e.g., a dermatological condition).
E. The disturbance causes clinically significant distress or impairment in social, occupational, or other important areas of functioning.

Associated Features and Disorders for 312.39 Trichotillomania (APA, 2000)

Examining the hair root, twirling it off, pulling the strand between the teeth, or trichophagia (eating hairs) may occur with Trichotillomania. Hair pulling does not usually occur in the presence of other people (except immediate family members), and social situations may be avoided. Individuals commonly deny their hair-pulling behavior and conceal or camouflage the resulting alopecia. Some individuals have urges to pull hairs from other people and may sometimes try to find opportunities to do so surreptitiously. They may pull hairs from pets, dolls, and other fibrous materials (e.g., sweaters or carpets). Nail biting, scratching, gnawing, and excoriation is often associated with Trichotillomania. Individuals with Trichotillomania may also have Mood Disorders, Anxiety Disorders (especially Obsessive–Compulsive Disorder), Substance Use Disorders, Eating Disorders, Personality Disorders, or Mental Retardation.

Diagnostic Criteria for 300.7 Body Dysmorphic Disorder (APA, 2000)

A. Preoccupation with an imagined defect in appearance. If a slight physical anomaly is present, the person's concern is markedly excessive.
B. The preoccupation causes clinically significant distress or impairment in social, occupational, or other important areas of functioning.
C. The preoccupation is not better accounted for by another mental disorder (e.g., dissatisfaction with body shape and size in Anorexia Nervosa).

Reprinted with permission from the *Diagnostic and Statistical Manual of Mental Disorders, Fourth Edition, Text Revision.* Copyright 2000 American Psychiatric Association.

Diagnostic Features for 300.7 Body Dysmorphic Disorder (APA, 2000)

Complaints commonly involve imagined or slight flaws of the face or head such as hair thinning, acne, wrinkles, scars, vascular markings, paleness or redness of the complexion, swelling, facial asymmetry or disproportion, or excessive facial hair. Other common preoccupations include the shape, size, or some other aspect of the nose, eyes, eyelids, eyebrows, ears, mouth, lips, teeth, jaw, chin, cheeks, or head. However, any other body part may be the focus of concern (e.g., the genitals, breasts, buttocks, abdomen, arms, hands, feet, legs, hips, shoulders, spine, larger body regions, overall body size, or body build and muscularity). The preoccupation may simultaneously focus on several body parts. Although the complaint is often specific (e.g., a "crooked" lip or a "bumpy" nose), it is sometimes vague (e.g., a "falling" face or "inadequately firm" eyes). Because of embarrassment over their concerns or for other reasons, some individuals with Body Dysmorphic Disorder avoid describing their "defects" in detail and may instead refer only to their general ugliness.

Most individuals with this disorder experience marked distress over their supposed deformity, often describing their preoccupations as "intensely painful,""tormenting," or "devastating." Most find their preoccupations difficult to control, and they may make little or no attempt to resist them. As a result, they often spend hours a day thinking about their "defect," to the point where these thoughts may dominate their lives. Significant impairment in many areas of functioning generally occurs. Feelings of self-consciousness about their "defect" may lead to avoidance of work, school, or public situations.

Associated Features and Disorders for 300.7
Body Dysmorphic Disorder (APA, 2000)

Frequent checking of the defect, either directly or in a reflecting surface (e.g., mirrors, store windows, car bumpers, watch faces) can consume many hours a day. Some individuals use special lighting or magnifying glasses to scrutinize their "defect." There may be excessive grooming behavior (e.g., excessive hair combing, hair removal, ritualized makeup application, or skin picking). Although the usual intent of checking and grooming is to diminish anxiety, be reassured about one's appearance, or temporarily improve one's appearance, these behaviors often intensify the preoccupation and associated anxiety. Consequently, some individuals avoid mirrors, sometimes covering them or removing them from their environment. Others alternate between periods of excessive mirror checking and avoidance. Other behaviors aimed at improving the "defect" include excessive exercise (e.g., weight lifting), dieting, and frequent changing of clothes. There may be frequent requests for reassurance about the "defect," but such reassurance leads to only temporary, if any, relief. Individuals with the disorder may also frequently compare their "ugly" body part with that of others. They may try to camouflage the "defect" (e.g., growing a beard to cover imagined facial scars, wearing a hat to hide imagined hair loss, stuffing their shorts to enhance a "small" penis). Some individuals may be excessively preoccupied with fears that the "ugly" body part will malfunction or is extremely fragile and in constant danger of being damaged. Insight about the perceived defect is often poor, and some individuals are delusional; that is, they are completely convinced that their view of the defect is accurate and undistorted, and they cannot be convinced otherwise. Ideas and delusions of reference related to the imagined defect are also common; that is, individuals with this disorder often think that others may be (or are) taking special notice of their supposed flaw, perhaps talking about it or mocking it.

Avoidance of usual activities may lead to extreme social isolation. In some cases, individuals may leave their homes only at night, when they cannot be seen, or become housebound, sometimes for years. Individuals with this disorder may drop out of school, avoid job interviews, work at jobs below their capacity, or not work at all. They may have few friends, avoid dating and other social interactions, have marital difficulties, or get divorced because of their symptoms. The distress and dysfunction associated with this disorder, although variable, can lead to repeated hospitalization and to suicidal ideation, suicide attempts, and completed suicide. Individuals with Body Dysmorphic Disorder often pursue and receive general medical (often dermatological), dental, or surgical treatments to rectify their imagined or slight defects. Occasionally, individuals may resort to extreme measures (e.g., self-surgery) to correct their perceived flaws.

Such treatment may cause the disorder to worsen, leading to intensified or new preoccupations, which may in turn lead to further unsuccessful procedures, so that individuals may eventually possess "synthetic" noses, ears, breasts, hips, or other body parts, which they are still dissatisfied with. Body Dysmorphic Disorder may be associated with Major Depressive Disorder, Delusional Disorder, Social Phobia, and Obsessive–Compulsive Disorder.

Reprinted with permission from the *Diagnostic and Statistical Manual of Mental Disorders, Fourth Edition, Text Revision.* Copyright 2000 American Psychiatric Association.

THE 11-PART KUNDALINI YOGA PROTOCOL FOR TREATING 300.3 OBSESSIVE–COMPULSIVE DISORDER OR THE OBSESSIVE–COMPULSIVE SPECTRUM DISORDERS (312.39 TRICHOTILLOMANIA AND 300.7 BODY DYSMORPHIC DISORDER)*

The 11-part protocol that is described below has now been tested in two clinical trials (Shannahoff-Khalsa, Ray, Levine, Gallen, Schwartz, & Sidorowich, 1999; Shannahoff-Khalsa, 1997, 2003, 2006; Shannahoff-Khalsa & Beckett, 1996). Each technique in this protocol can lead to a profound experience toward reducing and eliminating the symptoms

*Copyright © David Shannahoff-Khalsa, 1992. No portion of this protocol may be reproduced without the express written permission of the author.

of OCD and OC spectrum disorders. Individuals with OCD, or any of the OC spectrum disorders, including both trichotillomania and body dysmophic disorder, should apply the whole protocol, regardless of their individual or combined diagnoses. If an individual has both OCD and an OC spectrum disorder, the protocol will lead to amelioration of both at about the same rate. In our clinical trials patients have made comments during their first experience with the protocol, such as, "I almost forgot that I had OCD, my mind is so quiet." The woman who made this comment did so after 15 minutes in her first session. She was thoroughly amazed, especially since she was in a doctoral program for clinical psychology and had suffered with OCD for years. In fact, once a person becomes experienced with the protocol, he or she can usually achieve some significant relief within several minutes. Knowing that this rapid relief is possible, based on personal experience, is itself a source of great relief. After this awareness, the person decides how much torture or relief he or she can tolerate or enjoy, respectively.

In our trials, some people made an early commitment to practice every day, some took weeks to commit, some took months, some practiced only when they came to the group—and, of course, some dropped out so that they would not have to test their own will to commit even after achieving relief while participating in the group. Extensive summaries of these trials, along with individual case histories, have been published (Shannahoff-Khalsa et al., 1999; Shannahoff-Khalsa, 1997, 2006; Shannahoff-Khalsa & Beckett, 1996).

This protocol also produces delightful feelings throughout the body. There is an increase in energy and a new sense of comfort devoid of the constant tension that leaves people with OCD feeling temperamental and tense. The person also experiences renewal and rejuvenation. Everyone who entered our clinical trials felt completely refreshed, even before we reached the halfway point in the protocol. Their sense of well-being, vitality, and experience of spirituality only increased after as the weeks of practice progressed.

This protocol includes eight primary techniques to be used on a daily or near-daily basis and three additional techniques to be used at one's personal discretion. Most people also found two of the three supplementary techniques (especially 9 and 10) to be useful adjuncts to their daily routine. They require very little extra effort, and the benefits are well worth a few additional minutes. I have also produced a video to aid those who prefer to learn in that mode. However, the figures that accompany the techniques below should suffice.

1. Technique to Induce a Meditative State: "Tuning In"

Sit with a straight spine and with the feet flat on the floor if sitting in a chair (see Figure 2.1). Put the hands together at the chest in "prayer pose"—the palms are pressed together with 10–15 pounds of pressure (a mild to medium pressure, nothing too intense). The area where the sides of the thumbs touch rests on the sternum with the thumbs pointing up (along the sternum), and the fingers are together and point up and out at a 60-degree angle to the ground. The eyes are closed and focused on the third eye (imagine a sun rising on the horizon, or the equivalent of the point between the eyebrows at the origin of the nose). A mantra is chanted out loud in a 1½-breath cycle:

"Ong Namo Guru Dev Namo"

Inhale first through the nose and chant "Ong Namo" with an equal emphasis on the *Ong* and the *Namo*. Then immediately follow with a half-breath inhalation through the mouth and chant "Guru Dev Namo" with approximately equal emphasis on each word. (The *o* in *Ong* and *Namo* is a long-*o* sound; *Dev* sounds like *Dave*, with a long-*a* sound.)

- *Ong Namo* means I bow with reverence to that infinite energy that is the basis of all creation.
- *Guru* means teacher or wisdom.
- *Dev* means divine or of God.

The practitioner should focus on the experience of the vibrations these sounds create on the upper palate and throughout the cranium, while letting the mind be carried by the sounds into a new and pleasant mental space. This sequence should be repeated a minimum of three times. We employed it in our group about 10–12 times. This technique helps to create a meditative state of mind and is *always* used as a precursor to the other techniques.

2. Spine-Flexing Technique for Vitality

This technique can be practiced while sitting either in a chair or on the floor in a cross-legged position. If you are in a chair, hold the knees with both hands for support and leverage. If you are sitting cross-legged, grasp the ankles in front with both hands. Begin by pulling the chest up and slightly forward, inhaling deeply through the nose at the same time. Then exhale as you relax the spine down into a slouching position. Keep the head up straight, as if you were looking forward, without allowing it to move much while flexing the spine. This position will help prevent a whip effect in the cervical vertebrae. Breathe only through the nose for both the inhalation and exhalation. The eyes are closed, as if you were looking at a central point on the horizon, the third eye. Your mental focus is kept on the sound of the breath while listening to the fluid movement of the inhalation and exhalation. Begin the technique slowly while loosening up the spine. Eventually, a very rapid movement can be achieved with practice, reaching a rate of one to two times per second for the entire movement. A few minutes are adequate in the beginning. Later, there is no upper time limit. Food should be avoided just prior to this exercise. Be careful to flex the spine *slowly* in the beginning. Relax for 1 minute when finished.

3. Shoulder-Shrug Technique for Vitality

While keeping the spine straight, rest the hands on the knees if sitting in a cross-legged position or with hands on the thighs if sitting in a chair. Inhale and raise the shoulders toward the ears, then exhale, relaxing them down. Again, breathe only through the nose. Keep eyes closed and focused on the third eye. Mentally focus on the sound of the inhalation and exhalation. Continue this action rapidly, building to three times per second for a maximum of 2 minutes. *Note*: This technique should not be practiced by individuals who are hyperactive.

4. First Technique for Reducing Anxiety, Stress, and Mental Tension: A Meditation for an Unstable Mind

Sit and maintain a straight spine. Relax the arms and the hands in the lap. Focus the eyes on the tip of the nose even though you cannot see it. When you are unsure about where this is, start by placing the tip of your index finger on the very end of your nose. You will not be able to see the tip of your finger, but this is the area of your visual focus. You can only see the sides of the nose, and they will appear blurred while you are focusing on the tip. Open the mouth as wide as possible, slightly stressing the temporal–mandibular joint, the jaw joint. Touch the tongue tip to the upper palate, where it is hard and smooth in the center. Breathe continuously through the nose only, while making the respirations slow and deep. Mentally focus on the sound of the breath; listen to the sound of the inhalation and exhalation. Remember to keep the eyes focused, the jaw stretched, and the tongue on the upper palate throughout.

In the beginning, remembering to do everything correctly is sometimes challenging. Maintain this pattern for at least 3–5 minutes with a maximum of 8 minutes on the first trial. With practice it can be maintained for 31 minutes maximum. However, 8 minutes is enough time when this technique is practiced in this protocol. This technique can be used to curb a restless mind and bring an inner stillness and an extraordinary experience of mental silence even if someone is feeling insane (Bhajan & Khalsa, 1975).

5. Second Technique for Reducing Anxiety, Stress, and Mental Tension and Healing the Heart Center

Sit and maintain a straight spine (see Figure 3.1). The hands are in front of the chest at heart level. The left hand is 2 inches away from the chest, and the right is about 2 inches behind the left (4 inches away from the chest); the left-hand fingers point to the right. The right palm faces the back of the left hand with the right-hand fingers pointing to the left. The thumbs of both hands point up without tension. The eyes are opened and focused on the tip of the nose (see Technique 4). All breathing is done through the nose only.

Inhale, then keep the breath in as long as possible; now exhale and keep the breath out as long as possible, without creating undo discomfort at any stage. The inhalation and exhalation phases are each short. Only the holding in and holding out stages are stressed. When finished, inhale while still maintaining the eye and hand posture and then tense every muscle in the body for about 10 seconds. Exhale and repeat two times. Build the capacity for this technique to a maximum time of 15 minutes. However, 8 minutes is enough when practiced as part of this protocol. Avoid this exercise if you have high blood pressure or are pregnant. This technique was taught for relaxing the mind when there is emotional stress or mental tension. This technique will also help heal and relieve the heart center when there is a build up of emotional stress and strain.

6. Third Technique for Reducing Anxiety, Stress, and Mental Tension

Sit as in Technique 5. Eyes are opened and focused on the tip of the nose during the *entire* exercise. Attempt to pull the nose down toward the upper lip by pulling the upper lip down over the upper front teeth, using the muscles of the upper lip. The mouth is left open dur-

Figure 3.1.
Second Technique for Reducing Anxiety, Stress, and Mental Tension
and Healing the Heart Center

ing this exercise while keeping constant tension on the upper lip. This upper-lip tension is maintained during, in between, and throughout all six rounds. There are three steps to this exercise:

a. Start with the hands and arms up and out to the sides at 45–60 degrees, then inhale deeply and tightly clench the fists (this also produces tension in the arms and shoulders) and slowly pull them down toward the abdomen, at the navel-point region like a moving isometric exercise.

b. Maintaining the tension in the fists, arms, and shoulders, bring the shoulders up toward the ears, tensing the shoulders and neck as they go up. (Keep the breath from Part A held in, eyes focused, and upper lip pulled down.)

c. Exhale and relax (but keep the upper lip pulled down and the eyes focused on the tip of the nose). Repeat the entire sequence 5 more times. Avoid this exercise if you have high blood pressure or are pregnant. This short exercise is claimed to be so effective that, if it is done correctly, it can relieve the tensest person.

7. Technique for Managing Fears

Sit with a straight spine (see Figure 3.2). Close the eyes. Place the left hand with the four fingertips and thumbtip grouped and pressed very lightly into the navel point, like a plug.

Figure 3.2.
Technique for Managing Fears

Place the fingertips of the right hand with the four fingers pointing left over the third eye point (on the forehead just above the root of the nose), as if feeling your temperature. Play the audio musical tape of Chattra Chakkra Varti (Kaur, 2006; K. Singh, 2006) for 3 minutes while imaging and assessing all your fears and consciously relating to the mental experience of each fear. This technique helps to manage acute states of fear and eliminate fearful images and negative emotions that have developed due to fearful experiences. The effect is that the negative emotions related to specific fears are replaced with positive emotions, thereby slowly creating a new and different mental association with the stimulus. Only the musical tape recommended here will actually produce this unique effect.

8. Technique for Treating Obsessive–Compulsive Disorders (OCD)

Sit with a straight spine in a comfortable position, either with the legs crossed while sitting on the floor or in a straight-back chair with both feet flat on the ground. Do not lean against the chair. Close the eyes. Use the right thumb tip to block the end of the right nostril, with other fingers pointing up straight. Allow the arm to relax (the elbow should not stick up or out, to the side, creating unnecessary tension). A small cork or secure plug made of wet tissue paper can also be used to plug the right nostril.

Inhale very slowly and deeply through the left nostril and hold the breath *in* for a long time. Exhale out slowly and completely through the same nostril only (left nostril), and hold the breath *out* for a long time. The mental focus should be on the sound of the breath. The length of time a person can hold his or her breath (both in and out) varies from person to person. Ideal time per complete breath cycle is 1 minute, wherein each section of the cycle lasts exactly 15 seconds. This rate of respiration can be achieved by most people within 5–6 months for the full 31-minute maximum with daily discipline.

Initially, begin with a comfortable rate and time for which the effort presents a fair challenge for each phase of the breath. Yogic experiments claim that 90 days of 31 minutes per day, using the perfected rate of one breath per minute with 15 seconds per phase, will completely eliminate all OC disorders (Yogi Bhajan, personal communication). The hold-out phase is always the most difficult. Starting with 5 seconds for each of the four phases (the inhalation, the hold-in, the exhalation, and the hold-out) is a reasonable beginning for most people after practicing the technique for a while. Then attempt 7.5 seconds per phase with slow gradations. You should not try to make any phase longer than 15 seconds to compensate for the difficulties with the other phases. The balance of the four phases is an important key to this technique.

9. *Technique for Meeting Mental Challenges: The Vic-tor-y Breath*

This technique can be used at any time; it does not require a sitting position. It can be employed while driving a car, while participating in a conversation, or while taking a test. The eyes can be open or closed, depending on the situation. Take a near-full breath through the nose. Hold this breath without straining or tensing the stomach muscles for exactly 3–4 seconds and only during this holding phase mentally say to yourself the three separate sounds *vic–tor–y*. Then exhale. Mentally creating the three separated sounds should take 3–4 seconds, no longer or less. The entire time of each repetition should take about 8–10 seconds. The breath should not be exaggerated to the extent that anyone would even notice that you are taking a deep breath. It can be employed multiple times until you achieve the desired relief. When employed in our therapy sessions, it was usually done for 3–5 minutes with the eyes closed and while sitting with a straight spine to maximize the benefits. This technique is very helpful as a "thought stopping" exercise for a patient with OCD who is "on the go." There is no upper time limit for its practice. It can be used to help resist obsessive thoughts and as an antidote for compulsive rituals.

10. *Technique to Turn Negative Thoughts into Positive Thoughts*

This technique should be employed while sitting with a straight spine and with the eyes closed in a peaceful environment. The mantra

"Ek Ong Kar Sat Gurprasad Sat Gurprasad Ek Ong Kar"

must be repeated a minimum of five times and is best practiced for 5–11 minutes. Chant it through rapidly up to five full repetitions of the entire mantra per breath.

The "Ek" sound is the same as the *eck* in *neck*.
"Ong" has a long-*o* (not *ung*).
"Kar" sounds like *car* but with an emphasis on the *k* sound.

"Sat" has a short-*a* sound, as in the English *sat* and sounds like the word sought. "Gurprasad" has short vowel sounds (*u* as in *urgent*; *a* as in *ahhh*).

Eventually, one no longer thinks about the order of the sounds, they come automatically. The mental focus should be on the vibration created against the upper palate and throughout the cranium. If performed correctly, a very peaceful and "healed" state of mind is achieved.

11. Technique for Tranquilizing an Angry Mind

Sit with a straight spine and eyes closed. Simply chant out loud

"Jeeo, Jeeo, Jeeo, Jeeo"

continuously and rapidly for 11 minutes without stopping (pronounced like the names for the letters *g* and *o*). Rapid chanting involves about 8–10 repetitions per 5 seconds. During continuous chanting, you do not stop to take long breaths, but continue with just enough short breaths to keep the sound going. Eleven minutes is all that is needed, no more or less. The effect can last for up to 3 days. If necessary, it can be chanted for 11 minutes twice a day. This technique is most suitable for treating a "red-hot" angry mind. It is not a required part of the protocol unless there is apparent anger.

FOUR

Treating Phobias

This chapter covers both specific phobias and social phobias. The latter are now also called "social anxiety disorders," and they are believed to have a lifetime prevalence rate of 14% in the United States (Kessler, Stein, & Berglund, 1998). The social phobias begin early in life and rarely remit (Davidson, Hughes, George, & Blazer, 1993). There are at least 500 different specific phobias that can be found in medical texts (but there is no single official list), and they cover nearly everything imaginable. The following DSM IV-TR diagnostic criteria, additional diagnostic features, and associated features and disorders cover the specific phobias in a general way.

DSM DISORDERS

Diagnostic Criteria for 300.29 Specific Phobia (APA, 2000)

A. Marked and persistent fear that is excessive or unreasonable, cued by the presence or anticipation of a specific object or situation (e.g., flying, heights, animals, receiving an injection, seeing blood).

B. Exposure to the phobic stimulus almost invariably provokes an immediate anxiety response, which may take the form of a situationally bound or situationally predisposed Panic Attack. **Note:** In children, the anxiety may be expressed by crying, tantrums, freezing, or clinging.

C. The person recognizes that the fear is excessive or unreasonable. **Note:** In children, this feature may be absent.

D. The phobic situation(s) is avoided or else is endured with intense anxiety or distress.

E. The avoidance, anxious anticipation, or distress in the feared situation(s) interferes significantly with the person's normal routine, occupational (or academic) functioning, or social activities or relationships, or there is marked distress about having the phobia.

F. In individuals under age 18 years, the duration is at least 6 months.

G. The anxiety, Panic Attacks, or phobic avoidance associated with the specific object or situation are not better accounted for by another mental disorder, such as Obsessive–Compulsive Disorder (e.g., fear of dirt in someone with an obsession about contamination), Posttraumatic Stress Disorder (e.g., avoidance of stimuli associated with a severe stressor), Separation Anxiety Disorder (e.g., avoidance of school), Social Phobia (e.g., avoidance of social situations because of fear of embarrassment), Panic Disorder With Agoraphobia, or Agoraphobia Without History of Panic Disorder.

Reprinted with permission from the *Diagnostic and Statistical Manual of Mental Disorders, Fourth Edition, Text Revision.* Copyright 2000 American Psychiatric Association.

Additional Diagnostic Features (APA, 2000)

The individual experiences a marked, persistent, and excessive or unreasonable fear when in the presence of, or when anticipating an encounter with, a specific object or situation. The focus of the fear may be anticipated harm from some aspect of the object or situation (e.g., an individual may fear air travel because of a concern about crashing, may fear dogs because of concerns about being bitten, or may fear driving because of concerns about being hit by other vehicles on the road). Specific Phobias may also involve concerns about losing control, panicking, somatic manifestations of anxiety and fear (such as increased heart rate or shortness of breath), and fainting that might occur on exposure to the feared object. For example, individuals afraid of blood and injury may also worry about the possibility of fainting; people afraid of heights may also worry about dizziness; and people afraid of closed-in situations may also worry about losing control and screaming. These concerns may be particularly strong in the Situational Type of Specific Phobia.

Anxiety is almost invariably felt immediately on confronting the phobic stimulus (e.g., a person with a Specific Phobia of cats will almost invariably have an immediate anxiety response when forced to confront a cat). The level of anxiety or fear usually varies as a function of both the degree of proximity to the phobic stimulus (e.g., fear intensifies as the cat approaches and decreases as the cat withdraws) and the degree to which escape from the phobic stimulus is limited (e.g., fear intensifies as the elevator approaches the midway point between floors and decreases as the doors open at the next floor). However, the intensity of the fear may not always relate predictably to the phobic stimulus (e.g., a person afraid of heights may experience variable amounts of fear when crossing the same bridge on different occasions). Sometimes full-blown Panic Attacks are experienced in response to the phobic stimulus, especially when the person must remain in the situation or believes that escape will be impossible. Occasionally, the Panic Attacks are delayed and do not occur immediately upon confronting the phobic stimulus. This delay is more likely in the Situational Type. Because marked anticipatory anxiety occurs if the person is confronted with the necessity of entering into the phobic situation, such situations are usually avoided. Less commonly, the person forces himself or herself to endure the phobic situation, but it is experienced with intense anxiety.

Adults with this disorder recognize that the phobia is excessive or unreasonable. The diagnosis would be Delusional Disorder instead of Specific Phobia for an individual who avoids an elevator because of a conviction that it has been sabotaged and who does not recognize that this fear is excessive and unreasonable. Moreover, the diagnosis should not be given if the fear is reasonable given the context of the stimuli (e.g., fear of being shot in a hunting area or a dangerous neighborhood). Insight into the excessive or unreasonable nature of the fear tends to increase with age and is not required to make the diagnosis in children.

Fears of circumscribed objects or situations are very common, especially in children, but in many cases the degree of impairment is insufficient to warrant a diagnosis. If the phobia does not significantly interfere with the individual's functioning or cause marked distress, the diagnosis is not made. For example, a person who is afraid of snakes to the point of expressing intense fear in the presence of snakes would not receive a diagnosis of Specific Phobia if he or she lives in an area devoid of snakes, is not restricted in activities by the fear of snakes, and is not distressed about having a fear of snakes.

Associated Features and Disorders (APA, 2000)

Specific Phobia may result in a restricted lifestyle or interference with certain occupations, depending on the type of phobia. For example, job promotion may be threatened by avoidance of air travel, and social activities may be restricted by fears of crowded or closed-in places. Specific Phobias frequently co-occur with other Anxiety Disorders, Mood Disorders, and Substance-Related Disorders. For example, in community samples, rates of co-occurrence with other disorders range from 50% to 80%, and these rates may be higher among individuals with early-onset Specific Phobias. In clinical settings, Specific Phobias are very common comorbid diagnoses with other disorders. However, Specific Phobias are rarely the focus of clinical attention in these situations. The Specific Phobia is usually associated with less distress or less interference with functioning than the comorbid main diagnosis. Overall, only 12%–30% are estimated to seek professional help for their Specific Phobias. In the absence of other diagnoses, help seeking for Specific Phobias is more likely with more functionally impairing phobias (e.g., phobias of objects or situations that are commonly encountered), multiple phobias, and Panic Attacks in the phobic context. In contrast, individuals with irrational fears of blood injury, medical procedures, and medical settings may be less likely to seek help for phobias.

THE FOUR-PART KUNDALINI YOGA PROTOCOL FOR TREATING 300.29 SPECIFIC PHOBIAS*

There is a variety of Kundalini meditation techniques that would be useful in treating phobias. This protocol includes three very different techniques and is highly likely to be a comprehensive means of treating a range of phobic severity, from the mild and to the most chronic and severe phobias. The first technique is the mantra "Ong Namo Guru Dev Namo" that is standard tuning-in practice for any Kundalini yoga meditation. The first disorder-specific technique is useful to help manage fears of any nature; this technique is also a component of the 11-part OCD protocol in Chapter 3. This technique works by establishing a positive emotional association with the phobia over time; it can be used in both acute and chronic circumstances. This technique is even useful when one has a fear of death. The second disorder-specific technique is a relatively simple one and can be learned and practiced quickly; it is very useful for social phobias that have resulted in part from an interaction with another person. The third technique, called "Tershula Kriya," is the most difficult but can work for all phobias. Note, the technique for treating addictions in Chapter 12 is also applicable to phobias. The idea here is not just to reduce the momentary anxiety, but to eliminate the causal underlying factors that are rooted in the psyche. Combining the three techniques appropriately is the best strategy.

1. Technique to Induce a Meditative State: "Tuning In"

Sit with a straight spine and with the feet flat on the floor if sitting in a chair (see Figure 2.1). Put the hands together at the chest in "prayer pose"—the palms are pressed together with 10–15 pounds of pressure (a mild to medium pressure, nothing too intense). The area where the sides of the thumbs touch rests on the sternum with the thumbs pointing up (along the sternum), and the fingers are together and point up and out at a 60-degree angle to the ground. The eyes are closed and focused on the third eye (imagine a sun rising on the horizon, or the equivalent of the point between the eyebrows at the origin of the nose). This mantra is chanted out loud in a 1½-breath cycle:

"Ong Namo Guru Dev Namo"

Inhale first through the nose and chant "Ong Namo" with an equal emphasis on the *Ong* and the *Namo*. Then immediately follow with a half-breath inhalation through the mouth and chant "Guru Dev Namo" with approximately equal emphasis on each word. (The *o* in *Ong* and *Namo* is a long-o sound; *Dev* sounds like *Dave*, with a long-a sound.)

- *Ong Namo* means I bow with reverence to that infinite energy that is the basis of all creation.

- *Guru* means teacher or wisdom.
- *Dev* means divine or of God.

The practitioner should focus on the experience of the vibrations these sounds create on the upper palate and throughout the cranium, while letting the mind be carried by the sounds into a new and pleasant mental space. This sequence should be repeated a minimum of three times. We employed it in our group about 10–12 times. This technique helps to create a meditative state of mind and is *always* used as a precursor to the other techniques.

2. Technique for Managing Fears

Sit with a straight spine (see Figure 3.2). Close the eyes. Place the left hand with the four fingertips and thumb grouped and pressed very lightly into the navel point, like a plug. Place the fingertips of the right hand with the four fingers pointing left over the third eye point (on the forehead just above the root of the nose), as if feeling your temperature. Play the audio musical tape of Chattra Chakkra Varti (Kaur, 2006; K. Singh, 2006) for 3 minutes while assessing all your fears and consciously relating to the mental experience of each fear. This technique helps to manage acute states of fear and eliminate fearful images and negative emotions that have developed due to fearful experiences. The effect is that the negative emotions related to specific fears are replaced with positive emotions, thereby slowly creating a new and different mental association with the stimulus. Only the musical tape recommended here will actually produce this unique effect.

3. A Meditation for Removing Haunting Thoughts

This technique was first published in the scientific literature in 2004 (Shannahoff-Khalsa, 2004). "This meditation can cure phobias, fears, and neuroses. It can remove unsettling thoughts from the past that surface into the present. And it can take difficult situations in the present and release them. All of this can be done in forty seconds!" (Yogi Bhajan, personal communication). In addition, it is very useful for patients with posttraumatic stress disorder (PTSD) who have been the victim of rape, incest, or physical torment. There are 10 steps:

1. Lower the eyelids until the eyes are only open one-tenth. Start by mentally concentrating on the tip of the nose. Then silently say "Wha Hay Guru" in the following manner:

Wha while mentally focusing on the right eye; *Hay* while mentally focusing on the left eye; and *Guru* while mentally focusing on the tip of the nose.

2. Remember the encounter or incident that happened to you.
3. Mentally say "Wha Hay Guru" as in the first step.
4. Visualize and reactivate the actual feelings of the encounter.
5. Again repeat "Wha Hay Guru" as in the first step.
6. Reverse the roles in the encounter you are remembering. Become the other person and experience that perspective.
7. Again repeat "Wha Hay Guru" as in the first step.
8. Forgive the other person and forgive yourself.
9. Repeat "Wha Hay Guru" as in the first step.
10. Let go of the incident and release it to the universe.

These are 10 steps to peace.

4. "Tershula Kriya": An Advanced Technique for Overcoming Phobias

Yogis were taught this technique in ancient times for "achieving self-mastery and learning to heal others at a distance" (Shannahoff-Khalsa, 2004), and it is one of the most advanced techniques in the system of Kundalini yoga. It was first taught by Yogi Bhajan in August 1989. "Tershula Kriya can make you into a perfect master" (Bhajan, personal communication). While it presents a challenge for learning, its benefits go far beyond the amelioration of phobias.

Sit in an easy pose (see Figures 4.1 and 4.2). Pull in your elbows next to the ribs, forearms extended in front of you, with the hands in front of the heart, right over left, palms up. The hands are approximately 10 degrees higher than the elbows. There is no bend in the wrists; the path from fingertips to elbows forms a straight line. The thumbs are extended out to the side of the hands; the fingertips and palms do not exactly line up but are slightly offset. The eyes are closed and gazing at the backs of the eyelids. For the inhale, pull back on the navel and inhale through the nostrils and hold. Mentally repeat the mantra

"Har Har Wha Hay Guru"

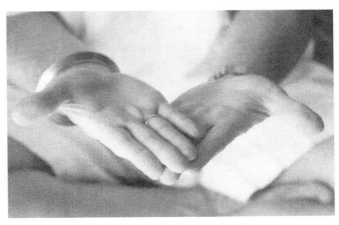

Figures 4.1 and 4.2.
Tershula Kriya

as long as you are able to retain the breath. While you are doing this, visualize your hands surrounded by white light. Exhale through the nostrils, and as you exhale, visualize lightning shooting out from your finger tips. When you have fully exhaled, pull in the mulbhand (tightening the muscles in the area of the rectum, sex organs, and navel), and hold for as long as you can, again mentally repeating the mantra "Har Har Wha Hay Guru." The maximum time for this technique is 62 minutes.

It has been suggested that this meditation be done in a cool room or at night when the temperature is cooler, because it stimulates the Kundalini directly and generates a great deal of heat in the body. The word *Tershula* relates to the thunderbolt of Shiva, the ultimate deliverer:

Tershula can heal everything. It is a self-healing process. This meditation is for the gunas. It brings the three nervous systems together. It also gives you the ability to heal at a distance, through your touch or through your projection. Many psychological disorders or imbalances in the personality can be cured through practice of this meditation. It is very helpful in getting rid of phobias and especially the "father phobia." (Bhajan & Khalsa, 1998; Shannahoff-Khalsa, 2004)

In addition, whenever a person with a phobia is confronted with the feared object, and he or she is not able to sit down and practice the entire protocol (or any part of the protocol, for that matter), he or she can easily employ Technique 9 in Chapter 3 for "Meeting Mental Challenges," called the *Vic-tor-y Breath*. This simple technique can be very useful if the person has confidence in its potency from past practice. Here the Vic-tor-y breath is like a band aid when you are on the run. It is not curative but it can give temporary help.

FIVE

Treating Panic Attacks and Panic Disorders

This chapter covers both panic attacks and panic disorders. It is important to note that the American Psychiatric Association's (2000) DSM IV-TR does not have a number code that is specific for only panic attacks. However, the criteria for panic attacks are listed immediately below. A diagnosis of Panic Disorder is usually given under "Panic Disorder without Agoraphobia" or "Panic Disorder with Agoraphobia," with the number codes of 300.01, and 300.21, resepctively. The criteria for each are also listed below, along with their important additional diagnostic features and associated features and disorders.

DSM DISORDERS

Diagnostic Criteria for Panic Attack (APA, 2000)

A discrete period of intense fear or discomfort, in which four (or more) of the following symptoms developed abruptly and reached a peak within 10 minutes:

1. palpitations, pounding heart, or accelerated heart rate
2. sweating
3. trembling or shaking
4. sensations of shortness of breath or smothering
5. feeling of choking

6. chest pain or discomfort
7. nausea or abdominal distress
8. feeling dizzy, unsteady, lightheaded, or faint
9. derealization (feelings of unreality) or depersonalization (being detached from oneself)
10. fear of losing control or going crazy
11. fear of dying
12. paresthesias (numbness or tingling sensations)
13. chills or hot flushes

Reprinted with permission from the *Diagnostic and Statistical Manual of Mental Disorders, Fourth Edition, Text Revision.* Copyright 2000 American Psychiatric Association.

Additional Features (APA, 2000)

The attack has a sudden onset and is often accompanied by a sense of imminent danger or impending doom and an urge to escape. The anxiety that is characteristic of a Panic Attack can be differentiated from generalized anxiety by its discrete, almost paroxysmal, nature and its typically greater severity. Attacks that meet all other criteria but that have fewer than 4 somatic or cognitive symptoms are referred to as limited-symptom attacks.

There are three characteristic types of Panic Attacks: unexpected (uncued), situationally bound (cued), and situationally predisposed. Each type of Panic Attack is defined by a different set of relationships between the onset of the attack and the presence or absence of situational triggers that can include cues that are either external (e.g., an individual with claustrophobia has an attack while in a elevator stuck between floors) or internal (e.g., catastrophic cognitions about the ramifications of heart palpitations). Unexpected (uncued) Panic Attacks are defined as those for which the individual does not associate onset with an internal or external situational trigger (i.e., the attack is perceived as occurring spontaneously "out of the blue"). Situationally bound (cued) Panic Attacks are defined as those that almost invariably occur immediately on exposure to, or in anticipation of, the situational cue or trigger (e.g., a person with Social Phobia having a Panic Attack upon entering into or thinking about a public speaking engagement). Situationally predisposed Panic Attacks are similar to situationally bound Panic Attacks but are not invariably associated with the cue and do not necessarily occur immediately after the exposure (e.g., attacks are more likely to occur while driving, but there are times when the individual drives and does not have a Panic Attack or times when the Panic Attack occurs after driving for a half hour).

Individuals seeking care for unexpected Panic Attacks will usually describe the fear as intense and report that they thought they were about to die, lose control, have a heart attack or stroke, or "go crazy." They also usually report an urgent desire to flee from wherever the attack is occurring. With recurrent unexpected Panic Attacks, over time the attacks typically become situationally bound or predisposed, although unexpected attacks may persist.

The occurrence of unexpected Panic Attacks is required for a diagnosis of Panic Disorder (with or without Agoraphobia). Situationally bound and situationally predisposed attacks are frequent in Panic Disorder but also occur in the context of other Anxiety Disorders and other mental disorders. For example, situationally bound Panic Attacks are experienced by a majority of individuals with Social Phobia (e.g., the person experiences a Panic Attack each and every time she must speak in public) and Specific Phobias (e.g., the person with a Specific Phobia of dogs experiences a Panic Attack each and every time he encounters a barking dog), whereas situationally predisposed Panic Attacks most typically occur in Generalized Anxiety Disorder (e.g., after watching television news programs that warn of an economic slowdown, the person becomes overwhelmed with worries about his finances and escalates into a Panic Attack) and Posttraumatic Stress Disorder (e.g., a rape victim sometimes experiences Panic Attacks when faced with reminders of the traumatic event, such as seeing a man who reminds her of the assailant).

In determining the differential diagnostic significance of a Panic Attack, it is important to consider the context in which the Panic Attack occurs. The distinction between unexpected Panic Attacks and both situationally bound and situationally predisposed Panic Attacks is critical, since recurrent unexpected attacks are required for a diagnosis of Panic Disorder (see Panic Disorder). Determining whether a history of Panic Attacks warrants a diagnosis of Panic Disorder is, however, complicated by the fact that an exclusive relationship does not always exist between the type of Panic Attack and the diagnosis. For instance, although a diagnosis of Panic Disorder definitionally requires that at least some of the Panic Attacks be unexpected, individuals with Panic Disorder frequently report also having situationally bound or situationally predisposed attacks. As such, careful consideration of the focus of anxiety associated with the Panic Attacks is also important in differential diagnosis.

To illustrate, consider a woman who has a Panic Attack prior to a public speaking engagement. If this woman indicates that the focus of her anxiety was that she might die from an impending heart attack, then assuming other diagnostic criteria are met, she may have Panic Disorder. If on the other hand, this woman identifies the focus of anxiety as not the Panic Attack itself, but of being embarrassed and humiliated, then she may be more likely to have Social Phobia.

Reprinted with permission from the *Diagnostic and Statistical Manual of Mental Disorders, Fourth Edition, Text Revision.* Copyright 2000 American Psychiatric Association.

Diagnostic Criteria for 300.01 Panic Disorder Without Agoraphobia (APA, 2000)

A. Both (1) and (2):
   1. recurrent unexpected Panic Attacks (see Criteria for Panic Attack)
   2. at least one of the attacks has been followed by 1 month (or more) of one (or more) of the following:
      a. persistent concern about having additional attacks
      b. worry about the implications of the attack or its consequences (e.g., losing control, having a heart attack, "going crazy")
      c. a significant change in behavior related to the attacks
B. Absence of Agoraphobia
C. The Panic Attacks are not due to the direct physiological effects of a substance (e.g., a drug of abuse, a medication) or a general medical condition (e.g., hyperthyroidism).
D. The Panic Attacks are not better accounted for by another mental disorder, such as Social Phobia (e.g., occurring on exposure to feared social situations), Specific Phobia (e.g., on exposure to a specific phobic situation), Obsessive–Compulsive Disorder (e.g., on exposure to dirt in someone with an obsession about contamination), Posttraumatic Stress Disorder (e.g., in response to stimuli associated with a severe stressor), or Separation Anxiety Disorder (e.g., in response to being away from home or close relatives).

Reprinted with permission from the *Diagnostic and Statistical Manual of Mental Disorders, Fourth Edition, Text Revision.* Copyright 2000 American Psychiatric Association.

Diagnostic Criteria for 300.21 Panic Disorder With Agoraphobia (APA, 2000)

A. Both (1) and (2):
    1. recurrent unexpected Panic Attacks (see Criteria for Panic Attack)
    2. at least one of the attacks has been followed by 1 month (or more) of one (or more) of the following:
        a. persistent concern about having additional attacks
        b. worry about the implications of the attack or its consequences (e.g., losing control, having a heart attack, "going crazy")
        c. a significant change in behavior related to the attacks
B. The presence of Agoraphobia (see Criteria for Agoraphobia below).
C. The Panic Attacks are not due to the direct physiological effects of a substance (e.g., a drug of abuse, a medication) or a general medical condition (e.g., hyperthyroidism).
D. The Panic Attacks are not better accounted for by another mental disorder, such as Social Phobia (e.g., occurring on exposure to feared social situations), Specific Phobia (e.g., on exposure to a specific phobic situation), Obsessive–Compulsive Disorder (e.g., on exposure to dirt in someone with an obsession about contamination), Posttraumatic Stress Disorder (e.g., in response to stimuli associated with a severe stressor), or Separation Anxiety Disorder (e.g., in response to being away from home or close relatives).

Diagnostic Criteria for Agoraphobia (APA, 2000)

A. Anxiety about being in places or situations from which escape might be difficult (or embarrassing) or in which help may not be available in the event of having an unexpected or situationally predisposed Panic Attack or panic-like symptoms. Agoraphobic fears typically involve characteristic clusters of situations that include being outside the home alone; being in a crowd or standing in a line; being on a bridge; and traveling in a bus, train, or automobile.
Note: Consider the diagnosis of Specific Phobia if the avoidance is limited to one or

only a few specific situations, or Social Phobia if the avoidance is limited to social situations.

B. The situations are avoided (e.g., travel is restricted) or else are endured with marked distress or with anxiety about having a Panic Attack or panic-like symptoms, or require the presence of a companion.

C. The anxiety or phobic avoidance is not better accounted for by another mental disorder, such as Social Phobia (e.g., avoidance limited to social situations because of fear of embarrassment), Specific Phobia (e.g., avoidance limited to a single situation like elevators), Obsessive–Compulsive Disorder (e.g., avoidance of dirt in someone with an obsession about contamination), Posttraumatic Stress Disorder (e.g., avoidance of stimuli associated with a severe stressor), or Separation Anxiety Disorder (e.g., avoidance of leaving home or relatives).

Reprinted with permission from the *Diagnostic and Statistical Manual of Mental Disorders, Fourth Edition, Text Revision.* Copyright 2000 American Psychiatric Association.

Additional Diagnostic Features (APA, 2000)

The frequency and severity of the Panic Attacks vary widely. For example, some individuals have moderately frequent attacks (e.g., once a week) that occur regularly for months at a time. Others report short bursts of more frequent attacks (e.g., daily for a week) separated by weeks or months without any attacks or with less frequent attacks (e.g., two each month) over many years. Limited-symptom attacks (i.e., attacks that are identical to "full" Panic Attacks except that the sudden fear or anxiety is accompanied by fewer than 4 of the 13 symptoms) are very common in individuals with Panic Disorder. Although the distinction between full Panic Attacks and limited-symptom attacks is somewhat arbitrary, full Panic Attacks are typically associated with greater morbidity (e.g., greater health care utilization, greater functional impairment, poorer quality of life). Most individuals who have limited-symptom attacks have had full Panic Attacks at some time during the course of the disorder.

Individuals with Panic Disorder display characteristic concerns or attributions about the implications or consequences of the Panic Attacks. Some fear that the attacks indicate the presence of an undiagnosed, life-threatening illness (e.g., cardiac disease, seizure disorder).

Despite repeated medical testing and reassurance, they may remain frightened and unconvinced that they do not have a life-threatening illness. Others fear that the Panic Attacks are an indication that they are "going crazy" or losing control or are emotionally weak. Some individuals with recurrent Panic Attacks significantly change their behavior (e.g., quit a job, avoid physical exertion) in response to the attacks, but deny either fear of having another attack or concerns about the consequences of their Panic Attacks. Concerns about the next attack, or its implications, are often associated with development of avoidant behavior that may meet criteria for Agoraphobia, in which case Panic Disorder With Agoraphobia is diagnosed.

Associated Features and Disorders (APA, 2000)

In addition to worry about Panic Attacks and their implications, many individuals with Panic Disorder also report constant or intermittent feelings of anxiety that are not focused on any specific situation or event. Others become excessively apprehensive about the outcome of routine activities and experiences, particularly those related to health or separation from loved ones. For example, individuals with Panic Disorder often anticipate a catastrophic outcome from a mild physical symptom or medication side effect (e.g., thinking that a headache indicates a brain tumor or a hypertensive crisis). Such individuals are also much less tolerant of medication side effects and generally need continued reassurance in order to take medication. In individuals whose Panic Disorder has not been treated or was misdiagnosed, the belief that they have an undetected life-threatening illness may lead to both chronic debilitating anxiety and excessive visits to health care facilities. This pattern can be both emotionally and financially disruptive.

In some cases, loss or disruption of important interpersonal relationships (e.g., leaving home to live on one's own, divorce) is associated with the onset or exacerbation of Panic Disorder. Demoralization is a common consequence, with many individuals becoming discouraged, ashamed, and unhappy about the difficulties of carrying out their normal routines. They often attribute this problem to a lack of "strength" or "character." This demoralization can become generalized to areas beyond specific panic-related problems. These individuals may frequently be absent from work or school for doctor and emergency-room visits, which can lead to unemployment or dropping out of school.

Reported rates for comorbid Major Depressive Disorder vary widely, ranging from 10%

to 65% in individuals with Panic Disorder. In approximately one-third of individuals with both disorders, the depression precedes the onset of Panic Disorder. In the remaining two-thirds, depression occurs coincident with or following the onset of Panic Disorder. A subset of individuals may treat their anxiety with alcohol or medications, and some of them may develop a Substance-Related Disorder as a consequence.

Comorbidity with other Anxiety Disorders is also common, especially in clinical settings and in individuals with more severe Agoraphobia. Social Phobia and Generalized Anxiety Disorder have been reported in 15%–30% of individuals with Panic Disorder, Specific Phobia in 2%–20%, and Obsessive–Compulsive Disorder in up to 10%. Although the literature suggests that Posttraumatic Stress Disorder has been reported in 2%–10% of those with Panic Disorder, some evidence suggests that rates may be much higher when posttraumatic symptoms are systematically queried. Separation Anxiety Disorder in childhood has been associated with this disorder. Comorbidity and symptom overlap with Hypochondriasis are common.

Reprinted with permission from the *Diagnostic and Statistical Manual of Mental Disorders, Fourth Edition, Text Revision.* Copyright 2000 American Psychiatric Association.

THE FOUR-PART KUNDALINI YOGA PROTOCOL FOR TREATING 300.01 PANIC DISORDER WITHOUT AGORAPHOBIA AND 300.21 PANIC DISORDER WITH AGORAPHOBIA*

The simplest and most immediate solution to minimize or stop a panic attack is to employ the Vic-tor-y Breath, described earlier in the 11-part protocol for OCD in Chapter 3. All of the other techniques in this chapter will also help to curb the attack. However, the most effective strategy that I have found employs the protocol below with technique number four that rebuilds what yogis call the *arcline*, also called the *halo*, and relates to functions of the brain involving the frontal lobes and other regions. When a person's arcline is strong, he or she is much more resilient to trauma. In images of saints we see the halo highlighted by

*Copyright © David Shannahoff-Khalsa, 2010. No portion of this protocol may be reproduced without the express written permission of the author.

brightness. The halo is, in effect, a shield for the psyche. The stronger and brighter the shield, the better. When the arcline is weak, whether through trauma, abuse, substance abuse, or other self-destructive habits, the mind can become subject to any kind of fear that can lead to a panic attack. The majority of people whom I have treated for panic attacks complain about the loss of their ability to drive on the freeway. I have found the following meditation technique to be very useful for people suffering from either frequent panic attacks or intermittent attacks that are induced only by well-defined circumstantial events. As always, we begin by tuning in . . .

1. Technique to Induce a Meditative State: "Tuning In"

Sit with a straight spine and with the feet flat on the floor if sitting in a chair (see Figure 2.1). Put the hands together at the chest in "prayer pose"—the palms are pressed together with 10–15 pounds of pressure (a mild to medium pressure, nothing too intense). The area where the sides of the thumbs touch rests on the sternum with the thumbs pointing up (along the sternum), and the fingers are together and point up and out at a 60-degree angle to the ground. The eyes are closed and focused on the third eye (imagine a sun rising on the horizon, or the equivalent of the point between the eyebrows at the origin of the nose). This mantra is chanted out loud in a 1½-breath cycle:

"Ong Namo Guru Dev Namo"

Inhale first through the nose and chant "Ong Namo" with an equal emphasis on the *Ong* and the *Namo*. Then immediately follow with a half-breath inhalation through the mouth and chant "Guru Dev Namo" with approximately equal emphasis on each word. (The *o* in *Ong* and *Namo* is a long-*o* sound; *Dev* sounds like *Dave*, with a long-*a* sound.)

- *Ong Namo* means I bow with reverence to that infinite energy that is the basis of all creation.
- *Guru* means teacher or wisdom.
- *Dev* means divine or of God.

The practitioner should focus on the experience of the vibrations these sounds create on the upper palate and throughout the cranium, while letting the mind be carried by the sounds into a new and pleasant mental space. This sequence should be repeated a minimum of three times. We employed it in our group about 10–12 times. This technique helps to create a meditative state of mind and is *always* used as a precursor to the other techniques.

2. Ganesha Meditation for Focus and Clarity

Sit with a straight spine, the eyes closed (see Figure 2.2). The left thumb and little finger are sticking out from the hand. The other fingers are curled into a fist with fingertips on the moon mound (the root of the thumb area that extends down to the wrist). The left hand and elbow are parallel to the floor, with the pad of the tip of the left thumb pressing on the curved notch of the nose between the eyes. The little finger is sticking out. With right hand and elbow parallel to the floor, grasp the left little finger with the right hand and close the right hand into a fist around it, so that both hands now extend straight out from your head. Push the notch with the tip of the left thumb to the extent that you feel some soreness as you breathe long and deep. (This soreness lessens with continued practice.) Do this for no longer than 3 minutes. To finish, inhale as you maintain the posture with eyes closed. Push a little more and pull the naval point in by tightening the abdominal muscles for 10 seconds, then exhale. Repeat one more time.

3. Technique for Managing Fears

Sit with a straight spine (see Figure 3.2). Close the eyes. Place the left hand with the four fingertips and thumb grouped and pressed very lightly into the navel point, like a plug. Place the fingertips of the right hand with the four fingers pointing left over the third eye point (on the forehead just above the root of the nose), as if feeling your temperature. Play the audio musical tape of Chattra Chakkra Varti (Kaur, 2006; K. Singh, 2006) for 3 minutes while imaging and assessing all your fears and consciously relating to the mental experience of each fear. This technique helps to manage acute states of fear and eliminate fearful images and negative emotions that have developed due to fearful experiences. The effect is that the negative emotions related to specific fears are replaced with positive emotions, thereby slowly creating a new and different mental association with the stimulus. Only the musical tape recommended here will actually produce this unique effect.

4. A Meditation to Rebuild the Arcline to Help Treat Panic Attacks and Panic Disorders

This technique has also been referred to as the *eight-stroke breath meditation* and has been taught as a therapy to strengthen and rebuild the arcline (Bhajan, 1981). Sit with a straight spine (see Figure 5.1). Extend the elbows out toward the sides and place the hands a few inches in front of the heart-center area of the chest. The two palms are about 4 inches apart,

Figure 5.1.
Rebuilding the Arcline

parallel to the ground. The left hand is on top and faces downward, and the right hand is directly underneath the left hand, with the right palm facing up. The eyes are opened and focused on the tip of the nose (the end you cannot see). Inhale only through the nose in eight rapid equal strokes, and exhale only through the nose in eight rapid equal strokes. This means that the inhalation–exhalation cycle is broken into 16 parts, eight equal parts for the inhale and eight for the exhale. To help clarify this procedure, imagine taking in about one-eighth volume of the lungs for each short inhalation, consecutively adding one more eighth or expelling one more eighth with each inhalation or exhalation, respectively. Try to start with small volumes so that you can reach eight strokes in and eight strokes out without filling the lungs prematurely. There is no pause once the inhale or exhale is complete. Simply continue breathing eight strokes in and eight strokes out where each complete breath cycle takes about 10 seconds.

When breathing, do not count the parts but mentally employ the use of the mantra

"Sa Ta Na Ma"

twice for the inhale and twice for the exhale. That is, for each segment of the breath, mentally hear with your "inner ear" one of the four sounds in sequence: for example, *Sa* with the first brief intake of air, *Ta* with the second, and so on, so that you go through two cycles of the mantra for the inhale and two cycles for the exhale (all short-*a* sounds). The time for this technique is only 11 minutes, no more or less.

When finished, inhale deeply and hold the breath for 35 seconds while maintaining the hand posture, then exhale and relax. This technique can be practiced more than once a day and is best practiced everyday until the panic attacks have subsided. Most of my patients completely overcome their panic attacks within 3–5 weeks with daily practice. Some patients have also included Gan Puttee Kriya (see Chapter 2). Usually the more techniques the patient includes, the quicker the results.

SIX

Treating Acute Stress Disorder

The condition of acute stress disorder (ASD) is very similar to posttraumatic stress disorder (PTSD) except that ASD lasts for at least 2 days and a maximum of 4 weeks, whereas PTSD lasts longer than the 4 weeks, indeed, often for a lifetime. The approach to treating ASD therefore requires immediate or near-immediate therapy to help prevent its evolution into PTSD. Below is the American Psychiatric Association's (2000) description of the diagnostic criteria and the diagnostic and associated features and disorders, followed by the Kundalini yoga meditation protocol for treatment.

DSM DISORDERS

Diagnostic Criteria for 308.3 Acute Stress Disorder (APA, 2000)

A. The person has been exposed to a traumatic event in which both of the following were present:
   1. the person experienced, witnessed, or was confronted with an event or events that involved actual or threatened death or serious injury, or a threat to the physical integrity of self or others
   2. the person's response involved intense fear, helplessness, or horror
B. Either while experiencing or after experiencing the distressing event, the individual has three (or more) of the following dissociative symptoms:

1. a subjective sense of numbing, detachment, or absence of emotional responsiveness
2. a reduction in awareness of his or her surroundings (e.g., "being in a daze")
3. derealization
4. depersonalization
5. dissociative amnesia (i.e., inability to recall an important aspect of the trauma)

C. The traumatic event is persistently reexperienced in at least one of the following ways: recurrent images, thoughts, dreams, illusions, flashback episodes, or a sense of reliving the experience; or distress on exposure to reminders of the traumatic event.

D. Marked avoidance of stimuli that arouse recollections of the trauma (e.g., thoughts, feelings, conversations, activities, places, people).

E. Marked symptoms of anxiety or increased arousal (e.g., difficulty sleeping, irritability, poor concentration, hypervigilance, exaggerated startle response, motor restlessness).

F. The disturbance causes clinically significant distress or impairment in social, occupational, or other important areas of functioning or impairs the individual's ability to pursue some necessary task, such as obtaining necessary assistance or mobilizing personal resources by telling family members about the traumatic experience.

G. The disturbance lasts for a minimum of 2 days and a maximum of 4 weeks and and occurs within 4 weeks of the traumatic event.

H. The disturbance is not due to the direct physiological effects of a substance (e.g., a drug of abuse, a medication) or a general medical condition, is not better accounted for by Brief Psychotic Disorder, and is not merely an exacerbation of a preexisting Axis I or Axis II disorder.

Reprinted with permission from the *Diagnostic and Statistical Manual of Mental Disorders, Fourth Edition, Text Revision.* Copyright 2000 American Psychiatric Association.

Diagnostic Features (APA, 2000)

As a response to the traumatic event, the individual develops dissociative symptoms. Individuals with Acute Stress Disorder may have a decrease in emotional responsiveness, often finding it difficult or impossible to experience pleasure in previously enjoyable activities, and frequently feel guilty about pursuing usual life tasks. They may experience difficulty concentrating, feel detached from their bodies, experience the world as unreal or dreamlike, or have increasing difficulty recalling specific details of the traumatic event (dissociative amnesia). In addition, at least one symptom from each of the symptom clusters required for Posttraumatic Stress Disorder is present. First, the traumatic event is persistently reexperienced (e.g., recurrent recollections, images, thoughts, dreams, illusions, flashback episodes, a sense of reliving the event, or distress on exposure to reminders of the event). Second, reminders of the trauma (e.g., places, people, activities) are avoided. Finally, hyperarousal in response to stimuli reminiscent of the trauma is present (e.g., difficulty sleeping, irritability, poor concentration, hypervigilance, an exaggerated startle response, and motor restlessness).

Associated Features and Disorders

Symptoms of despair and hopelessness may be experienced in Acute Stress Disorder and may be sufficiently severe and persistent to meet criteria for a Major Depressive Episode, in which case an additional diagnosis of Major Depressive Disorder may be warranted. If the trauma led to another's death or to serious injury, survivors may feel guilt about having remained intact or about not providing enough help to others. Individuals with this disorder often perceive themselves to have greater responsibility for the consequences of the trauma than is warranted. Problems may result from the individual's neglect of basic health and safety needs associated with the aftermath of the trauma. Individuals with this disorder are at increased risk for the development of Posttraumatic Stress Disorder. Rates of Posttraumatic Stress Disorder of approximately 80% have been reported for motor vehicle crash survivors and victims of violent crime whose response to the trauma initially met criteria for Acute Stress Disorder. Impulsive and risk-taking behavior may occur after the trauma.

THE SIX-PART KUNDALINI YOGA MEDITATION PROTOCOL FOR TREATING ACUTE STRESS DISORDER*

1. Technique to Induce a Meditative State: "Tuning In"

Sit with a straight spine and with the feet flat on the floor if sitting in a chair (see Figure 2.1). Put the hands together at the chest in "prayer pose"—the palms are pressed together with 10–15 pounds of pressure (a mild to medium pressure, nothing too intense). The area where the sides of the thumbs touch rests on the sternum with the thumbs pointing up (along the sternum), and the fingers are together and point up and out at a 60-degree angle to the ground. The eyes are closed and focused on the third eye (imagine a sun rising on the horizon, or the equivalent of the point between the eyebrows at the origin of the nose). This mantra is chanted out loud in a 1½-breath cycle:

"Ong Namo Guru Dev Namo"

Inhale first through the nose and chant "Ong Namo" with an equal emphasis on the *Ong* and the *Namo*. Then immediately follow with a half-breath inhalation through the mouth and chant "Guru Dev Namo" with approximately equal emphasis on each word. (The *o* in *Ong* and *Namo* is a long-*o* sound; *Dev* sounds like *Dave*, with a long-*a* sound.)

- *Ong Namo* means I bow with reverence to that infinite energy that is the basis of all creation.
- *Guru* means teacher or wisdom.
- *Dev* means divine or of God.

The practitioner should focus on the experience of the vibrations these sounds create on the upper palate and throughout the cranium, while letting the mind be carried by the sounds into a new and pleasant mental space. This sequence should be repeated a minimum of three times. We employed it in our group about 10–12 times. This technique helps to create a meditative state of mind and is *always* used as a precursor to the other techniques.

2. Spine-Flexing Technique for Vitality

This technique can be practiced while sitting either in a chair or on the floor in a cross-legged position. If you are in a chair, hold the knees with both hands for support and leverage. If you are sitting cross-legged, grasp the ankles in front with both hands. Begin by pulling the chest up and slightly forward, inhaling deeply through the nose at the same time. Then exhale as you relax the spine down into a slouching position. Keep the head up straight, as if you were looking forward, without allowing it to move much while flexing the spine. This position will help prevent a whip effect in the cervical vertebrae. Breathe only through the nose for both the inhalation and exhalation. The eyes are closed, as if you were looking at a central point on the horizon, the third eye. Your mental focus is kept on the sound of the breath while listening to the fluid movement of the inhalation and exhalation. Begin the technique slowly while loosening up the spine. Eventually, a very rapid movement can be achieved with practice, reaching a rate of one to two times per second for the entire movement. A few minutes are adequate in the beginning. Later, there is no upper time limit. Food should be avoided just prior to this exercise. Be careful to flex the spine *slowly* in the beginning. Relax for 1 minute when finished.

3. Shoulder-Shrug Technique for Vitality

While keeping the spine straight, rest the hands on the knees if sitting in a cross-legged position or with hands on the thighs if sitting in a chair. Inhale and raise the shoulders toward the ears, then exhale, relaxing them down. Again, breathe only through the nose. Keep eyes closed and focused on the third eye. Mentally focus on the sound of the inhalation and exhalation. Continue this action rapidly, building to three times per second for a maximum of 2 minutes. *Note*: This technique should not be practiced by individuals who are hyperactive.

4. Ganesha Meditation for Focus and Clarity

Sit with a straight spine, the eyes closed (see Figure 2.2). The left thumb and little finger are sticking out from the hand. The other fingers are curled into a fist with fingertips on the moon mound (the root of the thumb area that extends down to the wrist). The left hand and elbow are parallel to the floor, with the pad of the tip of the left thumb pressing on the curved notch of the nose between the eyes. The little finger is sticking out. With right hand

and elbow parallel to the floor, grasp the left little finger with the right hand and close the right hand into a fist around it, so that both hands now extend straight out from your head. Push the notch with the tip of the left thumb to the extent that you feel some soreness as you breathe long and deep. (This soreness lessens with continued practice.) Do this for no longer than 3 minutes. To finish, inhale as you maintain the posture with eyes closed. Push a little more and pull the naval point in by tightening the abdominal muscles for 10 seconds, then exhale. Repeat one more time.

5. Gan Puttee Kriya: A Technique to Eliminate the Negativity from the Past, the Present, and the Future

Gan Puttee Kriya has also been called the "Kriya to Make the Impossible Possible." Yogi Bhajan originally taught this meditation technique on November 2, 1988 (Bhajan, 1998). Yogis disovered this technique as a tool for eliminating the blocks that form in the subconscious mind and stifle growth, frequently leading to destructive, neurotic, and self-defeating patterns of mental activity.

Sit with a straight spine, either on the floor or in a chair. The backs of your hands are resting on your knees with the palms facing upward. The eyes are nine-tenths closed (one-tenth open, but looking straight ahead into the darkness, not the light below), focused on the third eye. Chant from your heart in a natural, relaxed manner, or chant in a steady, relaxed monotone:

"Sa Ta Na Ma Ra Ma Da Sa Sa Say So Hung"

More specifically:

Chant out loud the sound "Sa" (the *a* sounds like *ahhh*), and touch your thumb tips and index fingertips together quickly and simultaneously with about 2 pounds of pressure.
Chant "Ta" and touch the thumb tips to the middle fingertips.
Chant "Na" and touch the thumb tips to the ring fingertips.
Chant "Ma" and touch the thumb tips to the little fingertips.
Chant "Ra" and touch your thumb tips and index fingertips.
Chant "Ma" and touch the thumb tips to the middle fingertips.

Chant "Da" and touch the thumb tips to the ring fingertips.
Chant "Sa" and touch the thumb tips to the little fingertips.
Chant "Sa" and touch your thumb tips and index fingertips.
Chant "Say" (sounds like the word *say* with a long-*a*) and touch the thumb tips to the middle-finger tips. Chant "So" and touch the thumb tips to the ring-finger tips.
Chant "Hung" and touch the thumb tips to the little-finger tips.

Chant at a rate of one sound per second. The thumb tip and fingertips touch with a very light (2–3 pounds) pressure with each connection. This light touch helps to consolidate the circuit created by each thumb–finger link. Start with 11 minutes and slowly work up to 31 minutes of practice. To finish, remain in the sitting posture and inhale, holding the breath for 20–30 seconds while you shake and move every part of your body (like a dog shaking off water). Exhale and repeat this shaking motion two more times to circulate the energy and to break the pattern of tapping the thumb and fingertips, which affects the brain. Then immediately proceed without rest to technique 6, "When You Do Not Know What to Do."

Each sound used in this meditation is unique, and they all have a powerful effect on both the conscious and subconscious minds:

"Sa" gives the mind the ability to expand to the infinite.
"Ta" gives the mind the ability to experience the totality of life.
"Na" gives the mind the ability to conquer death.
"Ma" gives the mind the ability to resurrect.
"Ra" gives the mind the ability to expand in radiance (this sound purifies and energizes).
"Da" gives the mind the ability to establish security on the earth plane, providing a ground for action.
"Say" gives the totality of experience.
"So" is the personal sense of identity.
"Hung" is the infinite as a vibrating and real force. Together, *So Hung* means "I am Thou."

The unique qualities of this 12-syllable mantra help cleanse and restructure the subconscious mind and help heal the conscious mind to ultimately experience the *super*conscious mind. All the blocks that result from traumatic or troubling events are eliminated over time with the practice of Gan Puttee Kriya. When doing the whole protocol, 11 minutes for this technique is often adequate; however, 31 minutes is even better, and the maximum time: *Do not go beyond 31 minutes*. When finished proceed immediately to technique 6.

6. *When You Do Not Know What to Do*

Sit straight and rest the back of one hand in the palm of the other, with the thumbs crossing each other in one palm (see Figure 2.3). If the right hand rests in the palm of the left hand, the left thumb rests in the right palm and the right thumb then crosses over the back of the left thumb. Either this hand orientation is acceptable or the reverse, with the left hand resting in the palm of the right hand, and then the right thumb is in the left palm and covered by the left thumb.

The hands are placed at heart-center level, about 2 inches *in front of* the chest (the hands *do not* touch the chest), and the elbows are resting against the ribs. The eyes are open but focused on the tip of the nose (which you cannot actually see). The breathing pattern has four parts that repeat in sequence:

1. Inhale and exhale slowly through the nose only.
2. Inhale through the mouth slowly with the lips puckered as if to kiss or make a whistle. After the inhalation, relax the lips and exhale through the mouth slowly.
3. Inhale through the nose and exhale through the mouth slowly.
4. Inhale through the puckered lips and exhale through the nose. Breathe slowly and deeply.

Continue this four-part cycle for 11–31 minutes. If Gan Puttee Kriya is practiced without following with Technique 6, then the very last part of Gan Puttee Kriya requires a 1-minute focus with the eyes open and gazing on the tip of the nose, with slow, deep breathing after the breath holding and body shaking. When practiced here, followed immediately with "When You Do Not Know What to Do," this step can be eliminated, since this breath technique employs the use of the eyes opened and focused on the tip of the nose.

Note, if desired, the multipart protocol for PTSD in the next chapter could also be employed to treat ASD.

SEVEN

Treating Posttraumatic Stress Disorder

First we consider the American Psychiatric Association's (2000) diagnostic criteria, diagnostic features, and associated features and disorders for PTSD. This is followed by the eight-part Kundalini yoga meditation protocol specific for PTSD, which is uniquely effective for treating war combat veterans, victims of war and calamity, rape and torture victims, and others suffering from PTSD.

DSM DISORDER

Diagnostic Criteria for 309.81 Posttraumatic Stress Disorder (APA, 2000)

A. The person has been exposed to a traumatic event in which both of the following were present:
   1. the person experienced, witnessed, or was confronted with an event or events that involved actual or threatened death or serious injury, or a threat to the physical integrity of self or others
   2. the person's response involved intense fear, helplessness, or horror. **Note:** In children, this may be expressed instead by disorganized or agitated behavior
B. The traumatic event is persistently reexperienced in one (or more) of the following ways:
   1. recurrent and intrusive distressing recollections of the event, including images, thoughts, or perceptions. **Note:** In young children, repetitive play may occur in which themes or aspects of the trauma are expressed.

2. recurrent distressing dreams of the event. **Note:** In children, there may be frightening dreams without recognizable content.
3. acting or feeling as if the traumatic event were recurring (includes a sense of reliving the experience, illusions, hallucinations, and dissociative flashback episodes, including those that occur on awakening or when intoxicated). **Note:** In young children, trauma-specific reenactment may occur.
4. intense psychological distress at exposure to internal or external cues that symbolize or resemble an aspect of the traumatic event
5. physiological reactivity on exposure to internal or external cures that symbolize or resemble an aspect of the traumatic event

C. Persistent avoidance of stimuli associated with the trauma and numbing of general responsiveness (not present before the trauma), as indicated by three (or more) of the following:
1. efforts to avoid thoughts, feelings, or conversations associated with the trauma
2. efforts to avoid activities, places, or people that arouse recollections of the trauma
3. inability to recall an important aspect of the trauma
4. markedly diminished interest or participation in significant activities
5. feeling of detachment or estrangement from others
6. restricted range of affect (e.g., unable to have loving feelings)
7. sense of a foreshortened future (e.g., does not expect to have a career, marriage, children, or a normal life span)

D. Persistent symptoms of increased arousal (not present before the trauma), as indicated by two (or more) of the following:
1. difficulty falling or staying asleep
2. irritability or outbursts of anger
3. difficulty concentrating
4. hypervigilance
5. exaggerated startle response

E. Duration of the disturbance (symptoms in Criteria B, C, and D) is more than 1 month.

F. The disturbance causes clinically significant distress or impairment in social, occupational, or other important areas of functioning.

Additional Diagnostic Features (APA, 2000)

Traumatic events that are experienced directly include, but are not limited to, military combat, violent personal assault (sexual assault, physical attack, robbery, mugging), being kidnapped, being taken hostage, terrorist attack, torture, incarceration as a prisoner of war or in a concentration camp, natural or manmade disasters, severe automobile accidents, or being diagnosed with a life-threatening illness. For children, sexually traumatic events may include developmentally inappropriate sexual experiences without threatened or actual violence or injury. Witnessed events include, but are not limited to, observing the serious injury or unnatural death of another person due to violent assault, accident, war, or disaster or unexpectedly witnessing a dead body or body parts. Events experienced by others that are learned about include, but are not limited to, violent personal assault, serious accident, or serious injury experienced by a family member or a close friend; learning about the sudden, unexpected death of a family member or a close friend; or learning that one's child has a life-threatening disease. The disorder may be especially severe or long lasting when the stressor is of human design (e.g., torture, rape). The likelihood of developing this disorder may increase as the intensity of and physical proximity to the stressor increase.

The traumatic event can be reexperienced in various ways. Commonly the person has recurrent and intrusive recollections of the event (Criterion B1) or recurrent distressing dreams during which the event can be replayed or otherwise represented (Criterion B2). In rare instances, the person experiences dissociative states that last from a few seconds to several hours, or even days, during which components of the event are relived and the person behaves as though experiencing the event at that moment (Criterion B3). These episodes, often referred to as "flashbacks," are typically brief but can be associated with prolonged distress and heightened arousal. Intense psychological distress (Criterion B4) or physiological reactivity (Criterion B5) often occurs when the person is exposed to triggering events that resemble or symbolize an aspect of the traumatic event (e.g., anniversaries of the traumatic event; cold, snowy weather or uniformed guards for survivors of death camps in cold climates; hot, humid weather for combat veterans of the South Pacific; entering any elevator for a woman who was raped in an elevator).

Stimuli associated with the trauma are persistently avoided. The person commonly makes deliberate efforts to avoid thoughts, feelings, or conversations about the traumatic event (Criterion C1) and to avoid activities, situations, or people who arouse recollections of it (Criterion C2). This avoidance of reminders may include amnesia for an important aspect of the traumatic event (Criterion C3). Diminished responsiveness to the external world, referred to as "psychic numbing" or "emotional anesthesia," usually begins soon after the traumatic event. The individual may complain of having markedly diminished interest or participation in previously enjoyed activities (Criterion C4), of feeling detached or estranged from other people (Criterion C5), or of having markedly reduced ability to feel emotions (especially those associated with intimacy, tenderness, and sexuality) (Criterion C6). The individual may have a sense of a foreshortened future (e.g., not expecting to have a career, marriage, children, or a normal life span) (Criterion C7).

The individual has persistent symptoms of anxiety or increased arousal that were not present before the trauma. These symptoms may include difficulty falling or staying asleep that may be due to recurrent nightmares during which the traumatic event is relived (Criterion D1), hypervigilance (Criterion D4), and exaggerated startle response (Criterion D5). Some individuals report irritability or outbursts of anger (Criterion D2) or difficulty concentrating or completing tasks (Criterion D3).

Associated Features and Disorders (APA, 2000)

Individuals with Posttraumatic Stress Disorder may describe painful guilt feelings about surviving when others did not survive or about the things they had to do to survive. Avoidance patterns may interfere with interpersonal relationships and lead to marital conflict, divorce, or loss of job. Auditory hallucinations and paranoid ideation can be present in some severe and chronic cases. The following associated constellation of symptoms may occur and are more commonly seen in association with an interpersonal stressor (e.g., childhood sexual or physical abuse, domestic battering): impaired affect modulation; self-destructive and impulsive behavior; dissociative symptoms; somatic complaints; feelings of ineffectiveness, shame, despair, or hopelessness; feeling permanently damaged; a loss of previously sustained beliefs; hostility; social withdrawal; feeling constantly threatened; impaired relationships with others; or a change from the individual's previous personality characteristics.

Posttraumatic Stress Disorder is associated with increased rates of Major Depressive Disorder, Substance-Related Disorders, Panic Disorder, Agoraphobia, Obsessive–Compulsive Disorder, Generalized Anxiety Disorder, Social Phobia, Specific Phobia, and Bipolar

Disorder. These disorders can either precede, follow, or emerge concurrently with the onset of Posttraumatic Stress Disorder.

Reprinted with permission from the *Diagnostic and Statistical Manual of Mental Disorders, Fourth Edition, Text Revision*. Copyright 2000 American Psychiatric Association.

THE EIGHT-PART KUNDALINI YOGA MEDITATION PROTOCOL FOR POSTTRAUMATIC STRESS DISORDER*

1. Technique to Induce a Meditative State: "Tuning In"

Sit with a straight spine and with the feet flat on the floor if sitting in a chair (see Figure 2.1). Put the hands together at the chest in "prayer pose"—the palms are pressed together with 10–15 pounds of pressure (a mild to medium pressure, nothing too intense). The area where the sides of the thumbs touch rests on the sternum with the thumbs pointing up (along the sternum), and the fingers are together and point up and out at a 60-degree angle to the ground. The eyes are closed and focused on the third eye (imagine a sun rising on the horizon, or the equivalent of the point between the eyebrows at the origin of the nose). This mantra is chanted out loud in a 1½-breath cycle:

"Ong Namo Guru Dev Namo"

Inhale first through the nose and chant "Ong Namo" with an equal emphasis on the *Ong* and the *Namo*. Then immediately follow with a half-breath inhalation through the mouth and chant "Guru Dev Namo" with approximately equal emphasis on each word. (The *o* in *Ong* and *Namo* is a long-*o* sound; *Dev* sounds like *Dave*, with a long-*a* sound.)

- *Ong Namo* means I bow with reverence to that infinite energy that is the basis of all creation.

*Copyright © David Shannahoff-Khalsa, 2005. No portion of this protocol may be reproduced without the express written permission of the author.

- *Guru* means teacher or wisdom.
- *Dev* means divine or of God.

The practitioner should focus on the experience of the vibrations these sounds create on the upper palate and throughout the cranium, while letting the mind be carried by the sounds into a new and pleasant mental space. This sequence should be repeated a minimum of three times. We employed it in our group about 10–12 times. This technique helps to create a meditative state of mind and is *always* used as a precursor to the other techniques.

2. Gan Puttee Kriya: A Technique to Eliminate the Negativity from the Past, the Present, and the Future

Gan Puttee Kriya has also been called the "Kriya to Make the Impossible Possible." Yogi Bhajan originally taught this meditation technique on November 2, 1988 (Bhajan, 1998). Yogis disovered this technique as a tool for eliminating the blocks that form in the subconscious mind and stifle growth, frequently leading to destructive, neurotic, and self-defeating patterns of mental activity.

Sit with a straight spine, either on the floor or in a chair. The backs of your hands are resting on your knees with the palms facing upward. The eyes are nine-tenths closed (one-tenth open, but looking straight ahead into the darkness, not the light below), focused on the third eye. Chant from your heart in a natural, relaxed manner, or chant in a steady, relaxed monotone

"Sa Ta Na Ma Ra Ma Da Sa Sa Say So Hung"

More specifically:

Chant out loud the sound "Sa" (the *a* sounds like *ahhh*), and touch your thumb tips and index fingertips together quickly and simultaneously with about 2 pounds of pressure.
Chant "Ta" and touch the thumb tips to the middle fingertips.
Chant "Na" and touch the thumb tips to the ring fingertips.
Chant "Ma" and touch the thumb tips to the little fingertips.
Chant "Ra" and touch your thumb tips and index fingertips.

Chant "Ma" and touch the thumb tips to the middle fingertips.
Chant "Da" and touch the thumb tips to the ring fingertips.
Chant "Sa" and touch the thumb tips to the little fingertips.
Chant "Sa" and touch your thumb tips and index fingertips.
Chant "Say" (sounds like the word *say* with a long-*a*) and touch the thumb tips to the middle-finger tips. Chant "So" and touch the thumb tips to the ring-finger tips.
Chant "Hung" and touch the thumb tips to the little-finger tips.

Chant at a rate of one sound per second. The thumb tip and fingertips touch with a very light (2–3 pounds) pressure with each connection. This light touch helps to consolidate the circuit created by each thumb–finger link. Start with 11 minutes and slowly work up to 31 minutes of practice. To finish, remain in the sitting posture and inhale, holding the breath for 20–30 seconds while you shake and move every part of your body (like a dog shaking off water). Exhale and repeat this shaking motion two more times to circulate the energy and to break the pattern of tapping the thumb and fingertips, which affects the brain. Then immediately proceed without rest to Technique 6, "When You Do Not Know What to Do."

Each sound used in this meditation is unique, and they all have a powerful effect on both the conscious and subconscious minds:

"Sa" gives the mind the ability to expand to the infinite.
"Ta" gives the mind the ability to experience the totality of life.
"Na" gives the mind the ability to conquer death.
"Ma" gives the mind the ability to resurrect.
"Ra" gives the mind the ability to expand in radiance (this sound purifies and energizes).
"Da" gives the mind the ability to establish security on the earth plane, providing a ground for action.
"Say" gives the totality of experience.
"So" is the personal sense of identity.
"Hung" is the infinite as a vibrating and real force. Together, *So Hung* means "I am Thou."

The unique qualities of this 12-syllable mantra help cleanse and restructure the subconscious mind and help heal the conscious mind to ultimately experience the *super*conscious mind. All the blocks that result from traumatic or troubling events are eliminated over time with the practice of Gan Puttee Kriya. When doing the whole protocol, 11 minutes for this technique is often adequate; however, 31 minutes is even better, and the maximum time: *Do not go beyond 31 minutes*. When finished proceed immediately to technique 3.

3. When You Do Not Know What to Do

Sit straight and rest the back of one hand in the palm of the other, with the thumbs crossing each other in one palm (see Figure 2.3). If the right hand rests in the palm of the left hand, the left thumb rests in the right palm and the right thumb then crosses over the back of the left thumb. Either this hand orientation is acceptable or the reverse, with the left hand resting in the palm of the right hand, and then the right thumb is in the left palm and covered by the left thumb.

The hands are placed at heart-center level, about 2 inches *in front of* the chest (the hands *do not* touch the chest), and the elbows are resting against the ribs. The eyes are open but focused on the tip of the nose (which you cannot actually see). The breathing pattern has four parts that repeat in sequence:

1. Inhale and exhale slowly through the nose only.
2. Inhale through the mouth slowly with the lips puckered as if to kiss or make a whistle. After the inhalation, relax the lips and exhale through the mouth slowly.
3. Inhale through the nose and exhale through the mouth slowly.
4. Inhale through the puckered lips and exhale through the nose. Breathe slowly and deeply.

Continue this cycle for 8 minutes and then take a 2- to 3-minute rest and then proceed to technique 4. The maximum time allowed for this technique is 31 minutes.

4. Meditation to Balance the Jupiter and Saturn Energies: A Technique for Treating Depression, Focusing the Mind, and Eliminating Self-Destructive Behavior

Sit with a straight spine either in a chair or on the floor (see Figure 7.1). The hands are facing forward with the ends of the Jupiter (index) and Saturn (middle) fingers pointing straight up near the sides of the body at the level of the chin. The elbows are relaxed down

Figure 7.1.
Meditation to Balance the Jupiter and Saturn Energies:
A Technique to Reduce Depression and Self-Destructive Behavior

by the sides and the hands are near the shoulders. Close the ring and little fingers down into the palm, using the thumbs, and keep them there against the palm during the meditation. The Jupiter (index) finger and the Saturn (middle) finger are spread open in a *V* shape (or closed). The eyes are closed.

For 8 minutes open and close the Jupiter and Saturn fingers about once or twice per second. Make sure the two fingers open completely and close completely during the exercise. Simultaneously imagine the planets of Jupiter and Saturn coming together in front of you and then again going apart in synch with the finger movement—the planets should appear to go back and forth along a straight line, in and out to the sides in front of you. It does not matter whether you visualize Jupiter or Saturn on the left or right side.

In the beginning, the visualization part may be difficult to do, but this should not slow down the pace of the fingers, which play a more important role here. After 8 minutes, while continuing the same exercise, begin to inhale and exhale through the nose only with this movement: Inhale as the fingers open, exhale as the fingers close. Continue visualizing the planets moving in synchrony with the fingers for 2 additional minutes. Note during the first 8 minutes the breath is not consciously regulated.

Then, for the last minute, spread the two fingers and hold them wide apart (now they do not open and close, they remain in the fixed *V* shape), keeping them very stiff (which requires considerable effort) while also keeping the mouth in an O, or ring, shape. Breathe in and out of the mouth using only the diaphragm (not the wall of the upper chest) with a rate of one to three breaths per second. After 1 minute, inhale, hold the breath in, and tense every muscle tightly (including the hands and fingers, with the *V* shape kept rigid, arms, back, stomach) in the body for 10 seconds. Exhale and repeat two more times for 10 seconds. Then relax.

The effects of this meditation help the mind to become very focused and clear and the brain becomes very energized (few other 11-minute techniques compare). This technique is said to help eliminate depression. The meditation is used to coordinate and balance the Jupiter and Saturn energies, and to reduce the possibility of self-destructive and aggressive behavior. In addition, when the Jupiter and Saturn energies (functional brain areas related to the index finger that stimulates the brain area related to awareness and middle finger that stimulates the brain area related to patience and temperament) are integrated, individuals are said to be able to overcome difficult challenges more easily. (*Note*: If a person feels dizzy during the meditation, he or she should stop and try it again on another occasion.)

5. Ganesha Meditation for Focus and Clarity

Sit with a straight spine, the eyes closed (see Figure 2.2). The left thumb and little finger are sticking out from the hand. The other fingers are curled into a fist with fingertips on the moon mound (the root of the thumb area that extends down to the wrist). The left hand and elbow are parallel to the floor, with the pad of the tip of the left thumb pressing on the curved notch of the nose between the eyes. The little finger is sticking out. With right hand and elbow parallel to the floor, grasp the left little finger with the right hand and close the right hand into a fist around it, so that both hands now extend straight out from your head. Push the notch with the tip of the left thumb to the extent that you feel some soreness as you breathe long and deep. (This soreness lessens with continued practice.) Do this for no longer than 3 minutes. To finish, inhale as you maintain the posture with eyes closed. Push a little more and pull the naval point in by tightening the abdominal muscles for 10 seconds, then exhale. Repeat one more time for 10 seconds. Immediately proceed to the next technique.

6. Meditation for Deep Relaxation

This technique was first taught by Yogi Bhajan on July 2, 1998, for improving health. Bhajan claimed: "There is no more powerful relaxation than this. When you are very nervous, and you have too many thoughts, and you are being ground up by everything, do this for 3 minutes. You will be shocked—things will disappear. There is nothing more relaxing."

Sit and maintain a straight spine on the floor, or if in a chair, keep both feet flat on the ground without crossing the legs. Open the mouth to make an O shape. Stick the tongue out of the right side of the mouth to form a Q shape with the tongue and mouth. Keep the tongue stretched out. If you have trouble holding the tongue out in this position, you can hold it slightly between the teeth. (*Note*: The tongue should not stick straight out, but extend out the right side of the mouth only.) Breathe slowly and deeply through the mouth, keeping the tongue stretched out the entire time. Keep the eyes closed. Any beautiful music can be played (or no music at all). The practice time here is only 3 minutes. To end, keeping the spine straight and eyes closed, inhale and hold the breath for 13 seconds, then squeeze the breath out with a powerful exhale through the mouth. Repeat this but hold the breath the second time for only 11 seconds. Again squeeze the breath out with a powerful exhale through the mouth, and one last time, inhale and hold for 7 seconds. Squeeze the breath out with a powerful exhale through the mouth. Bhajan commented: "Karma will be over. It is called 'pre-experience.' Your 'Q' should be perfect."

The first part of the protocol is now complete. These techniques help take the patient through the shock, anger, fear, and guilt that is common for many patients with PTSD. Now immediately begin the second part with the next meditation.

7. A Tantric Meditation Technique to Create a Normal and Supernormal State of Consciousness

This technique (Shannahoff-Khalsa, 2003) is said to be a very powerful healing meditation that helps to organize and normalize the various regions of the brain. It is called a tantric meditation because of the hand posture, although it is not a "White Tantric yoga" meditation technique. This is a very sacred technique because of its power to produce rapid changes in brain states.

Sit with a straight spine (see Figure 7.2). The eyes are closed and focused at the third

Figure 7.2.
A Tantric Meditation to Create a Normal and Supernormal State of Consciousness

eye point, where the nose meets the forehead. The hands are interlocked, with the right thumb over the left thumb; all the fingers are interlaced, and the left little finger is on the bottom. (This finger-to-finger relationship is to be used even if one is naturally left-thumb-dominant with the right little finger on the bottom.) The right middle (or Saturn) finger is brought into the space between the hands, and points toward the wrists. The hands are then closed and the right Saturn finger becomes enclosed in a cave-like structure. The hands are held at the heart-center level, about 9 inches in front of the chest with the elbows resting at the sides.

Relax in this posture for 3–5 minutes with the breath regulating itself. Then keeping everything the same, begin to consciously regulate the breath so that the inhale, the holding of the breath, and the exhale are of equal lengths of time (there is no holding the breath out). The breath cycle can approach 1 minute, with the inhale, holding in, and exhale each lasting 20 seconds in duration. However, 5 seconds for the three phases is a good starting time. Have a conscious relationship with the experience of the sensations of the hand posture and the sensations in the head simultaneously. (This technique frequently produces unique physical sensations in the head.) Practice this technique for a total of 11 minutes.

Depending on the health of the patient, a break of 5 minutes is recommended here, before going on to the final meditation.

8. Meditation for When You Want to Command Your Own Consciousness to a Higher Consciousness

Sit in an easy, crossed-legged pose and maintain a straight spine, or sit in a chair and keep both feet flat on the ground without crossing the legs (see Figure 7.3). The hands are relaxed in the lap. Grasp the left thumb with the right hand and wrap the fingers of the left hand around the back of the right hand. The eyes are nine-tenths closed and focused on the tip of the nose (the end not visible to the practitioner's eye). This eye posture is called *ajna bond* and translates to "mind lock." The effect of this eye posture is to help stabilize the activity of the frontal lobes. The following mantra is chanted three times in one breath:

"Hari Nam Tat Sat Tat Sat Hari"

Figure 7.3.
Meditation for When You Want to Command Your Own Consciousness
to Higher Consciousness

Three times in one breath may be difficult for some beginners, but with practice and good lungs it can easily be achieved. Chant more rapidly if necessary to complete the three cycles. Specifically:

"Hari" is pronounced like the name *Harvey*, minus the *v*-sound.
"Nam" sounds like *Nam* in *Viet Nam*, with a short-*a* sound.
The "a" in "Tat" and "Sat" sounds like *ah*.

This mantra is said to awaken the infinite creative power within. The time for practice is 11 minutes. For a few minutes immediately after the 11 minutes, chant

"Sat Nam Sat Nam Sat Nam Sat Nam Sat Nam Sat Nam Whahay Guru"

in an eight-beat rhythm (one beat for each "Sat Nam," one beat for "Whahay," and one beat for "Guru"). The sounds of "Sat" and "Nam" are the same as in the first mantra. For "Wha-hay":

"Wha" as in the *wa* of *water*
"-hay" as in "*hey*!"

EIGHT

Treating the Abused and Battered Psyche

This chapter includes 10 special Kundalini yoga meditation techniques for treating the abused and battered psyche that can be useful for children, adolescents, and adults. There is no special American Psychiatric Association definition or coding for the abused and battered psyche. The choice of technique here is often best determined by the ability of the individual to perform a simple or more complex technique, and often this is determined or greatly affected by age and health.

As with all Kundalini yoga meditation practices, we begin with the "tuning in" technique. (Note that while it is listed first among the techniques here, technique 1 is included for all meditations and therefore isn't technically one of the 10 techniques of this particular group.) This technique helps to create a meditative state of mind and is always used as a precursor to the other techniques. There is no upper time limit for this technique—the longer the better.

10 KUNDALINI YOGA MEDITATION TECHNIQUES FOR THE ABUSED AND BATTERED PSYCHE

1. Technique to Induce a Meditative State: "Tuning In"

Sit with a straight spine and with the feet flat on the floor if sitting in a chair (see Figure 2.1). Put the hands together at the chest in "prayer pose"—the palms are pressed together with 10–15 pounds of pressure (a mild to medium pressure, nothing too intense). The area where the sides of the thumbs touch rests on the sternum with the thumbs pointing up (along the sternum), and the fingers are together and point up and out at a 60-degree angle to the ground. The eyes are closed and focused on the third eye (imagine a sun rising on the horizon, or the equivalent of the point between the eyebrows at the origin of the nose). This mantra is chanted out loud in a 1½-breath cycle:

"Ong Namo Guru Dev Namo"

Inhale first through the nose and chant "Ong Namo" with an equal emphasis on the *Ong* and the *Namo*. Then immediately follow with a half-breath inhalation through the mouth and chant "Guru Dev Namo" with approximately equal emphasis on each word. (The *o* in *Ong* and *Namo* is a long-o sound; *Dev* sounds like *Dave*, with a long-a sound.)

- *Ong Namo* means I bow with reverence to that infinite energy that is the basis of all creation.
- *Guru* means teacher or wisdom.
- *Dev* means divine or of God.

The practitioner should focus on the experience of the vibrations these sounds create on the upper palate and throughout the cranium, while letting the mind be carried by the sounds into a new and pleasant mental space. This sequence should be repeated a minimum of three times. We employed it in our group about 10–12 times. This technique helps to create a meditative state of mind and is *always* used as a precursor to the other techniques.

2. Meditation for Self-Worth and Achievement for the Very Young

The child sits on his or her heels with the knees together in front and the ankles out in back, with the tops of the feet resting flat on the floor (see Figure 8.1). The arms are up, with the upper arms parallel to the ground and the forearms straight up, palms open wide and facing forward. The child bows to the ground with closed eyes and says "I am," then moves up to the original sitting position, opening the eyes, and says "somebody." This is practiced for 3–11 minutes.

Figure 8.1.
Meditation for Self-Worth and Achievement for the Very Young

3. Meditation for Abused and Battered Children for Developing a Balanced Psyche: The Jupiter Finger Chakra Meditation

This meditation was originally taught by Yogi Bhajan as a "children's meditation," but it can also be practiced by adolescents and adults. Anyone with past trauma resulting from abuse and victimization will benefit from this practice. Even someone without past trauma can improve the balance of their personality by its use. This meditation helps to balance the chakras and meridians in the body. It will evoke many feelings that have stuck with the individual since childhood. It will help adults get rid of the "childhood syndrome," a condition wherein they cling to something that is already finished. This syndrome can easily limit and even ruin a person's life.

Sit with a straight spine either on the floor or in a chair. If in a chair, place the feet flat on the ground, uncrossed. Place the left hand on the chest at the heart center with the fingers pointing toward the right. Use the index (Jupiter) finger of the right hand (keep the other fingers closed in a relaxed fist, with the thumb over the other fingers) to touch, in sequence, the following points:

1. The middle of the lower lip
2. The tip (end) of the nose
3. The outer skin area or edge/corner of the eye socket (the region of the skull bone near the outside of the eye)
4. A point about three-fourths of an inch above the indent of the nose, which is near the bottom of the forehead (the midline point between the eyebrows).

Chant the mantra

"Sa Ta Na Ma"

out loud in sequence with the touching of the respective points. Chant

"Sa" when touching the lower lip
"Ta" when touching the tip of the nose
"Na" when touching the outer edge of the eye socket
"Ma" when touching the forehead point.

Since there are two eyes and thus two outer edges of the eye socket, the practitioner alternates sides with each sequence. Start by touching the right side first. Each round of touching the points and chanting the mantra through takes about 4–5 seconds. Keep the eyes closed when doing this meditation. The maximum time is 33 minutes, and it can be practiced for the full amount of time the first time it is used. Younger children may have to start with 11 minutes, or even less. When ending the technique, inhale deeply and hold the breath, then while holding the breath feel the "inner child" via self-hypnosis. The practitioner exhales, inhales, and hypnotizes him- or herself to picture him- or herself as a child in his or her own heart, where the left hand has been resting. Then the pracitioner concentrates, exhales, inhales, and repeats the picture of him- or herself. Bless that child, be that child, and let the breath go.

4. A Sitting Posture to Help Reduce Aggressive Tendencies, to Be Used for "Time-Outs"

A common problem with younger children who have been abused is their enactment of behavior that requires some restrictions. This technique can be used to help them learn to manage their behavior while reflecting on, and recovering from, their actions. This technique is a more effective way of having a child sit for a "time-out."

The child should sit with the knees in front of the body and the feet behind, but he or she must sit *in between* the heels instead of on the heels. This is called sitting in "celibate pose." The eyes are kept opened and focused on the tip of the nose while the child inhales slowly through the mouth with a curled tongue (sticking out slightly and held in a *U* shape), and then slowly exhales through the nose while closing the mouth. If the tongue cannot be curled, which is a genetic ability, it should be mimicked as best as possible. Begin with 3 minutes and build to 11 minutes.

5. Meditation for the Abused and Battered Psyche: A Technique for Children, Adolescents, and Adults

Sit either on the floor with the legs crossed or on a firm chair with feet flat on the floor, uncrossed (see Figure 8.2). The arms are extended out to the sides and up at a 60-degree angle from the ground. Curl the fingers so that the fingertips touch the area of the palm that is closest to where the fingers emerge from the hand—the pads where calluses frequently develop. Keep the thumb out and pointed straight up. Now roll the hands (and arms) in a 12-inch-diameter circle; the right hand goes in a counterclockwise direction and the left hand goes in a clockwise direction. With the circular movement of the hands the spine will move from top to bottom during the rotation of the arms. The eyes are closed and focused on what would be the tip of the chin if the eyes were open. There is no mantra or breathing

Figure 8.2.
Meditation for the Abused and Battered Psyche:
A Technique for Children, Adolescents, and Adults

pattern, although all breathing is through the nose. This technique can be practiced for 3–11 minutes.

6. Meditation for the Abused and Battered Psyche: An Advanced Technique for Adolescents and Adults

Sit either on the floor with the legs crossed or on a chair with feet flat on the floor, uncrossed. Both arms are extended straight out in front and parallel to the ground. The left palm faces up and the right palm faces down. The eyes are opened and focused on the tip of the nose, the end that cannot be seen. The tongue is pressed against the soft lower palate. Breathe only through the nose by inhaling in four equal parts, and exhaling in one full breath. This meditation is to be practiced for 11 minutes.

7. Meditation Technique for Dyslexia

In yogic medicine, dyslexia and other learning disabilities were known to develop occasionally as a result of abuse. This meditation (Shannahoff-Khalsa, 2004) was known to be effective in the treatment of dyslexia, which is understood by yogis to be a problem of information processing in general, not simply of letters or words or mathematical symbols. The retarded processing of emotions is also included in this more general view of dyslexia.

Sit in an easy pose (see Figure 8.3). The eyes are opened and focused on the tip of the nose. The arms are in front of the body and extended slightly out toward the sides with the palms up, the hands at the level of the solar plexus. The fingertips touch the thumb tip in the following order with a light but definite touch:

- First touch the little fingertip (the Mercury finger) to the thumb tip and mentally chant "Sa."
- Then touch the index fingertip (the Jupiter finger) to the thumb tip and mentally chant "Ta."
- Touch the ring fingertip (the Sun finger) to the thumb tip and mentally chant "Na."
- Again touch the Jupiter fingertip to the thumb tip and mentally chant "Ma."
- Touch the middle fingertip (the Saturn finger) to the thumb tip and mentally chant "Wha."
- Again touch the Mercury fingertip to the thumb tip and mentally chant "Hay."
- Open the hands completely (palms are almost flat and no fingers touch) and mentally chant "Guru."

During the entire exercise the tongue tip is held touching the upper palate in the top center, where the palate is hard and smooth; the tongue does not move. The breath has a six-part broken-breath inhale and 1-part exhale, all through the nose only. The six parts of the broken breath of the inhale correspond to the six mental sounds of "Sa," "Ta," "Na," "Ma," "Wha," and "Hay," and the exhale corresponds to the mental sound "Guru." You mentally

Figure 8.3.
Meditation Technique for Dsylexia

hear these sounds with each corresponding segment of the breath. End the meditation by closing the eyes, inhaling deeply, and stretching the hands up in the air above the head. Shake the arms and hands and fingers vigorously for about 30–60 seconds.

The rate of thumb–finger tapping can increase to one complete round (going through the whole series of thumb tip to fingertips) in 2-3 seconds. It takes some time to reach this rate, which is achieved once the practice becomes second nature—that is, when it happens automatically without thinking about the sequence. The time for this extremely powerful technique can be anywhere from 11 to 31 minutes, maximum. It is acceptable to start with less than 11 minutes, and most people may have to do so in the beginning. Slowly build the time up to 31 minutes. Eventually, try to complete 40–120 days at 31 minutes per sitting and marvel at the extraordinary effects. Individuals vary in dyslexic severity, and thus each may vary in the time required to attain all benefits. At 120 days of perfected practice, virtually all of one's processing skills are said to be very much healed, with the brain attaining a near-perfect balance.

This technique would also be excellent for people with attention-deficit disorder (ADD) or attention-deficit/hyperactivity disorder (ADHD). In addition, it would be helpful for those with a battered and abused psyche to employ either or both of the following two techniques (from Chapter 15) prior to this technique for dyslexia:

- Meditation to Balance and Synchronize the Cerebral Hemispheres
- Meditation to Balance the Jupiter and Saturn Energies: A Technique to Help Reduce Depression and Self-Destructive Behavior (also in Chapter 7).

The learning curve for this dyslexia technique is relatively long, but well worth the effort. This technique is very stimulating and powerful. As noted, the yogic definition of dyslexia is broad and includes the inability to process information and sensory feedback. Thus, we are all *dyslexic* to some degree. This technique helps the brain function at a much higher level of efficiency by organizing all of the major and minor regions of the brain. This efficiency will only increase with practice over time. Once a person practices this technique for an extended time, he or she will begin to realize just how "dyslexic" a life he or she has been living.

8. Meditation for Eliminating Deep, Long-Lasting Anger

Sit with a straight and erect spine, with the lower back pushed forward as if you are sitting "at attention" (see Figure 8.4), with both hands curled into fists. The starting posture is with the forearms parallel to the ground at the elbow level. The left fist moves with force toward the center of the chest area, near the heart center, and the right fist moves with force toward the center of the chest also, but under the left fist. Both fists stop abruptly in front of the chest without touching the chest or touching each other. The movement is more like a hard hitting motion using full strength. Note that the hands do not hit anything, but move toward each other, with the left on top. The elbows are out to the sides and the arms move in and out, with the elbows remaining at the level of the fists.

Figure 8.4.
Meditation for Eliminating Deep, Long-Lasting Anger

As the eyes remain closed, chant the mantra

"Har"

loudly and with force from the navel region, with each hard "hitting" motion. Repeat the action rapidly at a rate of about once every 2 seconds. The time for this segment of the meditation is 6½ minutes. To end this part of the meditation, inhale through the nose and hold the hands and arms tight near the chest, like an iron rod, making the body stiff, then exhale powerfully through the mouth, like an explosion. Repeat the sequence—inhale, tense, and powerful exhale—two more times. Place both hands over the heart center, but now touching the chest, with the left hand closer to the chest and the right hand touching the back of the left hand. Close the eyes and go into a state of "nonexistence"; feel and imagine nonexistence, a state of no thoughts, for an additional 8 minutes. Then relax.

This meditation can take a patient from anger to ecstasy, and it is helpful for all those who have been abused in their past. This meditation replaces the power of anger with the state of the "neutral self," a state from which all goodness comes to that person. When a person is without anger, he or she lives within a state of wisdom. One effect of anger is that it weakens one's intellectual caliber, and then when the intellect tells that person something useful, he or she does not have the capacity to receive and process the information—which then leads to failure, and failure leads to more anger.

9. *Meditation for Treating Impulsive Behavior in Youth and Others*

Sit with a straight spine and place the left arm in front of the body, with the left hand facing down and straight out in front of the heart center. The left arm and hand are parallel to the ground. The right arm is extended straight out parallel to the left arm and in front of the body, right palm facing up (see Figure 8.5). The eyes are closed. Chant the mantra

"Whahay Guru Whahay Guru Whahay Guru Whahay Jeeo"

with at least one entire round of the mantra per breath cycle. Chant/pronounce as follows:

"Wha" is like *wa* in *water*.
"Hay" sounds just like the food for horses.
"Jeeo" sounds like the two letters, *g* and *o*, run together.

Practice for 18 minutes maximum, then place both hands on the chest at the heart center. The left hand is touching the chest and the palm of the right hand is on the back of the left hand. Continue chanting the mantra, but in a whisper, for 2 more minutes, then remain silent for 1 minute with the hands on the chest. To end, inhale deeply and hold the breath, tightening the muscles of the arms, hands (pressing against the chest), and spine. Then ex-

Figure 8.5.
Meditation for Treating Impulsive Behavior

hale out powerfully through the mouth like a cannon. Repeat the inhalation, tightening, and exhalation sequence two more times.

This meditation will also balance the "earth" and "ether" elements of the psyche. This is a useful meditation for young children who sometimes go miserably astray in life. It will increase their ability to remain stable and secure and help develop their temperament, tolerance, and restraint.

10. Meditation for Treating Grief (Especially Useful for PTSD Patients)

Most abused and battered individuals, including those with PTSD, suffer from grief. Yogis claim that grief, anger, and anxiety play a major role in the onset of a wide range of diseases. This technique would be most beneficial when practiced with the first three techniques listed in the OCD protocol in Chapter 3. For text see pp. 105–108 in chapter 10 and see Figures 10.1 and 10.2 (p. 107).

11. Gan Puttee Kriya: A Technique to Eliminate the Negativity from the Past, the Present, and the Future

Gan Puttee Kriya has also been called the "Kriya to Make the Impossible Possible." Yogi Bhajan originally taught this meditation technique on November 2, 1988 (Bhajan, 1998). Yogis disovered this technique as a tool for eliminating the blocks that form in the subconscious mind and stifle growth, frequently leading to destructive, neurotic, and self-defeating patterns of mental activity.

Sit with a straight spine, either on the floor or in a chair. The backs of your hands are resting on your knees with the palms facing upward. The eyes are nine-tenths closed (one-tenth open, but looking straight ahead into the darkness, not the light below), focused on the third eye. Chant from your heart in a natural, relaxed manner, or chant in a steady, relaxed monotone:

"Sa Ta Na Ma Ra Ma Da Sa Sa Say So Hung"

More specifically:

Chant out loud the sound "Sa" (the *a* sounds like *ahhh*), and touch your thumb tips and index fingertips together quickly and simultaneously with about 2 pounds of pressure.
Chant "Ta" and touch the thumb tips to the middle fingertips.
Chant "Na" and touch the thumb tips to the ring fingertips.
Chant "Ma" and touch the thumb tips to the little fingertips.
Chant "Ra" and touch your thumb tips and index fingertips.

Chant "Ma" and touch the thumb tips to the middle fingertips.
Chant "Da" and touch the thumb tips to the ring fingertips.
Chant "Sa" and touch the thumb tips to the little fingertips.
Chant "Sa" and touch your thumb tips and index fingertips.
Chant "Say" (sounds like the word *say* with a long-*a*) and touch the thumb tips to the middle fingertips.
Chant "So" and touch the thumb tips to the ring fingertips.
Chant "Hung" and touch the thumb tips to the little-finger tips.

Chant at a rate of one sound per second. The thumb tip and fingertips touch with a very light (2–3 pounds) pressure with each connection. This light touch helps to consolidate the circuit created by each thumb–finger link. Start with 11 minutes and slowly work up to 31 minutes of practice. To finish, remain in the sitting posture and inhale, holding the breath for 20–30 seconds while you shake and move every part of your body (like a dog shaking off water). Exhale and repeat this shaking motion two more times to circulate the energy and to break the pattern of tapping the thumb and fingertips, which affects the brain. Finally, after the shaking, sit in absolute calmness and focus the eyes on the tip of the nose with slow deep breathing through the nose for one more minute.

Each sound used in this meditation is unique, and they all have a powerful effect on both the conscious and subconscious minds:

"Sa" gives the mind the ability to expand to the infinite.
"Ta" gives the mind the ability to experience the totality of life.
"Na" gives the mind the ability to conquer death.
"Ma" gives the mind the ability to resurrect.
"Ra" gives the mind the ability to expand in radiance (this sound purifies and energizes).
"Da" gives the mind the ability to establish security on the earth plane, providing a ground for action.
"Say" gives the totality of experience.
"So" is the personal sense of identity.
"Hung" is the infinite as a vibrating and real force. Together, *So Hung* means "I am Thou."

The unique qualities of this 12-syllable mantra help cleanse and restructure the subconscious mind and help heal the conscious mind to ultimately experience the *super*conscious mind. All the blocks that result from traumatic or troubling events are eliminated over time with the practice of Gan Puttee Kriya. When doing this technique in the beginning, 11 minutes for this technique is often adequate; however, 31 minutes is even better, and the maximum time: *Do not go beyond 31 minutes.*

NINE

Treating the Major Depressive Disorders

Major depressive disorder, or what is more commonly called *depression*, can involve a single episode or have recurrent episodes. The American Psychiatric Association's (2000) DSM-IV-TR definitions are given below. *Note that the depression that is part of bipolar disorder is treated differently and is addressed in Chapter 11*. However, the criteria for a mixed episode is also described below since it is related to the definition of a major depressive episode. The diagnostic criteria, diagnostic features, and associated disorders are reproduced from the DSM IV-TR. However, the issues of clinical status and/or features are not included here, due to their complexity, which goes beyond the scope of this chapter.

DSM DISORDERS

Diagnostic Criteria for 296.2 Major Depressive Disorder, Single Episode (APA, 2000)

A. Presence of a single Major Depressive Episode (see Criteria for Major Depressive Episode below).
B. The Major Depressive Episode is not better accounted for by Schizoaffective Disorder and is not superimposed on Schizophrenia, Schizophreniform Disorder, Delusional Disorder, or Psychotic Disorder Not Otherwise Specified.
C. There has never been a Manic Episode [see Criteria for Manic Episode in Chapter 11, pp. 110–111; see Criteria for Mixed Episode in Chapter 11, p. 112], or a Hypomanic Episode [see Criteria for Hypomanic Episode in Chapter 11, pp. 114–115]. **Note:** This

exclusion does not apply if all of the manic-like, mixed-like, or hypomanic-like episodes are substance or treatment induced or are due to the direct physiological effects of a general medical condition.

Criteria for Major Depressive Episode (APA, 2000)

A. Five (or more) of the following symptoms have been present during the same 2-week period and represent a change from previous functioning; at least one of the symptoms is either (1) depressed mood or (2) loss of interest or pleasure. **Note:** Do not include symptoms that are clearly due to a general medical condition, or mood-incongruent delusions or hallucinations.
    1. depressed mood most of the day, nearly every day, as indicated by either subjective report (e.g., feels sad or empty) or observation made by others (e.g., appears tearful). **Note:** In children and adolescents, can be irritable mood.
    2. markedly diminished interest or pleasure in all, or almost all, activities most of the day, nearly every day (as indicated by either subjective account or observation made by others)
    3. significant weight loss when not dieting or weight gain (e.g., a change of more than 5% of body weight in a month), or decrease or increase in appetite nearly every day. **Note:** In children, consider failure to make expected weight gains.
    4. insomnia or hypersomnia nearly every day
    5. psychomotor agitation or retardation nearly every day (observable by others, not merely subjective feelings of restlessness or being slowed down)
    6. fatigue or loss of energy nearly every day
    7. feelings of worthlessness or excessive or inappropriate guilt (which may be delusional) nearly every day (not merely self-reproach or guilt about being sick)
    8. diminished ability to think or concentrate, or indecisiveness, nearly every day (either by subjective account or as observed by others)
    9. recurrent thoughts of death (not just fear of dying), recurrent suicidal ideation without a specific plan, or a suicide attempt or a specific plan for committing suicide
B. The symptoms do not meet criteria for a Mixed Episode (see Criteria for Mixed Episode below).

C. The symptoms cause clinically significant distress or impairment in social, occupational, or other important areas of functioning.
D. The symptoms are not due to the direct physiological effects of a substance (e.g., a drug of abuse, a medication) or a general medical condition (e.g., hypothyroidism).
E. The symptoms are not better accounted for by Bereavement, i.e., after the loss of a loved one, the symptoms persist for longer than 2 months or are characterized by marked functional impairment, morbid preoccupation with worthlessness, suicidal ideation, psychotic symptoms, or psychomotor retardation.

Criteria for Mixed Episode (APA, 2000)

A. The criteria are met both for a Manic Episode [see Criteria for Manic Episode in Chapter 11, pp. 110–111] and for a Major Depressive Episode [see Criteria for Major Depressive Episode in this chapter, pp. 96–97] (except for duration) nearly every day during at least a 1-week period.
B. The mood disturbance is sufficiently severe to cause marked impairment in occupational functioning or in usual social activities or relationships with others, or to necessitate hospitalization to prevent harm to self or others, or there are psychotic features.
C. The symptoms are not due to the direct physiological effects of a substance (e.g., a drug of abuse, a medication, or other treatment) or a general medical condition (e.g., hyperthyroidism).

Note: Mixed-like episodes that are clearly caused by somatic antidepressant treatment (e.g., medication, electroconvulsive therapy, light therapy) should not count toward a diagnosis of Bipolar I Disorder.

Diagnostic Criteria for 296.3 Major Depressive Disorder, Recurrent (APA, 2000)

A. Presence of two or more Major Depressive Episodes [see Criteria for Major Depressive Episode, above].

Note: To be considered separate episodes, there must be an interval of at least 2 consecutive months in which criteria are not met for a Major Depressive Episode.

B. The Major Depressive Episodes are not better accounted for by Schizoaffective Disorder and are not superimposed on Schizophrenia, Schizophreniform Disorder, Delusional Disorder, or Psychotic Disorder Not Otherwise Specified.

C. There has never been a Manic Episode [see Criteria for Manic Episode in Chapter 11, pp. 110–111], a Mixed Episode [see Criteria for Mixed Episode in this chapter, p. 97], or a Hypomanic Episode [see Criteria for Hypomanic Episode in Chapter 11, pp. 114–115]. **Note:** This exclusion does not apply if all of the manic-like, mixed-like, or hypomanic-like episodes are substance or treatment induced or are due to the direct physiological effects of a general medical condition.

Reprinted with permission from the *Diagnostic and Statistical Manual of Mental Disorders, Fourth Edition, Text Revision.* Copyright 2000 American Psychiatric Association.

Diagnostic Features (APA, 2000)

The fourth digit in the diagnostic code for Major Depressive Disorder indicates whether it is a Single Episode (used only for first episodes) or Recurrent. It is sometimes difficult to distinguish between a single episode with waxing and waning symptoms and two separate episodes. For purposes of this manual, an episode is considered to have ended when the full criteria for the Major Depressive Episode have not been met for at least 2 consecutive months. During this 2-month period, there is either complete resolution of symptoms or the presence of depressive symptoms that no longer meet the full criteria for a Major Depressive Episode (In Partial Remission).

Associated Features and Disorders (APA, 2000)

Major Depressive Disorder is associated with high mortality. Up to 15% of individuals with severe Major Depressive Disorder die by suicide. Epidemiological evidence also suggests that there is a fourfold increase in death rates in individuals with Major Depressive Disorder who are over age 55 years. Individuals with Major Depressive Disorder admitted to nursing homes may have a markedly increased likelihood of death in the first year. Among individuals seen in general medical settings, those with Major Depressive Disorder have more pain and physical illness and decreased physical, social, and role functioning.

Major Depressive Disorder may be preceded by Dysthymic Disorder (10% in epidemiological samples and 15%–25% in clinical samples). It is also estimated that each year approximately 10% of individuals with Dysthymic Disorder alone will go on to have a first Major Depressive Episode. Other mental disorders frequently co-occur with Major Depressive Disorder (e.g., Substance-Related Disorders, Panic Disorder, Obsessive–Compulsive Disorder, Anorexia Nervosa, Bulimia Nervosa, Borderline Personality Disorder).

THE SIX-PART KUNDALINI YOGA MEDITATION PROTOCOL FOR TREATING MAJOR DEPRESSIVE DISORDERS*

1. Technique to Induce a Meditative State: "Tuning In"

Sit with a straight spine and with the feet flat on the floor if sitting in a chair (see Figure 2.1). Put the hands together at the chest in "prayer pose"—the palms are pressed together with 10–15 pounds of pressure (a mild to medium pressure, nothing too intense). The area where the sides of the thumbs touch rests on the sternum with the thumbs pointing up (along the sternum), and the fingers are together and point up and out at a 60-degree angle to the ground. The eyes are closed and focused on the third eye (imagine a sun rising on the horizon, or the equivalent of the point between the eyebrows at the origin of the nose). This mantra is chanted out loud in a 1½-breath cycle:

"Ong Namo Guru Dev Namo"

Inhale first through the nose and chant "Ong Namo" with an equal emphasis on the *Ong* and the *Namo*. Then immediately follow with a half-breath inhalation through the mouth and chant "Guru Dev Namo" with approximately equal emphasis on each word. (The *o* in *Ong* and *Namo* is a long-*o* sound; *Dev* sounds like *Dave*, with a long-*a* sound.)

- *Ong Namo* means I bow with reverence to that infinite energy that is the basis of all creation.
- *Guru* means teacher or wisdom.
- *Dev* means divine or of God.

The practitioner should focus on the experience of the vibrations these sounds create on the upper palate and throughout the cranium, while letting the mind be carried by the sounds into a new and pleasant mental space. This sequence should be repeated a minimum of three times. This technique helps to create a meditative state of mind and is *always* used as a precursor to the other techniques.

2. Spine-Flexing Technique for Vitality

This technique can be practiced while sitting either in a chair or on the floor in a cross-legged position. If you are in a chair, hold the knees with both hands for support and leverage. If you are sitting cross-legged, grasp the ankles in front with both hands. Begin by pulling the chest up and slightly forward, inhaling deeply through the nose at the same time. Then exhale as you relax the spine down into a slouching position. Keep the head up straight, as if you were looking forward, without allowing it to move much while flexing the spine. This position will help prevent a whip effect in the cervical vertebrae. Breathe only through the nose for both the inhalation and exhalation. The eyes are closed, as if you were looking at a central point on the horizon, the third eye. Your mental focus is kept on the sound of the breath while listening to the fluid movement of the inhalation and exhalation. Begin the technique slowly while loosening up the spine. Eventually, a very rapid movement can be achieved with practice, reaching a rate of one to two times per second for the entire movement. A few minutes are adequate in the beginning. Later, there is no upper time limit. Food should be avoided just prior to this exercise. Be careful to flex the spine *slowly* in the beginning. Relax for 1 minute when finished.

3. Shoulder-Shrug Technique for Vitality

While keeping the spine straight, rest the hands on the knees if sitting in a cross-legged position or with hands on the thighs if sitting in a chair. Inhale and raise the shoulders toward the ears, then exhale, relaxing them down. Again, breathe only through the nose. Keep eyes closed and focused on the third eye. Mentally focus on the sound of the inhalation and exhalation. Continue this action rapidly, building to three times per second for a maximum of 2 minutes. *Note*: This technique should not be practiced by individuals who are hyperactive.

4. Ganesha Meditation for Focus and Clarity

Sit with a straight spine, the eyes closed (see Figure 2.2). The left thumb and little finger are sticking out from the hand. The other fingers are curled into a fist with fingertips on the moon mound (the root of the thumb area that extends down to the wrist). The left hand and elbow are parallel to the floor, with the pad of the tip of the left thumb pressing on the curved notch of the nose between the eyes. The little finger is sticking out. With right hand and elbow parallel to the floor, grasp the left little finger with the right hand and close the right hand into a fist around it, so that both hands now extend straight out from your head. Push the notch with the tip of the left thumb to the extent that you feel some soreness as you breathe long and deep. (This soreness lessens with continued practice.) Do this for no longer than 3 minutes. To finish, inhale as you maintain the posture with eyes closed. Push a little more and pull the naval point in by tightening the abdominal muscles for 10 seconds, then exhale. Repeat one more time.

5. Technique for Fighting Brain Fatigue

This technique was originally taught by Yogi Bhajan on March 27, 1995 (Bhajan, 2000), and was later published in the scientific literature (Shannahoff-Khalsa, 2004). This technique has been used to help prevent depression as well as to treat it, and it is especially beneficial if any form of anxiety is accompanied by depression or fatigue.

■ *Part I*. Sit with a straight spine either in a chair or on the floor with your elbows bent and your upper arms near your rib cage (see Figure 2.4). Your forearms point straight out in front of your body, parallel to the floor. The right palm faces downward and the left palm faces upward. Breathing through your nose, inhale and exhale in eight equal parts. On each part or stroke of the breath, alternate moving either hand up and down, one hand moving up as the other moves down. The movement of the hands is approximately 6–8 inches, as if you were bouncing a ball. Breathe powerfully. Continue for 3 minutes and then change the hand position so that the left palm faces downward and the right palm faces upward. Continue for another 3 minutes and then change the hand position again, so that the right palm faces downward and the left palm faces upward for the last 3 minutes. (The total time is 9 minutes.) The eyes can be either open or closed in Part I.

 ■ *Part II.* Begin slow and deep breathing (again, only through the nose), ceasing the movement and relaxing the hands in the lap. Close your eyes and visually focus them on the center point of the chin. This requires pulling the eyes downward. Keep the body perfectly still and set the intention that the body should heal itself. Keep the mind quiet, stilling all thoughts. (The total time for this part is 5½ minutes.)

 To finish:

- Inhale deeply and hold your breath, making your hands into fists and pressing the fists strongly against the chest for 15 seconds. Exhale.
- Inhale deeply again and hold your breath, this time pressing both fists against the navel point for 15 seconds. Exhale.
- Inhale again then hold the breath. Bend your elbows and bring your fists near your shoulders, pressing your arms strongly against your rib cage for 15 seconds as if you are using the upper arms to crush the chest. Then exhale.

Now relax. "This exercise balances the diaphragm and fights brain fatigue. It renews the blood supply to the brain and moves the serum in the spine. It also benefits the liver, navel point, spleen, and lymphatic system" (Bhajan, 2000).

6. Meditation to Balance the Jupiter and Saturn Energies: A Technique Useful for Treating Depression, Focusing the Mind, and Eliminating Self-Destructive Behavior

Sit with a straight spine either in a chair or on the floor (see Figure 7.1). The hands are facing forward with the ends of the Jupiter (index) and Saturn (middle) fingers pointing straight up near the sides of the body at the level of the chin. The elbows are relaxed down by the sides and the hands are near the shoulders. Close the ring and little fingers down into the palm, using the thumbs, and keep them there against the palm during the meditation. The Jupiter (index) finger and the Saturn (middle) finger are spread open in a *V* shape (or closed). The eyes are closed.

For 8 minutes open and close the Jupiter and Saturn fingers about once or twice per second. Make sure the two fingers open completely and close completely during the exercise. Simultaneously imagine the planets of Jupiter and Saturn coming together in front of you and then again going apart in synch with the finger movement—the planets should appear to go back and forth along a straight line, in and out to the sides in front of you. It does not matter whether you visualize Jupiter or Saturn on the left or right side.

In the beginning, the visualization part may be difficult to do, but this should not slow down the pace of the fingers, which play a more important role here. After 8 minutes, while continuing the same exercise, begin to inhale and exhale through the nose only with this movement: Inhale as the fingers open, exhale as the fingers close. Continue visualizing the planets moving in synchrony with the fingers for 2 additional minutes. Note, during the first 8 minutes the breath is not consciously regulated.

Then, for the last minute, spread the two fingers and hold them wide apart (now they do not open and close, they remain in the fixed *V* shape), keeping them very stiff (which requires considerable effort) while also keeping the mouth in an O, or ring, shape. Breathe in and out of the mouth using only the diaphragm (not the wall of the upper chest) with a rate of one to three breaths per second. After 1 minute, inhale, hold the breath in, and tense every muscle tightly (including the hands and fingers, with the *V* shape kept rigid, arms, back, stomach) in the body for 10 seconds. Exhale and repeat two more times for 10 seconds. Then relax.

Yogi Bhajan noted the following:

This meditation will help increase a person's ability to focus and concentrate and also increase the IQ of an individual over several months of practice. The mind becomes very focused and clear, the brain becomes very energized. This technique will also help eliminate depression. This technique can also enhance math skills for those who have difficulties with math. The Jupiter and Saturn energies become balanced (the brain is balanced) and this allows one to overcome any challenge, including mastery of the self. This technique also helps to eliminate self-destructive behavior and undesirable acting out behavior toward others. In addition, during the beginning of the technique, around the 4- to 8-minute mark, a person can feel very irritable and sometimes it can bring out deep-seated anger. (Bhajan, 1995)

Note: If a person feels dizzy during the meditation, he or she should stop and try it again on another occasion.

TEN

Treating Grief

Grief per se is not defined as a disorder for treatment by the American Psychiatric Association's (2000) DSM-IV-TR. However, the topic of bereavement is listed in a category called "Other Conditions That May Be a Focus of Clinical Attention." Although there is a code for bereavement (V62.82), there is no listing of the diagnostic criteria, diagnostic features, and associated mental disorders that occurs with the other disorders covered in the DSM-IV-TR. Grief (bereavement) following the death of a loved one often requires therapy, and many symptoms are similar to those of Major Depressive Disorder. Frequently, there is an intense state of sadness that is accompanied by insomnia, poor appetite, and weight loss. These symptoms can warrant professional help. The American Psychiatric Association differentiates between bereavement and depression by stating that "The diagnosis of Major Depressive Disorder is generally not given unless the symptoms are still present 2 months after the loss" (APA, 2000).

KUNDALINI YOGA THERAPY FOR TREATING GRIEF

The technique described here is effective by itself, but will yield even more effective results when practiced with Techniques 2 through 4 described in the Six-Part Protocol for Treating Major Depressive Disorders in Chapter 9 (pp. 100–101). As always, the first technique to be employed is called "Tuning In" (see Chapter 2: "1. Technique to Induce a Meditative State: "Tuning In," and Figure 2.1, p. 10).

Following the Tuning In technique is this three-part technique to maximize the overall benefits; however, Part I can be done alone. The suggested music for each part is optional, though the benefits of the music will only add to the therapeutic value.

■ *Part I: Siddh Shiva*. "Whenever you have grief, do this exercise. It gets rid of centuries-old grief" (Bhajan, 1990) . In Position A (see Figure 10.1), sit with a straight spine in a cross-legged position. The eyes are wide open (do not meditate). The elbows are bent by the sides, and the upper arms are kept by the sides. The forearms are parallel to the ground just above each leg, with the palms open and facing up and placed about 6 inches above the knees.

In Position B (see Figure 10.2), raise the arms up so the hands quickly bounce up to the shoulders. As you do this, the tongue sticks out as far as possible (this is important because it affects the subconscious mind and helps get rid of the grief). Then return to Position A. The tongue goes back into the mouth, the mouth closes, and the arms go back down to the position above the legs. Do this movement powerfully with the breath. Inhale through the nose as you go into Position A and exhale through the mouth as you go into Position B. Breathe heavily and practice this movement at a rate of two times per second. Listen to the song "Se Saraswati" by Nirinjan Kaur and Guru Prem Singh (available at the Ancient Healing Ways website: www.a-healing.com). Do this technique for 7 minutes total. To end, inhale and hold the breath while pressing the tongue against the upper palate as hard as you can for 20 seconds. Exhale. Repeat this tongue process two more times (three times total), then relax for 3 minutes.

■ *Part II.* A second technique here is optional (taught as a companion technique by Yogi Bhajan on May 17, 1990). This exercise helps to create an inner balance that then helps to further induce healing. Stretch the arms up over the head, elbows straight, palms very flat and stiff, facing forward with the fingers together and the thumbs extended stiffly to the sides of the hands. Begin moving the left arm in a clockwise circle overhead and over the left side of the body. Move the right arm in a counterclockwise direction overhead and over the right side of the body. The movements of the two arms do not seem to be related in any fashion. One arm gets into a certain rhythm of a circular movement while the other arm does the same. (*Note*: You can reverse directions, if you wish.) The song "Heal Me" by Nirinjan Kaur is played (available at the Ancient Healing Ways website: www.a-healing.com). Do this for 11 minutes and then rest for 5 minutes. Bhajan said: "The idea of the movement is that the armpits get stimulated, so make the movement of the arms just an extension of

Figures 10.1 and 10.2.
Meditation for Treating Grief

the movement of the armpits and the sides of the rib cage. Usually we condemn ourselves and we have to feel guilty to be happy. This completely breaks through that" (Bhajan, 1990).

■ *Part III*. The third part of this exercise begins by inhaling through the left nostril by blocking the right nostril with the right thumb, then exhale only through the right nostril by blocking the left nostril with the right index finger, continuing with this pattern for 3 minutes (do not reverse nostrils). Then firmly grasp the knees by placing the palms flat down on top of them. Begin swaying your body forward approximately 1 foot and then backward approximately 1 foot in a rhythmic fashion. The grip of the hands should be so firm that it keeps you from tilting over when you go backward. Keep your spine "tight" while doing the exercise. Play the song "Humee Hum Tumee Tum" by Livtar Singh (available at the Ancient Healing Ways website: www.a-healing.com).

Do this technique for 3 minutes. To end, inhale deeply and tighten the whole body, then shake the body as much as possible. Do this five times total, holding the breath approximately 20 seconds the first time and 15 seconds the other four times. "It is said that this posture increases the circulation in the area of the breasts for females so they will not develop breast cancer. It will develop your automatic concentration, so you can concentrate whenever you want. It will also help expel the dead cells out of the physical body" (Bhajan, 1990).

ELEVEN

Treating the Bipolar Disorders

Bipolar disorders are much more complex than most psychiatric diorders and often very difficult to treat because they are a combination of both manic pathology and its polar state of depressed pathology. Treatment providers must be careful that medication does not lead to the polar condition. Antidepressants can lead to mania, and drugs for treating mania can lead to depression. In addition, the possible combinations of the amount and severity of mania and hypomania compared to depression within individuals also leads to a relative greater complexity in both the diagnosis and treatment of the bipolar condition.

The DSM-IV-TR lists four major categories for the bipolar disorders which include Bipolar I Disorder, Bipolar II Disorder, Cyclothymia, and Bipolar Disorder Not Otherwise Specified. In addition, the complexity of this disorder is further differentiated by the DSM IV-TR's listing of "six separate criteria sets for Bipolar I Disorder: Single Manic Episode, Most Recent Episode Hypomanic, Most Recent Episode Manic, Most Recent Episode Mixed, Most Recent Episode Depressed, and Most Recent Episode Unspecified. Bipolar I Disorder, Single Manic Episode, is used to describe individuals who are having a first episode of mania. The remaining criteria sets are used to specify the nature of the current (or most recent) episode in individuals who have had recurrent mood episodes" (APA, 2000) .

Instead of listing all of the diagnostic criteria, diagnostic features, and associated features and disorders for the many variants of the bipolar condition, only the following variants are described below with their respective diagnostic criteria, diagnostic features, and associated features and disorders:

- 296.4x Bipolar I Disorder, Most Recent Manic Episode (including criteria for Manic Episode, Major Depressive Episode, and Mixed Episode)
- 296.89 Bipolar II Disorder (Recurrent Major Depressive Episodes With Hypomanic Episodes)
- 296.80 Bipolar Disorder Not Otherwise Specified.

DSM DISORDERS

Diagnostic Criteria for 296.4x Bipolar I Disorder, Most Recent Episode Manic (APA, 2000)

A. Currently (or most recently) in a Manic Episode [see below Criteria for Manic Episode].
B. There has previously been at least one Major Depressive Episode [see Criteria for Major Depressive Episode], Manic Episode [see Criteria for Manic Episode], or Mixed Episode [see Criteria for Mixed Episode].
C. The mood episodes in Criteria A and B are not better accounted for by Schizoaffective Disorder and are not superimposed on Schizophrenia, Schizophreniform Disorder, Delusional Disorder, or Psychotic Disorder Not Otherwise Specified.

Criteria for Manic Episode (APA, 2000)

A. A distinct period of abnormally and persistently elevated, expansive, or irritable mood, lasting at least 1 week (or any duration if hospitalization is necessary).
B. During the period of mood disturbance, three (or more) of the following symptoms have persisted (four if the mood is only irritable) and have been present to a significant degree:
   1. inflated self-esteem or grandiosity
   2. decreased need for sleep (e.g., feels rested after only 3 hours of sleep)
   3. more talkative than usual or pressure to keep talking
   4. flight of ideas or subjective experience that thoughts are racing
   5. distractibility (i.e., attention too easily drawn to unimportant or irrelevant external stimuli)

6. increase in goal-directed activity (either socially, at work or school, or sexually) or psychomotor agitation
7. excessive involvement in pleasurable activities that have a high potential for painful consequences (e.g., engaging in unrestrained buying sprees, sexual indiscretions, or foolish business investments)
C. The symptoms do not meet criteria for a Mixed Episode [see below Criteria for Mixed Episode].
D. The mood disturbance is sufficiently severe to cause marked impairment in occupational functioning or in usual social activities or relationships with others, or to necessitate hospitalization to prevent harm to self or others, or there are psychotic features.
E. The symptoms are not due to the direct physiological effects of a substance (e.g., a drug of abuse, a medication, or other treatment) or a general medical condition (e.g., hyperthyroidism).

Criteria for Major Depressive Episode (APA, 2000)

A. Five (or more) of the following symptoms have been present during the same 2-week period and represent a change from previous functioning; at least one of the symptoms is either (1) depressed mood or (2) loss of interest or pleasure. **Note:** Do not include symptoms that are clearly due to a general medical condition, or mood-incongruent delusions or hallucinations.
   1. depressed mood most of the day, nearly every day, as indicated by either subjective report (e.g., feels sad or empty) or observation made by others (e.g., appears tearful). **Note:** In children and adolescents, can be irritable mood.
   2. markedly diminished interest or pleasure in all, or almost all, activities most of the day, nearly every day (as indicated by either subjective account or observation made by others)
   3. significant weight loss when not dieting or weight gain (e.g., a change of more than 5% of body weight in a month), or decrease or increase in appetite nearly every day. **Note:** In children, consider failure to make expected weight gains.
   4. insomnia or hypersomnia nearly every day
   5. psychomotor agitation or retardation nearly every day (observable by others, not merely subjective feelings of restlessness or being slowed down)

6. fatigue or loss of energy nearly every day
7. feelings of worthlessness or excessive or inappropriate guilt (which may be delusional) nearly every day (not merely self-reproach or guilt about being sick)
8. diminished ability to think or concentrate, or indecisiveness, nearly every day (either by subjective account or as observed by others)
9. recurrent thoughts of death (not just fear of dying), recurrent suicidal ideation without a specific plan, or a suicide attempt or a specific plan for committing suicide

B. The symptoms do not meet criteria for a Mixed Episode [see below Criteria for Mixed Episode].
C. The symptoms cause clinically significant distress or impairment in social, occupational, or other important areas of functioning.
D. The symptoms are not due to the direct physiological effects of a substance (e.g., a drug of abuse, a medication) or a general medical condition (e.g., hypothyroidism).
E. The symptoms are not better accounted for by Bereavement, i.e., after the loss of a loved one, the symptoms persist for longer than 2 months or are characterized by marked functional impairment, morbid preoccupation with worthlessness, suicidal ideation, psychotic symptoms, or psychomotor retardation.

Criteria for a Mixed Episode (APA, 2000)

A. The criteria are met both for a Manic Episode [see above Criteria for Manic Episode] and for a Major Depressive Episode [see above Criteria for Major Depressive Episode] (except for duration) nearly every day during at least a 1-week period.
B. The mood disturbance is sufficiently severe to cause marked impairment in occupational functioning or in usual social activities or relationships with others, or to necessitate hospitalization to prevent harm to self or others, or there are psychotic features.
C. The symptoms are not due to the direct physiological effects of a substance (e.g., a drug of abuse, a medication, or other treatment) or a general medical condition (e.g., hyperthyroidism). **Note:** Mixed-like episodes that are clearly caused by somatic antidepressant treatment (e.g., medication, electroconvulsive therapy, light therapy) should not count toward a diagnosis of Bipolar I Disorder.

Diagnostic Features for Bipolar I Disorder (APA, 2000)

The essential feature of Bipolar I Disorder is a clinical course that is characterized by the occurrence of one or more Manic Episodes or Mixed Episodes. Often individuals have also had one or more Major Depressive Episodes. Episodes of Substance-Induced Mood Disorder (due to the direct effects of a medication, other somatic treatments for depression, a drug of abuse, or toxin exposure) or of Mood Disorder Due to a General Medical Condition do not count toward a diagnosis of Bipolar I Disorder. In addition, the episodes are not better accounted for by Schizoaffective Disorder and are not superimposed on Schizophrenia, Schizophreniform Disorder, Delusional Disorder, or Psychotic Disorder Not Otherwise Specified. Bipolar I Disorder is subclassified in the fourth digit of the code according to whether the individual is experiencing a first episode (i.e., Single Manic Episode) or whether the disorder is recurrent. Recurrence is indicated by either a shift in the polarity of the episode or an interval between episodes of at least 2 months without manic symptoms. A shift in polarity is defined as a clinical course in which a Major Depressive Episode evolves into a Manic Episode or a Mixed Episode or in which a Manic Episode or a Mixed Episode evolves into a Major Depressive Episode. In contrast, a Hypomanic Episode that evolves into a Manic Episode or a Mixed Episode, or a Manic Episode that evolves into a Mixed Episode (or vice versa), is considered to be only a single episode. For recurrent Bipolar I Disorders, the nature of the current (or most recent) episode can be specified (Most Recent Episode Hypomanic, Most Recent Episode Manic, Most Recent Episode Mixed, Most Recent Episode Depressed, Most Recent Episode Unspecified).

Associated Features and Disorders (APA, 2000)

Completed suicide occurs in 10%–15% of individuals with Bipolar I Disorder. Suicidal ideation and attempts are more likely to occur when the individual is in a depressive or mixed state. Child abuse, spouse abuse, or other violent behavior may occur during severe Manic Episodes or during those with psychotic features. Other associated problems include school truancy, school failure, occupational failure, divorce, or episodic antisocial behavior. Bipolar Disorder is associated with Alcohol and other Substance Use Disorders in many individuals. Individuals with earlier onset of Bipolar I Disorder are more likely to have a history of current alcohol or other substance use problems. Concomitant alcohol and other substance use is associated with an increased number of hospitalizations and a worse course of illness. Other associated mental disorders include Anorexia Nervosa, Bulimia Nervosa, Attention-Deficit/Hyperactivity Disorder, Panic Disorder, and Social Phobia.

Reprinted with permission from the *Diagnostic and Statistical Manual of Mental Disorders, Fourth Edition, Text Revision.* Copyright 2000 American Psychiatric Association.

Diagnostic Criteria for 296.89 Bipolar II Disorder (Recurrent Major Depressive Episodes With Hypomanic Episodes) (APA, 2000)

A. Presence (or history) of one or more Major Depressive Episodes [see above Criteria for Major Depressive Episode].
B. Presence (or history) of at least one Hypomanic Episode [see below Criteria for Hypomanic Episode].
C. There has never been a Manic Episode [see above Criteria for Manic Episode] or a Mixed Episode [see above Criteria for Mixed Episode].
D. The mood symptoms in Criteria A and B are not better accounted for by Schizoaffective Disorder and are not superimposed on Schizophrenia, Schizophreniform Disorder, Delusional Disorder, or Psychotic Disorder Not Otherwise Specified.
E. The symptoms cause clinically significant distress or impairment in social, occupational, or other important areas of functioning.

Criteria for Hypomanic Episode (APA, 2000)

A. A distinct period of persistently elevated, expansive, or irritable mood, lasting throughout at least 4 days, that is clearly different from the usual nondepressed mood.
B. During the period of mood disturbance, three (or more) of the following symptoms have persisted (four if the mood is only irritable) and have been present to a significant degree:
   1. inflated self-esteem or grandiosity
   2. decreased need for sleep (e.g., feels rested after only 3 hours of sleep)
   3. more talkative than usual or pressure to keep talking

4. flight of ideas or subjective experience that thoughts are racing
5. distractibility (i.e., attention too easily drawn to unimportant or irrelevant external stimuli)
6. increase in goal-directed activity (either socially, at work or school, or sexually) or psychomotor agitation
7. excessive involvement in pleasurable activities that have a high potential for painful consequences (e.g., the person engages in unrestrained buying sprees, sexual indiscretions, or foolish business investments)

C. The episode is associated with an unequivocal change in functioning that is uncharacteristic of the person when not symptomatic.

D. The disturbance in mood and the change in functioning are observable by others.

E. The episode is not severe enough to cause marked impairment in social or occupational functioning, or to necessitate hospitalization, and there are no psychotic features.

F. The symptoms are not due to the direct physiological effects of a substance (e.g., a drug of abuse, a medication, or other treatment) or a general medical condition (e.g., hyperthyroidism).

Note: Hypomanic-like episodes that are clearly caused by somatic antidepressant treatment (e.g., medication, electroconvulsive therapy, light therapy) should not count toward a diagnosis of Bipolar II Disorder.

Diagnostic Features (APA, 2000)

Individuals with Bipolar II Disorder may not view the Hypomanic Episodes as pathological, although others may be troubled by the individual's erratic behavior. Often individuals, particularly when in the midst of a Major Depressive Episode, do not recall periods of hypomania without reminders from close friends or relatives. Information from other informants is often critical in establishing the diagnosis of Bipolar II Disorder.

Associated Features and Disorders (APA, 2000)

Completed suicide (usually during Major Depressive Episodes) is a significant risk, occurring in 10%–15% of persons with Bipolar II Disorder. School truancy, school failure, occupational failure, or divorce may be associated with Bipolar II Disorder. Associated mental disorders include Substance Abuse or Dependence, Anorexia Nervosa, Bulimia Nervosa, Attention-Deficit/Hyperactivity Disorder, Panic Disorder, Social Phobia, and Borderline Personality Disorder.

296.80 Bipolar Disorder Not Otherwise Specified (APA, 2000)

The Bipolar Disorder Not Otherwise Specified category includes disorders with bipolar features that do not meet criteria for any specific Bipolar Disorder. Examples include

1. Very rapid alternation (over days) between manic symptoms and depressive symptoms that meet symptom threshold criteria but not minimal duration criteria for Manic, Hypomanic, or Major Depressive Episodes
2. Recurrent Hypomanic Episodes without intercurrent depressive symptoms
3. A Manic or Mixed Episode superimposed on Delusional Disorder, residual Schizophrenia, or Psychotic Disorder Not Otherwise Specified
4. Hypomanic Episodes, along with chronic depressive symptoms, that are too infrequent to qualify for a diagnosis of Cyclothymic Disorder
5. Situations in which the clinician has concluded that a Bipolar Disorder is present but is unable to determine whether it is primary, due to a general medical condition, or substance induced

THE KUNDALINI YOGA MEDITATION PROTOCOL SPECIFIC FOR THE TREATMENT OF BIPOLAR DISORDERS*

Below is a protocol that includes three Kundalini yoga meditation techniques specific for the treatment of bipolar disorders. Two are phase-specific meditations—one for the depressed phase and one for the manic phase. The third is phase-independent and can be used to help resolve the condition when the patient is not depressed or manic as well as during either the manic or depressed phase. However, when the patient is clearly manic, the manic-specific technique is recommended, and of course the one specific for the depressed phase is only recommended for times when the patient is clearly depressed.

The phase-independent technique is more difficult than the other two, and is also less likely to be employed when a patient is suffering in deep depression. In fact, most patients find it requires significant rigor, but in time they develop the skill for the full practice time of 31 minutes, even if this takes several months. While the phase-appropriate techniques can be employed independently of the suggested protocol, there is one addition here (Gan Puttee Kriya), along with the required Tuning In technique, which I have used to help patients who want to resolve the condition in general. Here Gan Puttee Kriya is employed as the technique immediately before the phase-independent technique because it can help clear the mind for the rigor to come. Gan Puttee Kriya is a useful technique at this point because it leads to mental balance without overstimulation—a concern with patients who have a bipolar disorder, whether they are being treated with medications or meditations.

1. Technique to Induce a Meditative State: "Tuning In"

This technique is a precursor to the protocol, as is the case with all other Kundalini yoga protocols or individual techniques in this book or any other book on Kundalini yoga as taught by Yogi Bhajan, and it should be practiced before any of the three state-specific techniques here for bipolar disorders, whether they are done independently or in the suggested series for resolving the condition in general. Technique 2 (Gan Puttee Kriya) can be omitted, but the patient will receive reduced overall benefits. Technique 2 would also add additional benefits to Techniques 4 and 5.

Sit with a straight spine and with the feet flat on the floor if sitting in a chair (see Figure 2.1). Put the hands together at the chest in "prayer pose"—the palms are pressed together with 10–15 pounds of pressure (a mild to medium pressure, nothing too intense). The area where the sides of the thumbs touch rests on the sternum with the thumbs pointing up (along the sternum), and the fingers are together and point up and out at a 60-degree angle to the ground. The eyes are closed and focused on the third eye (imagine a sun rising on the horizon, or the equivalent of the point between the eyebrows at the origin of the nose). This mantra is chanted out loud in a 1½-breath cycle:

"Ong Namo Guru Dev Namo"

Inhale first through the nose and chant "Ong Namo" with an equal emphasis on the *Ong* and the *Namo*. Then immediately follow with a half-breath inhalation through the mouth and chant "Guru Dev Namo" with approximately equal emphasis on each word. (The *o* in *Ong* and *Namo* is a long-o sound; *Dev* sounds like *Dave*, with a long-a sound.)

- *Ong Namo* means I bow with reverence to that infinite energy that is the basis of all creation.
- *Guru* means teacher or wisdom.
- *Dev* means divine or of God.

The practitioner should focus on the experience of the vibrations these sounds create on the upper palate and throughout the cranium, while letting the mind be carried by the sounds into a new and pleasant mental space. This sequence should be repeated a minimum of three times.

2. Gan Puttee Kriya: A Technique to Eliminate the Negativity from the Past, the Present, and the Future

Gan Puttee Kriya has also been called the "Kriya to Make the Impossible Possible." Yogi Bhajan originally taught this meditation technique on November 2, 1988 (Bhajan, 1998). Yogis disovered this technique as a tool for eliminating the blocks that form in the subconscious mind and stifle growth, frequently leading to destructive, neurotic, and self-defeating patterns of mental activity.

Sit with a straight spine, either on the floor or in a chair. The backs of your hands are resting on your knees with the palms facing upward. The eyes are nine-tenths closed (one-tenth open, but looking straight ahead into the darkness, not the light below), focused on the third eye. Chant from your heart in a natural, relaxed manner, or chant in a steady, relaxed monotone:

"Sa Ta Na Ma Ra Ma Da Sa Sa Say So Hung"

More specifically:

Chant out loud the sound "Sa" (the *a* sounds like *ahhh*), and touch your thumb tips and index fingertips together quickly and simultaneously with about 2 pounds of pressure.

Chant "Ta" and touch the thumb tips to the middle fingertips.

Chant "Na" and touch the thumb tips to the ring fingertips.

Chant "Ma" and touch the thumb tips to the little fingertips.

Chant "Ra" and touch your thumb tips and index fingertips.

Chant "Ma" and touch the thumb tips to the middle fingertips.

Chant "Da" and touch the thumb tips to the ring fingertips.

Chant "Sa" and touch the thumb tips to the little fingertips.

Chant "Sa" and touch your thumb tips and index fingertips.

Chant "Say" (sounds like the word *say* with a long-*a*) and touch the thumb tips to the middle fingertips.

Chant "So" and touch the thumb tips to the ring fingertips.

Chant "Hung" and touch the thumb tips to the little-finger tips.

Chant at a rate of one sound per second. The thumb tip and fingertips touch with a very light (2–3 pounds) pressure with each connection. This light touch helps to consolidate the circuit created by each thumb–finger link. Start with 11 minutes and slowly work up to 31 minutes of practice. To finish, remain in the sitting posture and inhale, holding the breath for 20–30 seconds while you shake and move every part of your body (like a dog shaking off water). Exhale and repeat this shaking motion two more times to circulate the energy and to break the pattern of tapping the thumb and fingertips, which affects the brain. Finally, after the shaking, sit in absolute calmness and focus the eyes on the tip of the nose with slow deep breathing through the nose for one minute.

Each sound used in this meditation is unique, and they all have a powerful effect on both the conscious and subconscious minds:

"Sa" gives the mind the ability to expand to the infinite.

"Ta" gives the mind the ability to experience the totality of life.

"Na" gives the mind the ability to conquer death.

"Ma" gives the mind the ability to resurrect.

"Ra" gives the mind the ability to expand in radiance (this sound purifies and energizes).

"Da" gives the mind the ability to establish security on the earth plane, providing a
 ground for action.
"Say" gives the totality of experience.
"So" is the personal sense of identity.
"Hung" is the infinite as a vibrating and real force. Together, *So Hung* means "I am Thou."

The unique qualities of this 12-syllable mantra help cleanse and restructure the subconscious mind and help heal the conscious mind to ultimately experience the *super*conscious mind. All the blocks that result from traumatic or troubling events are eliminated over time with the practice of Gan Puttee Kriya. When doing the whole protocol, 11 minutes for this technique is often adequate; however, 31 minutes is even better, and the maximum time: *Do not go beyond 31 minutes.*

3. Phase-Independent Technique for the Resolution of the Bipolar Condition in General

The posture involves four 90-degree angles (see Figure 11.1):

- Sit on the floor with both legs extended straight out in front, side by side, with the thighs and heels touching.
- The first 90-degree angle is with the feet slightly pulled back (flexed) with the toes pointing straight up.
- The second 90-degree angle is formed with the spine perpendicular to the floor—that is, with the torso and legs at right angles.
- The third 90-degree angle is formed by extending the two upper arms straight in front of the body parallel to the ground and at right angles to the torso.
- The last 90-degree angle is formed by positioning the forearms at a 90-degree angle to the upper arms; the forearms are side by side, and the hands are pressed together, with the thumbs side by side and tucked inside the palms up to the first joint (see Figure 11.2).
- The middle fingers fold over and touch the back of the opposite hand, and the remaining three fingers extend up straight.
- The eyes remain opened and focused on the triangle that is formed by the two index fingers and tops of the thumbs.

Figure 11.1.
Phase-Independent Technique for the Resolution of the Bipolar Condition in General

In this position, now inhale and exhale deeply through the nose (the mouth remains closed). During the exhale, mentally "hear" a deep heart-felt sighing sound. Listen to the sound of the breath and become lost in it. Practice this technique for 11–31 minutes, then lay down and relax for 5–15 minutes.

4. Technique for Treating the Manic Phase of the Disorder

This technique is not recommended as a follow-up directly after Technique 3, unless the person feels that he or she is in a manic phase—which would be very unlikely after practic-

Figure 11.2.

ing the three previous techniques. Note that if the person is in a manic phase, he or she should first *tune in* (Technique 1). The person can also do Gan Puttee Kriya (Technique 2, above) and then skip to this technique.

Squat in "crow pose" and hold the head up straight. During the inhale, curl the hands into fists in front of the body, so that they are almost touching (see Figure 11.3). Keep the forearms parallel to the ground and the eyes closed. During the exhale, open the eyes and spread the fingers open, with the hands palm to palm (see Figure 11.4). The fingers point up and out at about a 60-degree angle. Continue the inhale and exhale rhythm with the eyes closed and open, respectively, for 3–11 minutes. Then relax on the back.

Figures 11.3 and 11.4.
Technique for Treating the Manic Phase of a Bipolar Disorder

5. Technique for Treating the Depressed Phase of the Disorder

This technique is not recommended as a follow-up directly after Technique 3, unless the person feels that he or she is depressed—which would be very unlikely after practicing techniques 1-3. Note that if the patient is in a depressed phase, he or she should first *tune in* (Technique 1) and then do this technique. The person can also do Gan Puttee Kriya (Technique 2, above) and then skip to this technique.

Sit with the buttocks on the ground and the bottoms of both feet touching, pulled close to the body (see Figure 11.5). The thumb tips touch the mounds on the palms just below the little finger on their respective hands throughout the entire exercise. The breathing pattern begins by inhaling through a curled tongue in four equal parts (four counts), holding the breath for four equal counts, then exhaling through the nose in four equal parts and holding the breath out for four counts. The hands are positioned by the ears with the palms facing backward. (Note that the hands in Figure 11.5 are shown facing forward so that the view of the thumb tip on the mound of the little finger is clear. However, the hands actually face *backward*.) The hands are stroked past the ears (6–9 inches) in rhythm with the count (so there are 16 strokes of the hands past the ears per breath). The eyes remain closed. Perform this technique for 3–11 minutes. Then relax on the back.

Figure 11.5.
Technique for Treating the Depressed Phase of a Bipolar Disorder

TWELVE

Treating The Addictive, Impulse Control, and Eating Disorders

This chapter covers several DSM-IV-TR diagnostic categories (American Psychiatric Association, 2000):

- The addictions, which include drugs and alcohol in the broad category called "Substance-Related Disorders"
- The Impulse Control Disorders (312.3) that are not covered in this book in other chapters and include Intermittent Explosive Disorder 312.34, Kleptomania 312.32, Pyromania 312.33, Pathological Gambling 312.31, Impulse Control Disorder Not Otherwise Specified 312.30
- The Eating Disorders (Anorexia Nervosa 307.1, Bulimia Nervosa 307.51, and Eating Disorder Not Otherwise Specified 307.50).

Trichotillomania (312.39) is also described in the DSM IV-TR as an Impulse Control Disorder; however, it is covered in this book in Chapter 3 as an OC spectrum disorder. All of the disorders listed above can be treated using the same seven-part protocol that follows the DSM material in this chapter. When it is perfected, this protocol is a "catch-all" treatment for minimizing, correcting, and curing these aberrant, "out-of-control" behaviors. The explanations and diagnostic criteria, diagnostic features, and associated features and disorders, as defined in the DSM IV-TR by the American Psychiatric Association (2000), are provided below.

DSM DISORDERS

The DSM-IV-TR groups the various substance-related disorders into 11 classes: alcohol; amphetamine or similarly acting sympathomimetics; caffeine; cannabis; cocaine; hallucinogens; inhalants; nicotine; opioids; phencyclidine (PCP) or similarly acting arylcyclohexylamines; and sedatives, hypnotics, or anxiolytics (APA, 2000). Polysubstance Dependence and Other or Unknown Substance-Related Disorders (304.80) are also classified in the DSM IV-TR. In addition, it is noted that over-the-counter medications can lead to substance abuse and dependence disorders. The following medication groups are also covered in the DSM IV-TR under Substance-Related Disorders:

> anesthetics and analgesics, anticholinergic agents, anticonvulsants, antihistamines, antihypertensive and cardiovascular medications, antimicrobial medications, antiparkinsonian medications, chemotherapeutic agents, corticosteroids, gastrointestinal medications, muscle relaxants, nonsteroidal anti-inflammatory medications, other over-the-counter medications, antidepressant medications, and disulfiram. (APA, 2000)

However, these latter medication groups are not the subject of treatment in this chapter, due to the possible medical complications. Also a note of extreme caution is warranted here. Some of these drugs (e.g., the barbituates, alcohol, anxiolytics) can have very serious side effects (including seizures and death) if discontinued abruptly, and established treatment plans must always be employed under the supervision and authority of a trained physician.

The DSM-IV-TR also divides the Substance-Related Disorders into two groups:

> the Substance Use Disorders (Substance Dependence and Substance Abuse) and the Substance-Induced Disorders (Substance Intoxication, Substance Withdrawal, Substance-Induced Delirium, Substance-Induced Persisting Dementia, Substance-Induced Persisting Amnestic Disorder, Substance-Induced Psychotic Disorder, Substance-Induced Mood Disorder, Substance-Induced Anxiety Disorder, Substance-Induced Sexual Dysfunction, and Substance-Induced Sleep Disorder). (APA, 2000)

The substance dependence and abuse disorders that include the 11 different classes, as stated above, are the general focus of treatment in this chapter with the seven-part protocol for the substance-related disorders. The substance-*induced* disorders are not covered here.

Criteria for Substance Dependence (APA, 2000)

A maladaptive pattern of substance use, leading to clinically significant impairment or distress, as manifested by three (or more) of the following, occurring at any time in the same 12-month period:

1. tolerance, as defined by either of the following:
   a. a need for markedly increased amounts of the substance to achieve intoxication or desired effect
   b. markedly diminished effect with continued use of the same amount of the substance
2. withdrawal, as manifested by either of the following:
   a. the characteristic withdrawal syndrome for the substance (refer to Criteria A and B of the criteria sets for Withdrawal from the specific substances)
   b. the same (or a closely related) substance is taken to relieve or avoid withdrawal symptoms
3. the substance is often taken in larger amounts or over a longer period than was intended
4. there is a persistent desire or unsuccessful efforts to cut down or control substance use
5. a great deal of time is spent in activities necessary to obtain the substance (e.g., visiting multiple doctors or driving long distances), use the substance (e.g., chain-smoking), or recover from its effects
6. important social, occupational, or recreational activities are given up or reduced because of substance use
7. the substance use is continued despite knowledge of having a persistent or recurrent physical or psychological problem that is likely to have been caused or exacerbated by the substance (e.g., current cocaine use despite recognition of cocaine-induced depression, or continued drinking despite recognition that an ulcer was made worse by alcohol consumption)

Reprinted with permission from the *Diagnostic and Statistical Manual of Mental Disorders, Fourth Edition, Text Revision.* Copyright 2000 American Psychiatric Association.

Criteria for Substance Abuse (APA, 2000)

A. A maladaptive pattern of substance use leading to clinically significant impairment or distress, as manifested by one (or more) of the following, occurring within a 12-month period:
    1. recurrent substance use resulting in a failure to fulfill major role obligations at work, school, or home (e.g., repeated absences or poor work performance related to substance use; substance-related absences, suspensions, or expulsions from school; neglect of children or household)
    2. recurrent substance use in situations in which it is physically hazardous (e.g., driving an automobile or operating a machine when impaired by substance use)
    3. recurrent substance-related legal problems (e.g., arrests for substance-related disorderly conduct)
    4. continued substance use despite having persistent or recurrent social or interpersonal problems caused or exacerbated by the effects of the substance (e.g., arguments with spouse about consequences of intoxication, physical fights)
B. The symptoms have never met the criteria for Substance Dependence for this class of substance.

Reprinted with permission from the *Diagnostic and Statistical Manual of Mental Disorders, Fourth Edition, Text Revision.* Copyright 2000 American Psychiatric Association.

303.90 Alcohol Dependence (APA, 2000)

Refer, in addition, to the text and criteria for Substance Dependence (see above Substance Dependence). Physiological dependence on alcohol is indicated by evidence of tolerance or symptoms of Withdrawal. Especially if associated with a history of withdrawal, physiological dependence is an indication of a more severe clinical course overall (i.e., earlier onset, higher levels of intake, more alcohol-related problems).

Alcohol Withdrawal (see 291.81 Alcohol Withdrawal in the DSM IV-TR) is characterized by withdrawal symptoms that develop 4–12 hours or so after the reduction of intake following prolonged, heavy, alcohol ingestion. Because Withdrawal from alcohol can be unpleasant and intense, individuals with Alcohol Dependence may continue to consume alcohol, despite adverse consequences, often to avoid or to relieve the symptoms of withdrawal. Some withdrawal symptoms (e.g., sleep problems) can persist at lower intensities for months. A substantial minority of individuals who have Alcohol Dependence never experience clinically relevant levels of alcohol withdrawal, and only about 5% of individuals with Alcohol Dependence ever experience severe complications of withdrawal (e.g., delirium, grand mal seizures). Once a pattern of compulsive use develops, individuals with Dependence may devote substantial periods of time to obtaining and consuming alcoholic beverages. These individuals often continue to use alcohol despite evidence of adverse psychological or physical consequences (e.g., depression, blackouts, liver disease, or other sequelae).

305.00 *Alcohol Abuse (APA, 2000)*

Refer, in addition, to the text and criteria for Substance Abuse (see above Substance Abuse). Alcohol Abuse requires fewer symptoms—and thus may be less severe—than Dependence and is only diagnosed once the absence of Dependence has been established. School and job performance may suffer either from the aftereffects of drinking or from actual intoxication on the job or at school; child care or household responsibilities may be neglected; and alcohol-related absences may occur from school or job. The person may use alcohol in physically hazardous circumstances (e.g., driving an automobile or operating machinery while intoxicated). Legal difficulties may arise because of alcohol use (e.g., arrests for intoxicated behavior or for driving under the influence). Finally, individuals with Alcohol Abuse may continue to consume alcohol despite the knowledge that continued consumption poses significant social or interpersonal problems for them (e.g., violent arguments with spouse while intoxicated, child abuse). When these problems are accompanied by evidence of tolerance, withdrawal, or compulsive behavior related to alcohol use, a diagnosis of Alcohol Dependence, rather than Alcohol Abuse, should be considered. However, since some symptoms of tolerance, withdrawal, or compulsive use can occur in individuals with Abuse but not Dependence, it is important to determine whether the full criteria for Dependence are met.

[Given the many different drugs/substances that are included in the 11 classes defined by the American Psychiatric Association, only the criteria for the abuse and dependence of the opioids are listed here as a model for the other substances. Reference to the DSM-IV-TR is encouraged for all other classes.]

304.00 Opioid Dependence (APA, 2000)

Refer, in addition, to the text and criteria for Substance Dependence (see above Substance Dependence). Most individuals with Opioid Dependence have significant levels of tolerance and will experience withdrawal on abrupt discontinuation of opioid substances. Opioid Dependence includes signs and symptoms that reflect compulsive, prolonged self-administration of opioid substances that are used for no legitimate medical purpose or, if a general medical condition is present that requires opioid treatment, that are used in doses that are greatly in excess of the amount needed for pain relief. Persons with Opioid Dependence tend to develop such regular patterns of compulsive drug use that daily activities are typically planned around obtaining and administering opioids. Opioids are usually purchased on the illegal market but may also be obtained from physicians by faking or exaggerating general medical problems or by receiving simultaneous prescriptions from several physicians. Health care professionals with Opioid Dependence will often obtain opioids by writing prescriptions for themselves or by diverting opioids that have been prescribed for patients or from pharmacy supplies.

305.50 Opioid Abuse (APA, 2000)

Refer, in addition, to the text and criteria for Substance Abuse (see above Substance Abuse). Legal difficulties may arise as a result of behavior while intoxicated with opioids or because an individual has resorted to illegal sources of supply. Persons who abuse opioids typically use these substances much less often than do those with dependence and do not develop significant withdrawal symptoms. When problems related to opioid use are accompanied by evidence of withdrawal or compulsive behavior related to the use of opioids, further information should be gathered to see if a diagnosis of Opioid Dependence, rather than Opioid Abuse, is more appropriate.

Impulse Control Disorders

In addition to the disorders described in this section, the problems of impulse control also exhibit with Substance-Related Disorders, Paraphilias, Antisocial Personality Disorder, Conduct Disorder, Schizophrenia, and Mood Disorders (APA, 2000):

> The essential feature of Impulse-Control Disorders is the failure to resist an impulse, drive, or temptation to perform an act that is harmful to the person or to others. . . . The individual feels an increasing sense of tension or arousal before committing the act and then experiences pleasure, gratification, or relief at the time of committing the act. Following the act there may or may not be regret, self-reproach, or guilt. (APA, 2000)

Following are short DSM descriptions of each disorder when these disorders are not the result of another disorder or the effects of a substance-induced delusional state of mind. For greater detail regarding the diagnostic criteria, associated features, and common concurrent mental disorders, see the DSM IV-TR (American Psychiatric Association, 2000).

Intermittent Explosive Disorder (312.34) is characterized by discrete episodes of failure to resist aggressive impulses resulting in serious assaults or destruction of property.

Kleptomania (312.32) is characterized by the recurrent failure to resist impulses to steal objects not needed for personal use or monetary value.

Pyromania (312.33) is characterized by a pattern of fire setting for pleasure, gratification, or relief of tension.

Pathological Gambling (312.31) is characterized by recurrent and persistent maladaptive gambling behavior.

Impulse-Control Disorder Not Otherwise Specified (312.30) is included for coding disorders of impulse control that do not meet the criteria for any of the specific Impulse-Control Disorders described above or in other sections of the manual.

The Eating Disorders (APA, 2000)

The Eating Disorders are characterized by severe disturbances in eating behavior. This section includes two specific diagnoses, Anorexia Nervosa and Bulimia Nervosa. **Anorexia Nervosa** is characterized by a refusal to maintain a minimally normal body weight. **Bulimia Nervosa** is characterized by repeated episodes of binge eating followed by inappropriate compensatory behaviors such as self-induced vomiting; misuse of laxatives, diuretics, or other medications; fasting; or excessive exercise. A disturbance in perception of body shape and weight is an essential feature of both Anorexia Nervosa and Bulimia Nervosa. An Eating Disorder Not Otherwise Specified category is also provided for coding disorders that do not meet criteria for a specific Eating Disorder.

Simple obesity is included in the *International Classification of Diseases* (WHO, 2007) as a general medical condition but does not appear in DSM-IV because it has not been established that it is consistently associated with a psychological or behavioral syndrome. However, when there is evidence that psychological factors are of importance in the etiology or course of a particular case of obesity, this can be indicated by noting the presence of Psychological Factors Affecting Medical Condition (316 Psychological Factor Affecting Medical Condition). Disorders of Feeding and Eating that are usually first diagnosed in infancy or early childhood (i.e., Pica, Rumination Disorder, and Feeding Disorder of Infancy or Early Childhood) are included in the section "Feeding and Eating Disorders of Infancy or Early Childhood" (Feeding and Eating Disorders of Infancy or Early Childhood).

Diagnostic Criteria for 307.1 Anorexia Nervosa (APA, 2000)

A. Refusal to maintain body weight at or above a minimally normal weight for age and height (e.g., weight loss leading to maintenance of body weight less than 85% of that expected; or failure to make expected weight gain during period of growth, leading to body weight less than 85% of that expected).

B. Intense fear of gaining weight or becoming fat, even though underweight.
C. Disturbance in the way in which one's body weight or shape is experienced, undue influence of body weight or shape on self-evaluation, or denial of the seriousness of the current low body weight.
D. In postmenarcheal females, amenorrhea, i.e., the absence of at least three consecutive menstrual cycles. (A woman is considered to have amenorrhea if her periods occur only following hormone, e.g., estrogen, administration.)

Specify type:
    Restricting Type: during the current episode of Anorexia Nervosa, the person has not regularly engaged in binge-eating or purging behavior (i.e., self-induced vomiting or the misuse of laxatives, diuretics, or enemas)
    Binge-Eating/Purging Type: during the current episode of Anorexia Nervosa, the person has regularly engaged in binge-eating or purging behavior (i.e., self-induced vomiting or the misuse of laxatives, diuretics, or enemas)

Reprinted with permission from the *Diagnostic and Statistical Manual of Mental Disorders, Fourth Edition, Text Revision.* Copyright 2000 American Psychiatric Association.

Additional Diagnostic Features (APA, 2000)

When Anorexia Nervosa develops in an individual during childhood or early adolescence, there may be failure to make expected weight gains (i.e., while growing in height) instead of weight loss. Criterion A provides a guideline for determining when the individual meets the threshold for being underweight. It suggests that the individual weigh less than 85% of that weight that is considered normal for that person's age and height (usually computed using one of several published versions of the Metropolitan Life Insurance tables or pediatric growth charts). An alternative and somewhat stricter guideline (used in the ICD-10 Diagnostic Criteria for Research) requires that the individual have a body mass index (BMI) (calculated as weight in kilograms/height in meters^2) equal to or below 17.5 kg/m^2. These cutoffs are provided only as suggested guidelines for the clinician, since it is unreasonable to specify a single standard for minimally normal weight that applies to all individuals of a given age and height. In determining a minimally normal weight, the clinician should consider not only such guidelines but also the individual's body build and weight history.

Usually weight loss is accomplished primarily through reduction in total food intake. Although individuals may begin by excluding from their diet what they perceive to be highly caloric foods, most eventually end up with a very restricted diet that is sometimes limited to only a few foods. Additional methods of weight loss include purging (i.e., self-induced vomiting or the misuse of laxatives or diuretics) and increased or excessive exercise.

Individuals with this disorder intensely fear gaining weight or becoming fat (Criterion B). This intense fear of becoming fat is usually not alleviated by the weight loss. In fact, concern about weight gain often increases even as actual weight continues to decrease.

The experience and significance of body weight and shape are distorted in these individuals (Criterion C). Some individuals feel globally overweight. Others realize that they are thin but are still concerned that certain parts of their bodies, particularly the abdomen, buttocks, and thighs, are "too fat." They may employ a wide variety of techniques to estimate their body size or weight, including excessive weighing, obsessive measuring of body parts, and persistently using a mirror to check for perceived areas of "fat." The self-esteem of individuals with Anorexia Nervosa is highly dependent on their body shape and weight. Weight loss is viewed as an impressive achievement and a sign of extraordinary self-discipline, whereas weight gain is perceived as an unacceptable failure of self-control. Though some individuals with this disorder may acknowledge being thin, they typically deny the serious medical implications of their malnourished state.

In postmenarcheal females, amenorrhea (due to abnormally low levels of estrogen secretion that are due in turn to diminished pituitary secretion of follicle-stimulating hormone [FSH] and luteinizing hormone [LH]) is an indicator of physiological dysfunction in Anorexia Nervosa (Criterion D). Amenorrhea is usually a consequence of the weight loss but, in a minority of individuals, may actually precede it. In prepubertal females, menarche may be delayed by the illness.

The individual is often brought to professional attention by family members after marked weight loss (or failure to make expected weight gains) has occurred. If individuals seek help on their own, it is usually because of their subjective distress over the somatic and psychological sequelae of starvation. It is rare for an individual with Anorexia Nervosa to complain of weight loss per se. Individuals with Anorexia Nervosa frequently lack insight into, or have considerable denial of, the problem and may be unreliable historians. It is therefore often necessary to obtain information from parents or other outside sources to evaluate the degree of weight loss and other features of the illness.

Associated Features and Disorders (APA, 2000)

When seriously underweight, many individuals with Anorexia Nervosa manifest depressive symptoms such as depressed mood, social withdrawal, irritability, insomnia, and diminished interest in sex. Such individuals may have symptomatic presentations that meet criteria for Major Depressive Disorder. Because these features are also observed in individuals without Anorexia Nervosa who are undergoing starvation, many of the depressive features may be secondary to the physiological sequelae of semistarvation. Symptoms of mood disturbance must therefore be reassessed after partial or complete weight restoration.

Obsessive–compulsive features, both related and unrelated to food, are often prominent. Most individuals with Anorexia Nervosa are preoccupied with thoughts of food. Some collect recipes or hoard food. Observations of behaviors associated with other forms of starvation suggest that obsessions and compulsions related to food may be caused or exacerbated by undernutrition. When individuals with Anorexia Nervosa exhibit obsessions and compulsions that are not related to food, body shape, or weight, an additional diagnosis of Obsessive–Compulsive Disorder may be warranted.

Other features sometimes associated with Anorexia Nervosa include concerns about eating in public, feelings of ineffectiveness, a strong need to control one's environment, inflexible thinking, limited social spontaneity, perfectionism, and overly restrained initiative and emotional expression. A substantial portion of individuals with Anorexia Nervosa have a personality disturbance that meets criteria for at least one Personality Disorder. Compared with individuals with Anorexia Nervosa, Restricting Type, those with the Binge-Eating/Purging Type are more likely to have other impulse-control problems, to abuse alcohol or other drugs, to exhibit more mood lability, to be sexually active, to have a greater frequency of suicide attempts in their history, and to have a personality disturbance that meets criteria for Borderline Personality Disorder.

Diagnostic Criteria for 307.51 Bulimia Nervosa (APA, 2000)

A. Recurrent episodes of binge eating. An episode of binge eating is characterized by both of the following:
   1. eating, in a discrete period of time (e.g., within any 2-hour period), an amount of food that is definitely larger than most people would eat during a similar period of time and under similar circumstances
   2. a sense of lack of control over eating during the episode (e.g., a feeling that one cannot stop eating or control what or how much one is eating)
B. Recurrent inappropriate compensatory behavior in order to prevent weight gain, such as self-induced vomiting; misuse of laxatives, diuretics, enemas, or other medications; fasting; or excessive exercise.
C. The binge eating and inappropriate compensatory behaviors both occur, on average, at least twice a week for 3 months.
D. Self-evaluation is unduly influenced by body shape and weight.
E. The disturbance does not occur exclusively during episodes of Anorexia Nervosa.

Specify type:
   Purging Type: during the current episode of Bulimia Nervosa, the person has regularly engaged in self-induced vomiting or the misuse of laxatives, diuretics, or enemas
   Nonpurging Type: during the current episode of Bulimia Nervosa, the person has used other inappropriate compensatory behaviors, such as fasting or excessive exercise, but has not regularly engaged in self-induced vomiting or the misuse of laxatives, diuretics, or enemas

Additional Diagnostic Features (APA, 2000)

Although the type of food consumed during binges varies, it typically includes sweet, high-calorie foods such as ice cream or cake. However, binge eating appears to be characterized more by an abnormality in the amount of food consumed than by a craving for a specific nutrient, such as carbohydrate. Although individuals with Bulimia Nervosa consume more calories during an episode of binge eating than persons without Bulimia Nervosa consume during a meal, the fractions of calories derived from protein, fat, and carbohydrate are similar.

Individuals with Bulimia Nervosa are typically ashamed of their eating problems and attempt to conceal their symptoms. Binge eating usually occurs in secrecy, or as inconspicuously as possible. An episode may or may not be planned in advance and is usually (but not always) characterized by rapid consumption. The binge eating often continues until the individual is uncomfortably, or even painfully, full. Binge eating is typically triggered by dysphoric mood states, interpersonal stressors, intense hunger following dietary restraint, or feelings related to body weight, body shape, and food. Binge eating may transiently reduce dysphoria, but disparaging self-criticism and depressed mood often follow.

An episode of binge eating is also accompanied by a sense of lack of control (Criterion A2). An individual may be in a frenzied state while binge eating, especially early in the course of the disorder. Some individuals describe a dissociative quality during, or following, the binge episodes. After Bulimia Nervosa has persisted for some time, individuals may report that their binge-eating episodes are no longer characterized by an acute feeling of loss of control, but rather by behavioral indicators of impaired control, such as difficulty resisting binge eating or difficulty stopping a binge once it has begun. The impairment in control associated with binge eating in Bulimia Nervosa is not absolute; for example, an individual may continue binge eating while the telephone is ringing, but will cease if a roommate or spouse unexpectedly enters the room.

Another essential feature of Bulimia Nervosa is the recurrent use of inappropriate compensatory behaviors to prevent weight gain (Criterion B). Many individuals with Bulimia Nervosa employ several methods in their attempt to compensate for binge eating. The most common compensatory technique is the induction of vomiting after an episode of binge eating. This method of purging is employed by 80%–90% of individuals with Bulimia Nervosa who present for treatment at eating disorders clinics. The immediate effects of vomiting include relief from physical discomfort and reduction of fear of gaining weight. In some cases, vomiting becomes a goal in itself, and the person will binge in order to vomit or will vomit after eating a small amount of food. Individuals with Bulimia Nervosa may use a variety of methods to induce vomiting, including the use of fingers or instruments to stimulate the gag reflex. Individuals generally become adept at inducing vomiting and are eventually able to vomit at will. Rarely, individuals consume syrup of ipecac to induce vomiting. Other purging behaviors include the misuse of laxatives and diuretics. Approximately one-third of those with Bulimia Nervosa misuse laxatives after binge eating. Rarely, individuals with the disorder will misuse enemas following episodes of binge eating, but this is seldom the sole compensatory method employed.

Individuals with Bulimia Nervosa may fast for a day or more or exercise excessively in an attempt to compensate for binge eating. Exercise may be considered to be excessive when it significantly interferes with important activities, when it occurs at inappropriate times or in inappropriate settings, or when the individual continues to exercise despite injury or other medical complications. Rarely, individuals with this disorder may take thyroid hormone in an attempt to avoid weight gain. Individuals with diabetes mellitus and Bulimia Nervosa may omit or reduce insulin doses in order to reduce the metabolism of food consumed during eating binges.

Individuals with Bulimia Nervosa place an excessive emphasis on body shape and weight in their self-evaluation, and these factors are typically the most important ones in determining self-esteem (Criterion D). Individuals with this disorder may closely resemble those with Anorexia Nervosa in their fear of gaining weight, in their desire to lose weight, and in the level of dissatisfaction with their bodies. However, a diagnosis of Bulimia Nervosa should not be given when the disturbance occurs only during episodes of Anorexia Nervosa (Criterion E).

Associated Features and Disorders (APA, 2000)

Individuals with Bulimia Nervosa typically are within the normal weight range, although some may be slightly underweight or overweight. The disorder occurs but is uncommon among moderately and morbidly obese individuals. There are suggestions that, prior to the onset of the Eating Disorder, individuals with Bulimia Nervosa are more likely to be overweight than their peers. Between binges, individuals with Bulimia Nervosa typically restrict their total caloric consumption and preferentially select low-calorie ("diet") foods while avoiding foods they perceive to be fattening or likely to trigger a binge.

There is an increased frequency of depressive symptoms (e.g., low self-esteem) or Mood Disorders (particularly Dysthymic Disorder and Major Depressive Disorder) in individuals with Bulimia Nervosa. In many or most individuals, the mood disturbance begins at the same time as or following the development of Bulimia Nervosa, and individuals often ascribe their mood disturbances to Bulimia Nervosa. However, in some individuals, the mood disturbance clearly precedes the development of Bulimia Nervosa. There may also be an increased frequency of anxiety symptoms (e.g., fear of social situations) or Anxiety Disorders. These mood and anxiety disturbances frequently remit following effective treatment of Bulimia Nervosa. The lifetime prevalence of Substance Abuse or Dependence, particularly involving alcohol or stimulants, is at least 30% among individuals with Bulimia Nervosa. Stimulant use often begins in an attempt to control appetite and weight. A substantial portion of individuals with Bulimia Nervosa also have personality features that meet criteria for one or more Personality Disorders (most frequently Borderline Personality Disorder).

Preliminary evidence suggests that individuals with Bulimia Nervosa, Purging Type, show more symptoms of depression and greater concern with shape and weight than individuals with Bulimia Nervosa, Nonpurging Type.

Reprinted with permission from the *Diagnostic and Statistical Manual of Mental Disorders, Fourth Edition, Text Revision.* Copyright 2000 American Psychiatric Association.

A SEVEN-PART MEDITATION PROTOCOL SPECIFIC FOR THE TREATMENT OF ADDICTIVE, IMPULSE CONTROL, AND EATING DISORDERS*

1. Technique to Induce a Meditative State: "Tuning In"

Sit with a straight spine and with the feet flat on the floor if sitting in a chair (see Figure 2.1). Put the hands together at the chest in "prayer pose"—the palms are pressed together with 10–15 pounds of pressure (a mild to medium pressure, nothing too intense). The area where the sides of the thumbs touch rests on the sternum with the thumbs pointing up (along the sternum), and the fingers are together and point up and out at a 60-degree angle to the ground. The eyes are closed and focused on the third eye (imagine a sun rising on the

*Copyright © David Shannahoff-Khalsa, 2005. No portion of this protocol may be reproduced without the express written permission of the author.

horizon, or the equivalent of the point between the eyebrows at the origin of the nose). This mantra is chanted out loud in a 1½-breath cycle:

"Ong Namo Guru Dev Namo"

Inhale first through the nose and chant "Ong Namo" with an equal emphasis on the *Ong* and the *Namo*. Then immediately follow with a half-breath inhalation through the mouth and chant "Guru Dev Namo" with approximately equal emphasis on each word. (The *o* in *Ong* and *Namo* is a long-*o* sound; *Dev* sounds like *Dave*, with a long-*a* sound.)

- *Ong Namo* means I bow with reverence to that infinite energy that is the basis of all creation.
- *Guru* means teacher or wisdom.
- *Dev* means divine or of God.

The practitioner should focus on the experience of the vibrations these sounds create on the upper palate and throughout the cranium, while letting the mind be carried by the sounds into a new and pleasant mental space. This sequence should be repeated a minimum of three times. We employed it in our group about 10–12 times. This technique helps to create a meditative state of mind and is always used as a precursor to the other techniques.

2. Spine-Flexing Technique for Vitality

This technique can be practiced while sitting either in a chair or on the floor in a cross-legged position. If you are in a chair, hold the knees with both hands for support and leverage. If you are sitting cross-legged, grasp the ankles in front with both hands. Begin by pulling the chest up and slightly forward, inhaling deeply through the nose at the same time. Then exhale as you relax the spine down into a slouching position. Keep the head up straight, as if you were looking forward, without allowing it to move much while flexing the spine. This position will help prevent a whip effect in the cervical vertebrae. Breathe only through the nose for both the inhalation and exhalation. The eyes are closed, as if you were looking at a central point on the horizon, the third eye. Your mental focus is kept on the sound of the breath while listening to the fluid movement of the inhalation and exhalation. Begin the technique slowly while loosening up the spine. Eventually, a very rapid movement can be achieved with practice, reaching a rate of one to two times per second for the entire movement. A few minutes are adequate in the beginning. Later, there is no upper time limit. Food should be avoided just prior to this exercise. Be careful to flex the spine *slowly* in the beginning. Relax for 1 minute when finished.

3. Shoulder-Shrug Technique for Vitality

While keeping the spine straight, rest the hands on the knees if sitting in a cross-legged position or with hands on the thighs if sitting in a chair. Inhale and raise the shoulders toward the ears, then exhale, relaxing them down. Again, breathe only through the nose. Keep eyes closed and focused on the third eye. Mentally focus on the sound of the inhalation and exhalation. Continue this action rapidly, building to three times per second for a maximum of 2 minutes. *Note*: This technique should not be practiced by individuals who are hyperactive.

4. Ganesha Meditation for Focus and Clarity

Sit with a straight spine, the eyes closed (see Figure 2.2). The left thumb and little finger are sticking out from the hand. The other fingers are curled into a fist with fingertips on the moon mound (the root of the thumb area that extends down to the wrist). The left hand and elbow are parallel to the floor, with the pad of the tip of the left thumb pressing on the curved notch of the nose between the eyes. The little finger is sticking out. With right hand and elbow parallel to the floor, grasp the left little finger with the right hand and close the right hand into a fist around it, so that both hands now extend straight out from your head. Push the notch with the tip of the left thumb to the extent that you feel some soreness as you breathe long and deep. (This soreness lessens with continued practice.) Do this for no longer than 3 minutes. To finish, inhale as you maintain the posture with eyes closed. Push a little more and pull the naval point in by tightening the abdominal muscles for 10 seconds, then exhale. Repeat one more time.

5. Gan Puttee Kriya: A Technique to Help Eliminate Negativity from the Past, the Present, and the Future

Gan Puttee Kriya has also been called the "Kriya to Make the Impossible Possible." Yogi Bhajan originally taught this meditation technique on November 2, 1988 (Bhajan, 1998).

Yogis disovered this technique as a tool for eliminating the blocks that form in the subconscious mind and stifle growth, frequently leading to destructive, neurotic, and self-defeating patterns of mental activity.

Sit with a straight spine, either on the floor or in a chair. The backs of your hands are resting on your knees with the palms facing upward. The eyes are nine-tenths closed (one-tenth open, but looking straight ahead into the darkness, not the light below), focused on the third eye. Chant from your heart in a natural, relaxed manner, or chant in a steady, relaxed monotone:

"Sa Ta Na Ma Ra Ma Da Sa Sa Say So Hung"

More specifically:

Chant out loud the sound "Sa" (the *a* sounds like *ahhh*), and touch your thumb tips and index fingertips together quickly and simultaneously with about 2 pounds of pressure.
Chant "Ta" and touch the thumb tips to the middle fingertips.
Chant "Na" and touch the thumb tips to the ring fingertips.
Chant "Ma" and touch the thumb tips to the little fingertips.
Chant "Ra" and touch your thumb tips and index fingertips.
Chant "Ma" and touch the thumb tips to the middle fingertips.
Chant "Da" and touch the thumb tips to the ring fingertips.
Chant "Sa" and touch the thumb tips to the little fingertips.
Chant "Sa" and touch your thumb tips and index fingertips.
Chant "Say" (sounds like the word *say* with a long-*a*) and touch the thumb tips to the middle fingertips.
Chant "So" and touch the thumb tips to the ring fingertips.
Chant "Hung" and touch the thumb tips to the little-finger tips.

Chant at a rate of one sound per second. The thumb tip and fingertips touch with a very light (2–3 pounds) pressure with each connection. This light touch helps to consolidate the circuit created by each thumb–finger link. Start with 11 minutes and slowly work up to 31 minutes of practice. To finish, remain in the sitting posture and inhale, holding the breath for 20–30 seconds while you shake and move every part of your body (like a dog shaking off water). Exhale and repeat this shaking motion two more times to circulate the energy and to break the pattern of tapping the thumb and fingertips, which affects the brain. Finally, after the shaking, sit in absolute calmness and focus the eyes on the tip of the nose with slow deep breathing through the nose for one minute.

Each sound used in this meditation is unique, and they all have a powerful effect on both the conscious and subconscious minds:

"Sa" gives the mind the ability to expand to the infinite.
"Ta" gives the mind the ability to experience the totality of life.
"Na" gives the mind the ability to conquer death.
"Ma" gives the mind the ability to resurrect.
"Ra" gives the mind the ability to expand in radiance (this sound purifies and energizes).
"Da" gives the mind the ability to establish security on the earth plane, providing a ground for action.
"Say" gives the totality of experience.
"So" is the personal sense of identity.
"Hung" is the infinite as a vibrating and real force. Together, *So Hung* means "I am Thou."

The unique qualities of this 12-syllable mantra help cleanse and restructure the subconscious mind and help heal the conscious mind to ultimately experience the *super*conscious mind. All the blocks that result from traumatic or troubling events are eliminated over time with the practice of Gan Puttee Kriya. When doing the whole protocol, 11 minutes for this technique is often adequate; however, 31 minutes is even better, and the maximum time: *Do not go beyond 31 minutes.*

6. *Medical Meditation for Habituation: A Technique to Cure Any Addiction*

Sit either in a chair or on the floor (see Figure 12.1) (Bhajan, 1976; Shannahoff-Khalsa, 2004). Straighten the spine and make sure that the first six lower vertebrae are locked forward. This means that the lower back is pushed forward as if you are "at attention." Make fists of both hands and extend the thumbs straight. Place the thumbs on the temples and find the niche where the thumbs just fit. (This is the lower anterior portion of the frontal

Figure 12.1.
Medical Meditation for Habituation: A Technique to Cure Any Addiction

bone above the temporal–sphenoidal suture.) This place is usually sensitive to the touch, so do not apply pressure per se; simply touching the area is adequate.

Now lock the back molars together and keep the lips closed. Vibrate the jaw muscles by alternating the pressure on the molars on both sides equally. A muscle will move in rhythm under the thumbs. Feel it massage the thumbs. Keep the eyes closed and look at the brow point, or third eye, the point where the top of the nose meets the forehead. Silently vibrate the five primal sounds

"Sa Ta Na Ma"

at the brow point, applying pressure to the molars with one pressure per sound (the fifth sound here is the sound "ah," which is basic to the other four sounds). The effects of the mantra are the following:

"Sa" gives the mind the ability to expand to the infinite.
"Ta" gives the mind the ability to experience the totality of life.
"Na" gives the mind the ability to conquer death.
"Ma" gives the mind the ability to resurrect under all circumstances.

In other words, the mantra puts one's consciousness through the cycle of infinity, life, death, and rebirth. This mantra cleanses and restructures the subconscious mind to help the individual live in a conscious state that is merged with the infinite. Continue 5–7 minutes and slowly build the practice to 31 minutes maximum.

Yogi Bhajan comments on this technique in this way:

> This meditation is one of a class of meditations that will become well-known to the future medical society. Meditation will be used to alleviate all kinds of mental and physical afflictions, but it may be as many as 500 years before the new medical science will understand the effects of this kind of meditation well enough to delineate all of its parameters in measurable factors. The pressure exerted by the thumbs triggers a rhythmic reflex current in the central brain. This current activates the brain area directly underneath the stem of the pineal gland. It is an imbalance in this area that makes mental and physical addictions seemingly unbreakable. In modern culture, the imbalance is pandemic. If we are not addicted to smoking, eating, drinking or drugs, then we are addicted subconsciously to acceptance, advancement, rejection, emotional love, etc. All these lead us to insecure and neurotic behavior patterns. The imbalance in this pineal area upsets the radiance of the pineal gland itself. It is this pulsating radiance that regulates the pituitary gland. Since the pituitary regulates the rest of the glandular system, the entire body and mind go out of balance. This meditation corrects the problem. It is excellent for everyone but particularly effective for rehabilitation efforts in drug dependence, mental illness, and phobic conditions. (Bhajan, 1976)

7. Meditation for Treating Impulsive Behavior

Sit with a straight spine and place the left arm in front of the body, with the left hand facing down and straight out in front of the heart center. The left arm and hand are parallel to the ground. The right arm is extended straight out parallel to the left arm and in front of the body, right palm facing up (see Figure 12.2). The eyes are closed. Chant the mantra

"Whahay Guru Whahay Guru Whahay Guru Whahay Jeeo"

Figure 12.2.
Meditation for Treating Impulsive Behavior

with at least one entire round of the mantra per breath cycle.

"Wha" is like *wa* in *water*.
"Hay" sounds just like the food for horses.
"Jeeo" sounds like the two letters, *g* and *o*, run together.

Practice for 18 minutes maximum, then place both hands on the chest at the heart center. The left hand is touching the chest and the palm of the right hand is on the back of the left hand. Continue chanting the mantra, but in a whisper, for 2 more minutes, then remain silent for 1 minute with the hands on the chest. To end, inhale deeply and hold the breath, tightening the muscles of the arms, hands (pressing against the chest), and spine. Then exhale out powerfully through the mouth like a cannon. Repeat the inhalation, tightening, and exhalation sequence two more times.

This meditation will also balance the "earth" and "ether" elements of the psyche. This is a useful meditation for young children who sometimes go miserably astray in life. It will increase their ability to remain stable and secure and help develop their temperament, tolerance, and restraint.

This seven-part protocol is designed to help overcome any substance abuse disorder: smoking; the impulse control disorders, including the paraphilias, intermittent explosive disorders, kleptomania, pyromania, and pathological gambling; conduct and antisocial personality disorders; and the eating disorders, including anorexia nervosa, bulimia nervosa, binge eating, and "overeating." One difficulty with this protocol is that both Techniques 6 and 7 require an arm posture that some individuals may find hard to hold for an extended amount of time. However, as with the practice of other difficult techniques, or for beginners in general, the times for these techniques can be reduced in the initial stages of practice. In time the practice can be extended to maximum times.

Usually people find that they can quickly lengthen the times for these two techniques if they persevere. Those who have a severe weakness in the shoulders may initially choose to omit Technique 7 until they are inclined to endure a greater challenge and have built greater strength through the use of Technique 6. In fact, the reason that Technique 7 is added here is only to expedite the rate of recovery overall. It is likely that all of the disorders in this chapter can be treated successfully with only Techniques 1 through 6. Once a person achieves the ability to practice Technique 6 for the full practice time of 31 minutes per day, he or she has overcome a major hurdle. Maintaining this daily practice will help keep the person on safe ground, and after 40 days he or she will likely remain in remission; 90–120 consecutive days would virtually guarantee complete remission. Including Technique 7 will further accelerate the person's overall progress. Both techniques work toward the same goal, however, through different pathways.

One virtue of this entire seven-part protocol is that it can be practiced while sitting in a chair. Sitting erect on the ground adds no significant advantages or additional benefits. The first four techniques are included to help prepare for the use, ease, and maximum benefit of Techniques 5 through 7, which are the key components for treating the disorders in this chapter. Technique 5 actually helps to set a "mental stage" for attempting the more arduous Techniques 6 and 7. Technique 5 helps to create an inner balance and clear negative thoughts from the subconscious mind that lead to self-defeat.

This seven-part protocol is a "catch-all protocol" that provides the greatest assurance and most rapid rate of relief for the entire spectrum of unique disorders in this chapter. However, there are possible substitutions with other meditation techniques that would also benefit people with these disorders. In addition, there are many "on-the-floor" Kundalini yoga exercise sets that would be helpful adjuncts to therapy, maintenance, and recovery.

THIRTEEN

Treating Insomnia and Other Sleep Disorders

According to the American Psychiatric Association's (2000) DSM-IV-TR there are four basic categories of sleep disorders: the Primary Sleep Disorders, which include the Dyssomnias and the Parasomnias; the Sleep Disorders Related to Another Mental Disorder; the Sleep Disorders Due to a General Medical Condition; and Substance-Induced Sleep Disorders. In the first category, the Dyssomnias are "characterized by abnormalities in the amount, quality, or timing of sleep," and the Parasomnias "are characterized by abnormal behavioral or physiological events occurring in association with sleep, specific sleep stages, or sleep-wake transitions" (APA, 2000) . The condition diagnosed as a "Sleep Disorder Related to Another Mental Disorder" can include Insomnia related to another mental condition (327.02) or Hypersomnia Related to Another Mental Condition (327.15). Although the techniques in this chapter may be useful for the two latter conditions, they are not the focus of treatment here. Often, the secondary sleep problem that evolves from "another mental condition" will dissipate when treated with another and more disorder-related protocol. For example, people suffering with depression or generalized anxiety disorder will find that their sleep problems are resolved when using the respective protocols described in this book.

The Sleep Disorder Due to a General Medical Condition (327.xx) "that results from the direct physiological effects of a general medical condition on the sleep–wake system" (APA, 2000) and what is called "Substance-Induced Sleep Disorders" that are directly related to substance use are also not addressed directly in this book. The techniques in this chapter may be relevant to their treatment; however, the sleep-related problems are only secondary to the medical problem.

The Dyssomnias include the common problems of falling asleep and staying asleep, or sleeping excessively, and "are characterized by a disturbance in the amount, quality, or timing of sleep" (APA, 2000) . The American Psychiatric Association lists these problems as Primary Insomnia, Primary Hypersomnia, Narcolepsy, Breathing-Related Sleep Disorder, Circadian Rhythm Sleep Disorder, and Dyssomnia Not Otherwise Specified.

The Parasomnias are defined as Nightmare Disorder (formerly Dream Anxiety Disorder [307.47]), Sleep Terror Disorder (307.46), Sleepwalking Disorder (307.46), and Parasomnia Not Otherwise Specified (307.47). The DSM-IV-TR describes this group of disorders as follows:

> Parasomnias are disorders characterized by abnormal behavioral or physiological events occurring in association with sleep, specific sleep stages, or sleep–wake transitions. Unlike dyssomnias, parasomnias do not involve abnormalities of the mechanisms generating sleep–wake states, nor of the timing of sleep and wakefulness. Rather, parasomnias represent the activation of physiological systems at inappropriate times during the sleep–wake cycle. In particular, these disorders involve activation of the autonomic nervous system, motor system, or cognitive processes during sleep or sleep–wake transitions. Different parasomnias occur at different times during sleep, and specific parasomnias often occur during specific sleep stages. Individuals with parasomnias usually present with complaints of unusual behavior during sleep rather than complaints of insomnia or excessive daytime sleepiness. (APA, 2000)

The diagnostic criteria, diagnostic features, and common co-occuring conditions are not described here for the parasomnias. However, it is likely that the technique listed below, "Shabd Kriya," would be a very useful meditation technique for treating these disorders.

Diagnostic Criteria for 307.42 Primary Insomnia (APA, 2000)

A. The predominant complaint is difficulty initiating or maintaining sleep, or nonrestorative sleep, for at least 1 month.
B. The sleep disturbance (or associated daytime fatigue) causes clinically significant distress or impairment in social, occupational, or other important areas of functioning.

C. The sleep disturbance does not occur exclusively during the course of Narcolepsy, Breathing-Related Sleep Disorder, Circadian Rhythm Sleep Disorder, or a Parasomnia.

D. The disturbance does not occur exclusively during the course of another mental disorder (e.g., Major Depressive Disorder, Generalized Anxiety Disorder, a delirium).

E. The disturbance is not due to the direct physiological effects of a substance (e.g., a drug of abuse, a medication) or a general medical condition.

Reprinted with permission from the *Diagnostic and Statistical Manual of Mental Disorders, Fourth Edition, Text Revision.* Copyright 2000 American Psychiatric Association.

Additional Diagnostic Features (APA, 2000)

Individuals with Primary Insomnia most often report a combination of difficulty falling asleep and intermittent wakefulness during sleep. The specific type of sleep complaint often varies over time. For instance, individuals who complain of difficulty falling asleep at one time may later complain of difficulty maintaining sleep, and vice versa. Less commonly, individuals with Primary Insomnia may complain only of nonrestorative sleep—that is, feeling that their sleep was restless, light, or of poor quality. Not all individuals with nighttime sleep disturbances are distressed or have functional impairment. A diagnosis of Primary Insomnia should be reserved for those individuals with significant distress or impairment.

Primary Insomnia is often associated with increased physiological, cognitive, or emotional arousal in combination with negative conditioning for sleep. A marked preoccupation with and distress due to the inability to sleep may contribute to the development of a vicious cycle: the more the individual strives to sleep, the more frustrated and distressed he or she becomes and the less he or she is able to sleep. Lying in a bed in which the individual has frequently spent sleepless nights may cause frustration and conditioned arousal. Conversely, the individual may fall asleep more easily when not trying to do so (e.g., while watching television, reading, or riding in a car). Some individuals with increased arousal and negative conditioning report that they sleep better away from their own bedrooms and their usual routines. Individuals with Primary Insomnia may thereby acquire maladaptive sleep habits (e.g., daytime napping, spending excessive time in bed, following an erratic sleep schedule, performing sleep-incompatible behaviors in bed) during the course of the disorder. Chronic insomnia may lead to decreased feelings of well-being during the day (e.g., deterioration of mood and motivation; decreased attention, energy, and concentration; and an increase in fatigue and malaise). Although individuals often have the subjective complaint of daytime fatigue, polysomnographic studies usually do not demonstrate an increase in physiological signs of sleepiness.

Associated Features and Disorders (APA, 2000)

Many individuals with Primary Insomnia have a history of "light" or easily disturbed sleep prior to the development of more persistent sleep problems. Other associated factors may include anxious overconcern with general health and increased sensitivity to the daytime effects of mild sleep loss. Symptoms of anxiety or depression that do not meet criteria for a specific mental disorder may be present. Interpersonal, social, and occupational problems may develop as a result of overconcern with sleep, increased daytime irritability, and poor concentration. Problems with inattention and concentration may also lead to accidents. Individuals with severe insomnia have greater functional impairment, lower productivity, and increased health care utilization compared with individuals without sleep complaints. Individuals with Primary Insomnia may also report interpersonal and work-related stress.

Individuals with Primary Insomnia may have a history of mental disorders, particularly Mood Disorders and Anxiety Disorders. Primary Insomnia also constitutes a risk factor for (or perhaps an early symptom of) subsequent Mood Disorders, Anxiety Disorders, and Substance Use Disorders. Individuals with Primary Insomnia sometimes use medications inappropriately: hypnotics or alcohol to help with nighttime sleep, anxiolytics to combat tension or anxiety, and caffeine or other stimulants to combat excessive fatigue. In some cases, this type of substance use may progress to Substance Abuse or Substance Dependence.

TREATING PRIMARY INSOMNIA

The techniques listed below are not necessarily meant to be practiced as a protocol, as is the case with the numbered techniques in most of the other chapters. However, the first technique, "Tuning In," should always be practiced before other techniques, as mentioned throughout this book. In addition to treating insomnia, a technique is included that is specific for helping to prevent nightmares, and another to deepen, shorten, and induce super efficient sleep.

Two techniques are included here for treating insomnia. One, "Shabd Kriya," is specific for treating sleep disorders that exhibit abnormal rhythmic sleep processes, including difficulties in falling asleep and in staying asleep (Bhajan & Khalsa, 1975; Shannahoff-Khalsa, 2004). Shabd Kriya is most useful for treating longstanding and severe cases of insomnia. The second technique, "Yuni Kriya," can be used to treat less problematic cases of insomnia. It is thought that nearly all primary physiological insomnia cases result from stress or hyperarousal. Therefore, stress is viewed as the leading cause of insomnia for the vast majority of people. When prolonged stress is combined with a poor knowledge of healthy sleep habits, insomnia is a frequent end result.

With initial use, Shabd Kriya can lead to a mild disruption of sleep processes and excess dreams that sometimes last 3–5 weeks prior to obtaining apparent day-to-day improvements. This does not mean that the patient is not benefiting at all from the practice, but only that there is an underlying process of change that can have unpleasant effects. These side effects do not happen in all cases, but in my experience the events happen in a significant number of cases and warrant another possible approach when they do occur. These same side effects can also occur when Shabd Kriya is practiced by those who do not suffer from insomnia, but simply choose to practice the technique for its restorative effects and for the supposed benefits toward mastery of the mental realm. One claimed benefit of Shabd Kriya is that it can be used to refine rhythmic brain processes and enhance the development of the personality (Bhajan & Khalsa, 1975).

The occasional side effects with Shabd Kriya have led me to first employ Yuni Kriya as a meditation technique for treating patients with less severe cases of shorter duration, and more often than not, I will start a client on Yuni Kriya before teaching them Shabd Kriya. Yuni Kriya leads to a very deep state of relaxation, and it is best employed immediately before sleep. However, it can also be used as a technique to reduce stress and anxiety during the day, but ample time (several hours) should be allotted for rest thereafter. Yuni Kriya can lead to a spacey state of mind, but one that is coupled with a deep state of relaxation. Thus this technique is a valuable tool for the early stages of insomnia for many patients.

Some of my patients have become annoyed by the side effects of Shabd Kriya in the beginning stages of treatment, and inevitably the switch to practicing Yuni Kriya leads to more satisfying results overall. Some patients are willing to do both, or to start with Shabd Kriya during the day for a while, and then use Yuni Kriya alone before bed. Patients differ in the severity of their sleep disturbance, their will and priority to overcome their condition, and in the occurrence of side effects. Many other Kundalini yoga meditation techniques and exercise sets would also be helpful in the treatment of insomnia. However, Shabd Kriya is likely to be the most effective tool for severe cases and when nothing else works. There is no reason not to employ Shabd Kriya first and then to gauge if side effects manifest. If so, the patient may prefer to start with a practice of Yuni Kriya, and then if needed eventually incorporate Shabd Kriya as the primary or single technique for treatment.

As with all other Kundalini yoga meditation techniques or protocols, the first step is to "tune in." If the patient is employing either Shabd Kriya or Yuni Kriya immediately before bed or within several hours beforehand, the other techniques that have been used frequently in this book as precursors, such as spine flexes and shoulder shrugs, should be avoided, as they act as stimulants.

1. Technique to Induce a Meditative State: "Tuning In"

Sit with a straight spine and with the feet flat on the floor if sitting in a chair (see Figure 2.1). Put the hands together at the chest in "prayer pose"—the palms are pressed together with 10–15 pounds of pressure (a mild to medium pressure, nothing too intense). The area where the sides of the thumbs touch rests on the sternum with the thumbs pointing up (along the sternum), and the fingers are together and point up and out at a 60-degree angle to the ground. The eyes are closed and focused on the third eye (imagine a sun rising on the horizon, or the equivalent of the point between the eyebrows at the origin of the nose). This mantra is chanted out loud in a 1½-breath cycle:

"Ong Namo Guru Dev Namo"

Inhale first through the nose and chant "Ong Namo" with an equal emphasis on the *Ong* and the *Namo*. Then immediately follow with a half-breath inhalation through the mouth and chant "Guru Dev Namo" with approximately equal emphasis on each word. (The *o* in *Ong* and *Namo* is a long-*o* sound; *Dev* sounds like *Dave*, with a long-*a* sound.)

- *Ong Namo* means I bow with reverence to that infinite energy that is the basis of all creation.
- *Guru* means teacher or wisdom.
- *Dev* means divine or of God.

The practitioner should focus on the experience of the vibrations these sounds create on the upper palate and throughout the cranium, while letting the mind be carried by the sounds into a new and pleasant mental space. This sequence should be repeated a minimum of three times. We employed it in our group about 10–12 times. This technique helps to create a meditative state of mind and is *always* used as a precursor to the other techniques.

2. Meditation for Treating Insomnia and Regulating Sleep Stages: Shabd Kriya

This technique was first reported in the scientific literature along with Yuni Kriya in an introduction to Kundalini yoga meditation techniques specific for the treatment of psychiatric disorders (Shannahoff-Khalsa, 2004).

Sit with a straight spine, with both feet flat on the floor if sitting in a chair. Place the hands in the lap, palms up, with the right hand over the left hand (see Figures 13.1 and 13.2). The thumb pads are touching together and point forward. Focus the eyes on the tip of the nose with the eyelids half closed. The tip of the nose is the point you cannot actually see, but if you use a fingertip to touch the end of the nose, this is where the eyes are focused. This is not an eyes-crossed posture but may seem like it initially. (The sides of the nose will look blurry during the focus, but having the eyes crossed makes the nose appear to balloon up, which is not the correct eye posture.) Inhale through the nose in four equal parts, mentally vibrating the mantra

"Sa Ta Na Ma"

with one syllable per each part of the four-part inhale. Hold the breath and mentally vibrate the four-syllable mantra four times, for a total of 16 "beats," then exhale through the nose in two equal parts, mentally vibrating the mantra

"Whahay Guru"

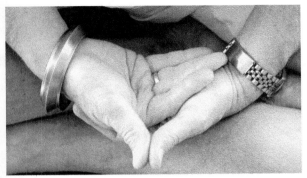

Figures 13.1 and 13.2.
Meditation for Treating Insomnia and Regulating Sleep Stages: Shabd Kriya

one word per part or beat on the exhale. This equals a 22-part, or 22-beat, cycle. Continue for at least 11–15 minutes, working up to 62 minutes. When finished, relax completely and go to sleep.

3. Meditation for Deep Relaxation: Yuni Kriya

Sit with a straight spine, with both feet flat on the floor if sitting in a chair (see Figure 13.3). The eyes are opened and focused on the tip of the nose (to know where this spot is, take the

Figure 13.3.
Meditation for Deep Relaxation: Yuni Kriya

index fingertip and touch the end of the nose, which is not a spot you can actually see, but the point that you attempt to see while keeping the eyes fixed in that position). Only the blurry sides of the nose and anything else that may be in front of you is visible. The elbows are relaxed against the sides. Both hands come up to meet in front of the body at the level of the solar plexus, about one foot in front of the body. The little finger, edges of the hand, and sides of the thumbs are touching. The thumbs are pointing up and the little fingers are pointing away from the body. No other parts of the hands are touching. The three other fingers (index, middle, and ring, are grouped together side by side and not touching the little fingers or thumbs) are pointed forward at about a 60-degree angle to each other. In this position, the hands form a cave-like structure pointing away from the body.

Inhale through the nose and exhale through the mouth, then inhale through the mouth and exhale through the nose, and so on, continuing the cycle for 11 minutes. When inhaling through the mouth, the lips are puckered as if one is about to whistle or kiss. When exhaling through the mouth, the lips are relaxed. In the beginning the hand posture is a little difficult to hold correctly for many people, but in time it becomes very easy to perform. This breath can take you into a very deep state of relaxation and should only be practiced right before going to bed or if you have nothing to do for several hours afterward. This technique should not be practiced for more than 11 minutes.

4. Meditation Breath to Prevent Nightmares

Sit with a straight spine and inhale quickly, like a panic breath; that is, very suddenly open the mouth, as if shocked. At that motion the navel point jerks as if contracted, the tailbone pulls up, the tongue comes forward to the teeth (but not out of the mouth), and the diaphragm is jerked to exchange oxygen maximally. This breath technique is to be practiced 20 times a day, one after the other in succession, to help prevent nightmares. It is also supposedly good for hysteria and paranoia.

5. Meditation Technique to Deepen, Shorten, and Induce Efficient Sleep

Sit with a straight spine, with the lower back pushed forward to attain a very alert posture (see Figure 13.4). The hands are in *ghyan mudra* (i.e., index fingertip touching the thumb tip, not the index nail touching the pad of the thumb tip). The palms face up (see Figure 13.5). The tips of the Mercury (little), Sun (ring), and Saturn (middle) fingers touch their respective counterparts on the opposite hand. The Mercury fingers are closest to the face, and you can see the six fingers grouped in their respective postures back to back. The Mercury fingers meet along their respective backsides, and the Sun and Saturn fingers touch only near the sides of their nails at the ends of the fingers. The six fingers point up and out at a 60-degree angle away from the body and are held at the heart-center level, with the elbows touching the ribs at the sides. The hands are about 9–12 inches in front of the body. The eyes are opened and focused down the nose tip, looking directly at the meeting point where the six finger tips meet. There is no breathing pattern; the breath will slowly adjust

Figures 13.4 and 13.5.
Meditation Technique to Deepen, Shorten, and Induce Efficient Sleep

and should not be consciously regulated. No mantras are to be used. The entire mental and visual focus is on the ends of the six finger tips as a group. The time should be no more than 11–15 minutes per sitting.

This meditation can make a person sleepy and should be done immediately before bed for best results. This meditation may lead to bizarre dreams and disrupt sleep patterns for the first 1–3 weeks. Also, visual hallucinations can occur while looking at the fingertips during the practice of this technique. These hallucinations should be ignored and the practitioner should continue with the practice, allowing the extraneous visual images to disappear.

Optimal results are achieved by practicing this technique every night for 15 minutes maximum, 90–180 nights in succession. This technique induces such a deep and efficient sleep that sleep time can be reduced to 2–4 hours for most healthy young people.

This technique was the very first Kundalini yoga meditation technique that I practiced on a regular daily basis with an intent to explore its long-term effects. At that time I was 26 years of age. After 90 days of perfect night-to-night practice for 15 minutes immediately before bed, I was sleeping from only 11 P.M. to 2 A.M. At this point I would get up and practice other techniques for 2 hours. However, after the 90 days, I quit the practice of this specific technique and eventually my sleep increased in length to 4 or 5 hours per night. Prior to the practice of this technique, I routinely slept for 6–7 hours per night.

At the age of 52, I again practiced the technique but found that I was only able to reduce my sleep to 3½ or 4 hours per night, and I practiced for 120 nights. No doubt the ultimate utility of this technique is dependent on one's age, health status, lifestyle, and how long one wants to employ it. It is claimed that this technique can increase the initial time spent in stage 4 nonrapid eye movement (NREM) sleep and adjust the central nervous system (CNS) to support a more efficient, deeper, and restorative sleep (Yogi Bhajan, personal communication). When I practiced this technique, I found that my dreams increased for several weeks. I also had the same experience with Shabd Kriya.

FOURTEEN

Treating Chronic Fatigue Syndrome

The American Psychiatric Association's (2000) DSM-IV-TR does not include a code or definition for chronic fatigue syndrome, nor does it provide diagnostic criteria or other information for the disorder. However, the Centers for Disease Control and Prevention provides the following information (CDC, 1994):

Chronic fatigue syndrome (CFS) is a debilitating and complex disorder characterized by intense fatigue that is not improved by bed rest and that may be worsened by physical or mental activity. People with CFS most often function at a substantially lower level of activity than they were capable of before the onset of illness. The cause or causes of CFS have not been identified and no specific diagnostic tests are available. Therefore, in order to be diagnosed with chronic fatigue syndrome, a patient must satisfy two criteria:

1. Have severe chronic fatigue for at least six months or longer with other known medical conditions (whose manifestation includes fatigue) excluded by clinical diagnosis; and

2. Concurrently have four or more of the following symptoms: post-exertional malaise, impaired memory or concentration, unrefreshing sleep, muscle pain, multi-joint pain without redness or swelling, tender cervical or axillary lymph nodes, sore throat, headache.

The symptoms must have persisted or recurred during six or more consecutive months of illness and must not have predated the fatigue.

According to the Centers for Disease Control (CDC; 1994), "Other Commonly Observed Symptoms" in CFS include abdominal pain, alcohol intolerance, bloating, chest pain, chronic cough, diarrhea, dizziness, dry eyes or mouth, earaches, irregular heartbeat, jaw pain, morning stiffness, nausea, night sweats, psychological problems (depression, irritability, anxiety, panic attacks), shortness of breath, skin sensations such as tingling, and weight loss. However, the CDC notes that "these symptoms do not contribute to the diagnosis of CFS."

The CDC (CDC, 1994) also lists "Conditions that Exclude a Diagnosis of CFS":

1. Any active medical condition that may explain the presence of chronic fatigue, such as untreated hypothyroidism, sleep apnea and narcolepsy, and iatrogenic conditions such as side effects of medication.

2. Some diagnosable illnesses may relapse or may not have completely resolved during treatment. If the persistence of such a condition could explain the presence of chronic fatigue, and if it cannot be clearly established that the original condition has completely resolved with treatment, then such patients should not be classified as having CFS. Examples of illnesses that can present such a picture include some types of malignancies and chronic cases of hepatitis B or C virus infection.

3. Any past or current diagnosis of major depressive disorder with psychotic or melancholic features, bipolar affective disorders, schizophrenia of any subtype, delusional disorders of any subtype, dementias of any subtype, anorexia nervosa, or bulimia nervosa.

4. Alcohol or other substance abuse, occurring within 2 years of the onset of chronic fatigue and any time afterward.

5. Severe obesity as defined by a body mass index [BMI; body mass index = (weight in kilograms) ÷ (height in meters)^2] equal to or greater than 45. Note: body mass index values vary considerably among different age groups and populations. No "normal" or "average" range of values can be suggested in a fashion that is meaningful. The range of 45 or greater was selected because it clearly falls within the range of severe obesity.]

Any unexplained abnormality detected on examination or other testing that strongly suggests an exclusionary condition must be resolved before attempting further classification.

A NINE-PART KUNDALINI YOGA PROTOCOL FOR TREATING CHRONIC FATIGUE SYNDROME*

1. Technique to Induce a Meditative State: "Tuning In"

Sit with a straight spine and with the feet flat on the floor if sitting in a chair (see Figure 2.1). Put the hands together at the chest in "prayer pose"—the palms are pressed together with 10–15 pounds of pressure (a mild to medium pressure, nothing too intense). The area where the sides of the thumbs touch rests on the sternum with the thumbs pointing up (along the sternum), and the fingers are together and point up and out at a 60-degree angle to the ground. The eyes are closed and focused on the third eye (imagine a sun rising on the horizon, or the equivalent of the point between the eyebrows at the origin of the nose). This mantra is chanted out loud in a 1½-breath cycle:

"Ong Namo Guru Dev Namo"

Inhale first through the nose and chant "Ong Namo" with an equal emphasis on the *Ong* and the *Namo*. Then immediately follow with a half-breath inhalation through the mouth and chant "Guru Dev Namo" with approximately equal emphasis on each word. (The *o* in *Ong* and *Namo* is a long-*o* sound; *Dev* sounds like *Dave*, with a long-*a* sound.)

- *Ong Namo* means I bow with reverence to that infinite energy that is the basis of all creation.
- *Guru* means teacher or wisdom.
- *Dev* means divine or of God.

The practitioner should focus on the experience of the vibrations these sounds create on the upper palate and throughout the cranium, while letting the mind be carried by the sounds into a new and pleasant mental space. This sequence should be repeated a minimum of three times. We employed it in our group about 10–12 times. This technique helps to

*Copyright © David Shannahoff-Khalsa, 2005. No portion of this protocol may be reproduced without the express written permission of the author.

create a meditative state of mind and is always used as a precursor to the other techniques. There is no upper time limit for this technique—the longer the better.

2. Rotating the Spine While Maintaining the Hips in a Steady Position

Sit in an easy pose (a cross-legged posture with knees relaxed down toward the floor as much as possible). Hold the knees with both hands and rotate the torso for 1 minute first in a clockwise direction and then again for 1 minute in a counterclockwise direction, with long, deep breathing through the nose only. (If this sitting posture is not comfortable, practice this technique while sitting in a chair.) Keep the head erect, focusing on the movement of the torso. Keep the eyes closed and focus on the sound of the breath as you inhale and exhale. Make one inhale and exhale for each rotation of the spine and torso. This exercise helps to loosen the spine, and you may even feel as if you are "grinding" the spine. However, it should not feel uncomfortable.

3. Spine-Flexing Technique in Rock Pose for Vitality

This technique increases metabolism, uplifts the spirit, and induces the healthy glandular changes that give an experience of vitality. For this technique, sit on the heels ("rock pose") with the knees coming together in front of the body and the hands resting on the thighs. (If this exercise position is difficult, the person can substitute spine flexing while sitting in a chair, as taught in Chapter 2, "Spine-Flexing Technique for Vitality," p. 11.) Begin by pulling the chest up and slightly forward, inhaling deeply at the same time. Then exhale and relax the spine down into a slouching position. Keep the head up straight, as if looking forward, without allowing it to move much with the flexing action of the spine. This will help prevent a whip action of the cervical vertebrae. All breathing should occur only through the nose for both the inhalation and exhalation. The eyes are closed and focused at a central point on the horizon, which is equivalent to the third eye, a point where the nose and eyebrows meet. The mental focus is kept on the sound of the breath while listening to the fluid movement of the inhalation and exhalation. Begin the technique slowly while loosening up the spine. Eventually a very rapid movement can be achieved with practice, reaching a rate of one to two times per second for the entire movement. Two minutes is adequate in the beginning. Later, there is no upper time limit. Food should be avoided just prior to this exercise. Be careful and flex the spine slowly in the beginning. Relax for 1 or 2 minutes when finished.

4. Third Exercise for the CFS Protocol

Begin by getting down on "all fours" on the floor. Place the chin on the floor (or the forehead if the chin is too difficult), use both hands to hold the right ankle (the right knee is under the chest) and balance on the arms with the left leg extended out behind, keeping the left foot at 90 degrees to the left leg (retracted in) (see Figure 14.1). The eyes are closed and focused at the crown of the head. Breathe slowly and deeply for 1 minute (building to three minutes over time), then relax on your back for 1 minute, and then repeat by reversing the exercise with the right leg up, and so on, for 1 to 3 minutes, followed again by 1 minute relaxing on your back.

Figure 14.1.
Third Exercise for the CFS Protocol

5. Fourth Exercise for the CFS Protocol

Lay on the back and bring the knees up to the chest with the hands in a venus lock (interlock the fingers) over the legs. Raise the head so that the nose is between the knees. Breathe slowly and deeply for 1 minute, then relax on the back for 1 minute. Repeat this exercise for 1 minute, and again follow with 1 minute of rest on the back.

6. Fifth Exercise for the CFS Protocol

Sit on the floor with the legs spread halfway out to the sides (45 degrees) and bend forward 30 degrees (60 degrees up from the ground) (see Figure 14.2). Keep the spine straight and

Figure 14.2.
Fifth Exercise for the CFS Protocol

the head in line with the spine. The arms are out to the sides, parallel to ground. The left hand has the palm facing up and the right hand has the palm facing down. With both hands, touch the tip of the ring finger to the tip of the thumb (sun mudra). When in this posture, breathe only through the nose, inhaling in four parts and exhaling in four parts for 3–5 minutes.

7. Sixth Exercise for the CFS Protocol

Sitting on the floor, lean back at a 30-degree angle as you raise both legs up, balancing on the buttocks and clasping the hands in a venus lock (interlaced fingers) under the legs at the knees. The legs and feet are held together about 30–45 degrees above the ground (see Figure 14.3). Lean back to create approximately a 120-degree angle between the legs and the torso. The head is held in line with the torso. Focus the eyes on the two big toes. Do slow deep breathing through the nose only for 2 minutes. Then relax flat on the back for 1 minute. If there is trouble holding this position, place a pillow behind the back, but maintain the angle; the posture is the important element in this exercise.

8. Seventh Exercise for the CFS Protocol

Sit on the floor with knees open far enough so that the soles of the feet touch in front of the body (see Figure 14.4). The feet are as close to the groin as possible. Bring the forearms together, side by side in front of the body with the elbows touching, in front of the solar plexus region. Both of the palms are flat, touching together with the fingers pointing up (in a prayer position). The eyes are opened and focused on the tip of the nose (the end you cannot see). Breathe slowly and deeply, with four parts segmented for the inhale and one part for the exhale, for 3 minutes. Then relax on the stomach for 2 minutes.

9. A Specific Meditation to Follow the Exercise Set for the CFS Protocol

This meditation is passing energy around the blocked solar plexus (part of the condition for CFS patients). Sit in an easy pose on the floor (or in a chair if necessary) (see Figure 14.5). The left palm is on the navel point (left fingers point right) and the right palm is on the heart center (right fingers point to the left). The eyes are closed, and the patient breathes

Figure 14.3.
Sixth Exercise for the CFS Protocol

Figure 14.4.
Seventh Exercise for the CFS Protocol

slowly and deeply, but inhales through a curled tongue and exhales through puckered lips, making a whistle. This is continued for 11 minutes (if the person cannot make the actual sound of the whistle, that is fine, but the effort should be made to exhale through puckered lips).

This series works on the lower triangle of the chakras (chakras one through three) and the related glands and organs. The final meditation bypasses the solar plexus as the energy is

Figure 14.5.
A Specific Meditation to Follow the Exercise Set for the CFS Protocol

moved from the lower triangle into the heart center. The glands and organs primarily affected in the exercise set are the adrenals, kidneys, liver, gall bladder, and spleen. The meditation (technique 9) also affects the thyroid, parathyroid, and pituitary. The four-part breath orders and organizes the glands (guardians of the body) to create a balanced blood chemistry. This protocol is the most efficient and direct Kundalini yoga routine for treating CFS.

FIFTEEN

Treating Attention-Deficit/Hyperactivity Disorder and Comorbid Disorders (Conduct Disorder and Oppositional Defiant Disorder)

The descriptions with diagnostic criteria and features are listed below, as defined by the American Psychiatric Association's (2000) DSM-IV-TR, for the three subtypes of Attention-Deficit/Hyperactivity Disorder—which include Predominantly Inattentive (314.00), Predominantly Hyperactive–Impulsive Type (314.01), and Combined Type (314.01)—and for the commonly comorbid disorders of Conduct Disorder and Oppositional Defiant Disorder.

DSM DISORDERS

Diagnostic Criteria for Attention-Deficit/Hyperactivity Disorder (APA, 2000)

A. Either (1) or (2):
1. six (or more) of the following symptoms of **inattention** have persisted for at least 6 months to a degree that is maladaptive and inconsistent with developmental level:
    Inattention
    a. often fails to give close attention to details or makes careless mistakes in schoolwork, work, or other activities

     b. often has difficulty sustaining attention in tasks or play activities
     c. often does not seem to listen when spoken to directly
     d. often does not follow through on instructions and fails to finish schoolwork, chores, or duties in the workplace (not due to oppositional behavior or failure to understand instructions)
     e. often has difficulty organizing tasks and activities
     f. often avoids, dislikes, or is reluctant to engage in tasks that require sustained mental effort (such as schoolwork or homework)
     g. often loses things necessary for tasks or activities (e.g., toys, school assignments, pencils, books, or tools)
     h. is often easily distracted by extraneous stimuli
     i. is often forgetful in daily activities

2. six (or more) of the following symptoms of **hyperactivity–impulsivity** have persisted for at least 6 months to a degree that is maladaptive and inconsistent with developmental level:

Hyperactivity

     a. often fidgets with hands or feet or squirms in seat
     b. often leaves seat in classroom or in other situations in which remaining seated is expected
     c. often runs about or climbs excessively in situations in which it is inappropriate (in adolescents or adults, may be limited to subjective feelings of restlessness)
     d. often has difficulty playing or engaging in leisure activities quietly
     e. is often "on the go" or often acts as if "driven by a motor"
     f. often talks excessively

Impulsivity

     g. often blurts out answers before questions have been completed
     h. often has difficulty awaiting turn
     i. often interrupts or intrudes on others (e.g., butts into conversations or games)

B. Some hyperactive–impulsive or inattentive symptoms that caused impairment were present before age 7 years.

C. Some impairment from the symptoms is present in two or more settings (e.g., at school [or work] and at home).

D. There must be clear evidence of clinically significant impairment in social, academic, or occupational functioning.

E. The symptoms do not occur exclusively during the course of a Pervasive Developmental Disorder, Schizophrenia, or other Psychotic Disorder and are not better accounted for by another mental disorder (e.g., Mood Disorder, Anxiety Disorder, Dissociative Disorder, or a Personality Disorder).

Code based on type:

    314.01 Attention-Deficit/Hyperactivity Disorder, Combined Type: if both Criteria A1 and A2 are met for the past 6 months

    314.00 Attention-Deficit/Hyperactivity Disorder, Predominantly Inattentive Type: if Criterion A1 is met but Criterion A2 is not met for the past 6 months

    314.01 Attention-Deficit/Hyperactivity Disorder, Predominantly Hyperactive–Impulsive Type: if Criterion A2 is met but Criterion A1 is not met for the past 6 months

Reprinted with permission from the *Diagnostic and Statistical Manual of Mental Disorders, Fourth Edition, Text Revision.* Copyright 2000 American Psychiatric Association.

Associated Features and Disorders (APA, 2000)

Associated features vary depending on age and developmental stage and may include low frustration tolerance, temper outbursts, bossiness, stubbornness, excessive and frequent insistence that requests be met, mood lability, demoralization, dysphoria, rejection by peers, and poor self-esteem. Academic achievement is often markedly impaired and devalued, typically leading to conflict with the family and with school authorities. Inadequate self-application to tasks that require sustained effort is often interpreted by others as indicating laziness, a poor sense of responsibility, and oppositional behavior. Family relationships are often characterized by resentment and antagonism, especially because variability in the individual's symptomatic status often leads others to believe that all the troublesome behavior is willful. Family discord and negative parent–child interactions are often present. Such negative interactions often diminish with successful treatment. On average, individuals with Attention-Deficit/Hyperactivity Disorder obtain less schooling than their peers and have poorer vocational achievement. Also, on average, intellectual level, as assessed by individual IQ tests, is several points lower in children with this disorder compared with peers. At the same time, great variability in IQ is evidenced: individuals with Attention-Deficit/Hyperactivity Disorder may show intellectual development in the above-average or gifted range. In its severe form, the disorder is markedly impairing, affecting social, familial, and scholastic adjustment. All three subtypes are associated with significant impairment. Academic deficits and school-related problems tend to be most pronounced in the types marked by inattention (Predominantly Inattentive and Combined Types), whereas peer rejection and, to a lesser extent, accidental injury are most salient in the types marked by hyperactivity and impulsivity (Predominantly Hyperactive–Impulsive and Combined Types). Individuals with the Predominantly Inattentive Type tend to be socially passive and appear to be neglected, rather than rejected, by peers.

A substantial proportion (approximately half) of clinic-referred children with Attention-Deficit/Hyperactivity Disorder also have Oppositional Defiant Disorder or Conduct Disorder. The rates of co-occurrence of Attention-Deficit/Hyperactivity Disorder with these other Disruptive Behavior Disorders are higher than with other mental disorders, and this co-occurrence is most likely in the two subtypes marked by hyperactivity–impulsivity (Hyperactive–Impulsive and Combined Types). Other associated disorders include Mood Disorders, Anxiety Disorders, Learning Disorders, and Communication Disorders in children with Attention-Deficit/Hyperactivity Disorder. Although Attention-Deficit/Hyperactivity Disorder appears in at least 50% of clinic-referred individuals with Tourette's Disorder, most individuals with Attention-Deficit/Hyperactivity Disorder do not have accompanying Tourette's Disorder. When the two disorders coexist, the onset of the Attention-Deficit/ Hyperactivity Disorder often precedes the onset of the Tourette's Disorder.

There may be a history of child abuse or neglect, multiple foster placements, neurotoxin exposure (e.g., lead poisoning), infections (e.g., encephalitis), drug exposure in utero, or Mental Retardation. Although low birth weight may sometimes be associated with Attention-Deficit/Hyperactivity Disorder, most children with low birth weight do not develop Attention-Deficit/Hyperactivity Disorder, and most children with Attention-Deficit/Hyperactivity Disorder do not have a history of low birth weight.

Diagnostic Criteria for 312. 8 Conduct Disorder (APA, 2000)

A. A repetitive and persistent pattern of behavior in which the basic rights of others or major age-appropriate societal norms or rules are violated, as manifested by the presence of three (or more) of the following criteria in the past 12 months, with at least one criterion present in the past 6 months:

   Aggression to people and animals
   (1) often bullies, threatens, or intimidates others
   (2) often initiates physical fights
   (3) has used a weapon that can cause serious physical harm to others (e.g., a bat, brick, broken bottle, knife, gun)
   (4) has been physically cruel to people
   (5) has been physically cruel to animals
   (6) has stolen while confronting a victim (e.g., mugging, purse snatching, extortion, armed robbery)
   (7) has forced someone into sexual activity

   Destruction of property
   (8) has deliberately engaged in fire setting with the intention of causing serious damage
   (9) has deliberately destroyed others' property (other than by fire setting)

   Deceitfulness or theft
   (10) has broken into someone else's house, building, or car
   (11) often lies to obtain goods or favors or to avoid obligations (i.e., "cons" others)
   (12) has stolen items of nontrivial value without confronting a victim (e.g., shoplifting, but without breaking and entering; forgery)

   Serious violations of rules
   (13) often stays out at night despite parental prohibitions, beginning before age 13 years
   (14) has run away from home overnight at least twice while living in parental or parental surrogate home (or once without returning for a lengthy period)

B. The disturbance in behavior causes clinically significant impairment in social, academic, or occupational functioning.

C. If the individual is age 18 years or older, criteria are not met for Antisocial Personality Disorder.

[There are also codes based on age at onset and all three can be graded as mild, moderate, or severe:]

312.81 Conduct Disorder, Childhood-Onset Type: onset of at least one criterion characteristic of Conduct Disorder prior to age 10 years

This subtype is defined by the onset of at least one criterion characteristic of Conduct Disorder prior to age 10 years. Individuals with Childhood-Onset Type are usually male, frequently display physical aggression toward others, have disturbed peer relationships, may have had Oppositional Defiant Disorder during early childhood, and usually have symptoms that meet full criteria for Conduct Disorder prior to puberty. Many children with this subtype also have concurrent Attention-Deficit/Hyperactivity Disorder. Individuals with Childhood-Onset Type are more likely to have persistent Conduct Disorder and to develop adult Antisocial Personality Disorder than are those with Adolescent-Onset Type.

312.82 Conduct Disorder, Adolescent-Onset Type: absence of any criteria characteristic of Conduct Disorder prior to age 10 years

This subtype is defined by the absence of any criteria characteristic of Conduct Disorder prior to age 10 years. Compared with those with the Childhood-Onset Type, these individuals are less likely to display aggressive behaviors and tend to have more normative peer relationships (although they often display conduct problems in the company of others). These individuals are less likely to have persistent Conduct Disorder or to develop adult Antisocial Personality Disorder. The ratio of males to females with Conduct Disorder is lower for the Adolescent-Onset Type than for the Childhood-Onset Type.

312.89 Conduct Disorder, Unspecified Onset: age at onset is not known

Reprinted with permission from the *Diagnostic and Statistical Manual of Mental Disorders, Fourth Edition, Text Revision.* Copyright 2000 American Psychiatric Association.

Associated Features and Disorders (APA, 2000)

Individuals with Conduct Disorder may have little empathy and little concern for the feelings, wishes, and well-being of others. Especially in ambiguous situations, aggressive individuals with this disorder frequently misperceive the intentions of others as more hostile and threatening than is the case and respond with aggression that they then feel is reasonable and justified. They may be callous and lack appropriate feelings of guilt or remorse. It can be difficult to evaluate whether displayed remorse is genuine because some of these individuals learn that expressing guilt may reduce or prevent punishment. Individuals with this disorder may readily inform on their companions and try to blame others for their own misdeeds. Self-esteem may be low, despite a projected image of "toughness." For other individuals, measured self-esteem may be overly inflated. Poor frustration tolerance, irritability, temper outbursts, and recklessness are frequent associated features. Accident rates appear to be higher in individuals with Conduct Disorder than in those without it.

Conduct Disorder is often associated with an early onset of sexual behavior, drinking, smoking, use of illegal substances, and reckless and risk-taking acts. Illegal drug use may increase the risk that Conduct Disorder will persist. Conduct Disorder behaviors may lead to school suspension or expulsion, problems in work adjustment, legal difficulties, sexually transmitted diseases, unplanned pregnancy, and physical injury from accidents or fights. These problems may preclude attendance in ordinary schools or living in a parental or foster home. Suicidal ideation, suicide attempts, and completed suicide occur at a higher-than-expected rate. Conduct Disorder may be associated with lower-than-average intelligence, particularly with regard to verbal IQ. Academic achievement, particularly in reading and other verbal skills, is often below the level expected on the basis of age and intelligence and may justify the additional diagnosis of a Learning or Communication Disorder. Attention-Deficit/Hyperactivity Disorder is common in children with Conduct Disorder. Conduct Disorder may also be associated with one or more of the following mental disorders: Learning Disorders, Anxiety Disorders, Mood Disorders, and Substance-Related Disorders. The following factors may predispose the individual to the development of Conduct Disorder: parental rejection and neglect, difficult infant temperament, inconsistent child-rearing practices with harsh discipline, physical or sexual abuse, lack of supervision, early institutional living, frequent changes of caregivers, large family size, history of maternal smoking during pregnancy, peer rejection, association with a delinquent peer group, neighborhood exposure to violence, and certain kinds of familial psychopathology (e.g., Antisocial Personality Disorder, Substance Dependence or Abuse).

Diagnostic Criteria for 313.81 Oppositional Defiant Disorder (APA, 2000)

A. A pattern of negativistic, hostile, and defiant behavior lasting at least 6 months, during which four (or more) of the following are present:
  1. often loses temper
  2. often argues with adults
  3. often actively defies or refuses to comply with adults' requests or rules
  4. often deliberately annoys people
  5. often blames others for his or her mistakes or misbehavior
  6. is often touchy or easily annoyed by others
  7. is often angry and resentful
  8. is often spiteful or vindictive

Note: Consider a criterion met only if the behavior occurs more frequently than is typically observed in individuals of comparable age and developmental level.

B. The disturbance in behavior causes clinically significant impairment in social, academic, or occupational functioning.
C. The behaviors do not occur exclusively during the course of a Psychotic or Mood Disorder.
D. Criteria are not met for Conduct Disorder, and, if the individual is age 18 years or older, criteria are not met for Antisocial Personality Disorder.

Associated Features and Disorders (APA, 2000)

Associated features and disorders vary as a function of the individual's age and the severity of the Oppositional Defiant Disorder. In males, the disorder has been shown to be more prevalent among those who, in the preschool years, have problematic temperaments (e.g., high reactivity, difficulty being soothed) or high motor activity. During the school years, there may be low self-esteem (or overly inflated self-esteem), mood lability, low frustration tolerance, swearing, and the precocious use of alcohol, tobacco, or illicit drugs. There are often conflicts with parents, teachers, and peers. There may be a vicious cycle in which the parent and child bring out the worst in each other. Oppositional Defiant Disorder is more prevalent in families in which child care is disrupted by a succession of different caregivers or in families in which harsh, inconsistent, or neglectful child-rearing practices are common. Attention-Deficit/Hyperactivity Disorder is common in children with Oppositional Defiant Disorder. Learning Disorders and Communication Disorders also tend to be associated with Oppositional Defiant Disorder.

Reprinted with permission from the *Diagnostic and Statistical Manual of Mental Disorders, Fourth Edition, Text Revision*. Copyright 2000 American Psychiatric Association.

THE 11-PART KUNDALINI YOGA MEDITATION PROTOCOL FOR ATTENTION-DEFICIT/ HYPERACTIVITY DISORDER AND COMORBID DISORDERS*

This 11-part protocol has been designed and tested for use with children, adolescents, and adults with ADHD and any combination of co-morbid disorders, including CD, ODD, depression, anxiety, and some learning disorders.

*Copyright © David Shannahoff-Khalsa, 2004. No portion of this protocol may be reproduced without the express written permission of the author.

1. Technique to Induce a Meditative State: "Tuning In"

Sit with a straight spine and with the feet flat on the floor if sitting in a chair (see Figure 2.1). Put the hands together at the chest in "prayer pose"—the palms are pressed together with 10–15 pounds of pressure (a mild to medium pressure, nothing too intense). The area where the sides of the thumbs touch rests on the sternum with the thumbs pointing up (along the sternum), and the fingers are together and point up and out at a 60-degree angle to the ground. The eyes are closed and focused on the third eye (imagine a sun rising on the horizon, or the equivalent of the point between the eyebrows at the origin of the nose). This mantra is chanted out loud in a 1½-breath cycle:

"Ong Namo Guru Dev Namo"

Inhale first through the nose and chant "Ong Namo" with an equal emphasis on the *Ong* and the *Namo*. Then immediately follow with a half-breath inhalation through the mouth and chant "Guru Dev Namo" with approximately equal emphasis on each word. (The *o* in *Ong* and *Namo* is a long-*o* sound; *Dev* sounds like *Dave*, with a long-*a* sound.)

- *Ong Namo* means I bow with reverence to that infinite energy that is the basis of all creation.
- *Guru* means teacher or wisdom.
- *Dev* means divine or of God.

The practitioner should focus on the experience of the vibrations these sounds create on the upper palate and throughout the cranium, while letting the mind be carried by the sounds into a new and pleasant mental space. This sequence should be repeated a minimum of three times. We employed it in our group about 10–12 times. This technique helps to create a meditative state of mind and is *always* used as a precursor to the other techniques. There is no upper time limit for this technique—the longer the better.

2. Spine-Flexing Technique for Vitality

This technique can be practiced while sitting either in a chair or on the floor in a cross-legged position. If you are in a chair, hold the knees with both hands for support and leverage. If you are sitting cross-legged, grasp the ankles in front with both hands. Begin by pulling the chest up and slightly forward, inhaling deeply through the nose at the same time. Then exhale as you relax the spine down into a slouching position. Keep the head up straight, as if you were looking forward, without allowing it to move much while flexing the spine. This position will help prevent a whip effect in the cervical vertebrae. Breathe only through the nose for both the inhalation and exhalation. The eyes are closed, as if you were looking at a central point on the horizon, the third eye. Your mental focus is kept on the sound of the breath while listening to the fluid movement of the inhalation and exhalation. Begin the technique slowly while loosening up the spine. Eventually, a very rapid movement can be achieved with practice, reaching a rate of one to two times per second for the entire movement. A few minutes are adequate in the beginning. Later, there is no upper time limit. Food should be avoided just prior to this exercise. Be careful to flex the spine *slowly* in the beginning. Relax for 1 minute when finished.

3. Spine Twists for Reducing Tension

This technique helps to reduce stress and tension and induce a change of mood by bringing a balance to the nervous system and electromagnetic field. Place the hands on the shoulders, right hand on the right shoulder, left hand on the left shoulder, with the fingers in the front and the thumbs pointing toward the back. Keep both elbows up and out toward the sides. Inhale and twist the spine–torso–head to the left, then exhale and twist to the right. Inhale and exhale only through the nose. Continue this motion while slowly warming up the spine and then picking up the pace for 1 minute. Keep the eyes closed and focused on the third eye to help prevent the possibility of becoming dizzy. When finished, inhale with eyes closed, sitting forward with the arms remaining up, and exhale. Relax for 30 seconds.

4. Ganesha Meditation for Focus and Clarity

Sit with a straight spine, the eyes closed (see Figure 2.2). The left thumb and little finger are sticking out from the hand. The other fingers are curled into a fist with fingertips on the moon mound (the root of the thumb area that extends down to the wrist). The left hand and elbow are parallel to the floor, with the pad of the tip of the left thumb pressing on the curved notch of the nose between the eyes. The little finger is sticking out. With right hand and elbow parallel to the floor, grasp the left little finger with the right hand and close the right hand into a fist around it, so that both hands now extend straight out from your head. Push the notch with the tip of the left thumb to the extent that you feel some soreness as you breathe long and deep. (This soreness lessens with continued practice.) Do this for no longer than 3 minutes. To finish, inhale as you maintain the posture with eyes closed. Push a little more and pull the naval point in by tightening the abdominal muscles for 10 seconds, then exhale. Repeat one more time.

5. Meditation for Learning Disabilities, ADD, and ADHD

Sit with a straight spine, either in a chair or on the floor, with the lower spine pushed forward, as if "standing at attention." The eyes are closed and focused at the third eye, the point where the nose emerges from the forehead. Use the thumb tip of the right hand (or a nasal plug) to block the right nostril and begin breathing only through the left nostril. The pattern of the breath is as follows: Inhale slowly for the count of 10, hold the breath for the count of 10, and exhale slowly for the count of 10. The "count of 10" can approximate 10 seconds once the practitioner has had some experience with this meditation, and eventually can reach 20 seconds. The time should be increased to a maximum time of 31 minutes, with a good beginning time of 11 minutes. Eventually build the practice to do it perfectly for 31 minutes for 120 days in a row. However, when combined here with the other techniques, 11–15 minutes is adequate.

When the ability to do this technique for the full time of 31 minutes is developed, the person should begin to notice that his or her receptive qualities (the ability to listen, the ability to retain what is heard, and the ability not to be reactive to what is heard and seen) are much improved. This technique is also excellent for the condition wherein things "go in one ear and out the other." The effects of this technique can help relax an individual both physically and mentally. When practicing this technique, always do it for at least 3–5 minutes; doing it for a minute or 2 can actually make the person slightly more active for a few minutes. However, most people would not notice the difference if they began the technique feeling agitated or overstimulated and had already practiced Techniques 1 through 4.

6. Meditation to Balance and Synchronize the Cerebral Hemispheres

Sit with a straight spine. The eyes are opened and focused on the tip of the nose (the very end, which is not visible to the practitioner). Both hands are at the shoulder level with palms facing forward and upward, with the hands loosely open, the fingers spread pointing up and not straight, as if holding a heavy ball in each hand (see Figure 15.1). Chant out loud

"Har Har Gur Gur"

and with each sound ("Har" or "Gur"), rotate the hands so that the palms face toward the back (see Figure 15.2) and then quickly return them to face the more forward–upward position. The left palm rotates in the clockwise direction and the right hand rotates in the counterclockwise direction (the only natural direction for rotation of each hand when starting with the palms facing upward). Make sure that the tongue quickly touches (flicks) the

Figures 15.1 and 15.2.
Meditation for Balancing and Synchronizing the Cerebral Hemispheres

upper palate on "Har" and the lower palate on "Gur." Also pump the navel point out lightly with each "Har" or "Gur." Chanting for the mantra and rotating the hands takes about 2 seconds per round. The time for practice is 11 minutes. The frontal lobes and other paired regions of the hemispheres are synchronized by this practice to bring clarity, peace, vitality, and intuition.

7. Meditation to Balance the Jupiter and Saturn Energies: A Technique for Treating Depression, Focusing the Mind, and Eliminating Self-Destructive Behavior

Sit with a straight spine either in a chair or on the floor (see Figure 7.1). The hands are facing forward with the ends of the Jupiter (index) and Saturn (middle) fingers pointing straight up near the sides of the body at the level of the chin. The elbows are relaxed down by the sides and the hands are near the shoulders. Close the ring and little fingers down into the palm, using the thumbs, and keep them there against the palm during the meditation. The Jupiter (index) finger and the Saturn (middle) finger are spread open in a *V* shape (or closed). The eyes are closed.

For 8 minutes open and close the Jupiter and Saturn fingers about once or twice per second. Make sure the two fingers open completely and close completely during the exercise. Simultaneously imagine the planets of Jupiter and Saturn coming together in front of you and then again going apart in synch with the finger movement—the planets should appear to go back and forth along a straight line, in and out to the sides in front of you. It does not matter whether you visualize Jupiter or Saturn on the left or right side.

In the beginning, the visualizatin part may be difficult to do, but this should not slow down the pace of the fingers, which play a more important role here. After 8 minutes, while continuing the same exercise, begin to inhale and exhale through the nose only with this movement: Inhale as the fingers open, exhale as the fingers close. Continue visualizing the planets for 2 additional minutes. Note during the first 8 minutes the breath is not consciously regulated.

Then, for the last minute, spread the two fingers and hold them wide apart (now they do not open and close, they remain in the fixed *V* shape), keeping them very stiff (which requires considerable effort) while also keeping the mouth in an O, or ring, shape. Breathe in and out of the mouth using only the diaphragm (not the wall of the upper chest) with a rate of one to three breaths per second. After 1 minute, inhale, hold the breath in, and tense every muscle tightly (including the hands and fingers, with the *V* shape kept rigid, arms, back, stomach) in the body for 10 seconds. Exhale and repeat two more times for 10 seconds. Then relax.

As previously noted in Chapter 9, Yogi Bhajan explained the effects of this meditation:

> This meditation will help increase a person's ability to focus and concentrate and also increase the IQ of an individual over several months of practice. The mind becomes very focused and clear, the brain becomes very energized. This technique will also help eliminate depression. This technique can also enhance math skills for those who have difficulties with math. The Jupiter and Saturn energies become balanced (the brain is balanced) and this allows one to overcome any challenge, including mastery of the self. This technique also helps to eliminate self-destructive behavior and undesirable (acting out) behavior toward others. In addition, during the beginning of the technique, around the 4 to 8 minute mark, a person can feel very irritable and sometimes it can bring out deep-seated anger. (Bhajan, 1995)

Note: If a person feels dizzy during the meditation, he or she should stop and try it again on another occasion.

8. Brain Exercise for Normalizing Frontal Lobes and Enhancing Focus, Clarity, and the Ability to Communicate (Listen and Articulate)

Sit straight and raise the hands to the shoulder level near the sides with the hands facing forward. The first three fingers (index, middle, and ring finger) are kept straight and point up (this is difficult for many in the beginning, and patients should simply do their best). The thumb tips and the tips of the little fingers continuously touch and let go at a very rapid pace (up to four to five times per second). The eyes remain closed. Continue the rapid contact and release of the thumb tips and little fingertips for 3 minutes, maximum. After 2 minutes, the person begins to create the effect he or she wants, but 3 minutes is ideal. The effects can last up to 4 hours. Once an individual develops the ability to do this technique easily for 3 minutes, he or she will begin to excel in communication skills.

Techniques 9, 10, and 11 are especially useful for patients with comorbid Conduct Disorder or Oppositional Defiant Disorder. And, of course, they can be used separately. A patient with "pure" ADHD or ADD (no comborbid disorders) can choose not to include Techniques 9 through 11.

9. Technique for Tranquilizing an Angry Mind

This technique is only used when people are experiencing significant anger. This is not a technique for latent or "cold" repressed, deep-seated anger. On the contrary, it is a wonderful option with which to tranquilize a "red-hot" angry mind. There are at least a half-dozen Kundalini yoga meditation techniques for anger, and this one, in my opinion, is by far the simplest and most effective and can easily be implemented with young children. The results can last up to 3 days in less severe cases, and may require two times per day for those with severe red-hot anger.

Sit with a straight spine and close the eyes. Simply chant out loud

"Jeeo, Jeeo, Jeeo, Jeeo"

(pronounced likes the names of the letters *g* and *o*) continuously and rapidly for 11 minutes without stopping. Rapid chanting involves about 8–10 repetitions per 5 seconds. During continuous chanting, the person does not stop to take long breaths, but continues with just enough short breaths to keep the sound going seamlessly. Eleven minutes is all that is needed. (This technique only has real benefit if anger is a clear and immediate problem.)

10. Brain Exercise for Patience and Temperament

Sit with a straight spine. Close the eyes nine-tenths and look straight ahead at the third eye point. Interlock the middle fingers only and bring this lock in front of the heart center, 2–3 inches in front of the chest. The right palm faces down and the left palm faces the chest. Make sure that only the middle fingers are touching and pull this lock with maximum capacity for 3 minutes while breathing slowly and deeply. This technique is usually a little painful in the middle fingers when done correctly.

11. Meditation for Releasing Childhood Anger

Sit straight and extend the arms out straight to the sides, with no bend in the elbows (see Figure 15.3). The thumb locks down the ring and little fingers and the index and middle

Figure 15.3.
Meditation for Releasing Childhood Anger

fingers are extended straight out to the sides, with the palms facing forward. Breathe deeply by sucking the air through closed teeth and exhale through the nose for 11 minutes. To end: Inhale deeply, hold the breath for 10 seconds, stretch the spine up and the arms out straight to the sides with maximum force, then exhale, repeat the inhale, hold, and stretch two more times. This technique can be done at any time with the intended effects, but the effects are most unique when practiced in the evening (Bhajan, 2002).

SIXTEEN

Treating Dyslexia and Other Learning Disorders

The American Psychiatric Association's (2000) DSM-IV-TR does not have a specific code and listing for the diagnostic criteria of dyslexia per se. However, they include a section called the Learning Disorders (formerly Academic Skills Disorder) that includes the following:

- Reading Disorder (315.00)
- Mathematics Disorder (315.1)
- Disorder of Written Expression (315.2)
- Learning Disorder Not Otherwise Specified (315.9).

The general features of the learning disorders are provided below. However, the diagnostic criteria for Reading, Mathematics, and Written Expression are not provided below (see the DSM IV-TR).

DSM DISORDERS

Diagnostic Features of Learning Disorders (APA, 2000)

Learning Disorders are diagnosed when the individual's achievement on individually administered, standardized tests in reading, mathematics, or written expression is substantially below that expected for age, schooling, and level of intelligence. The learning problems significantly interfere with academic achievement or activities of daily living that require reading, mathematical, or writing skills. A variety of statistical approaches can be used to establish that a discrepancy is significant. *Substantially below* is usually defined as a discrepancy of more than 2 standard deviations between achievement and IQ. A smaller discrepancy between achievement and IQ (i.e., between 1 and 2 standard deviations) is sometimes used, especially in cases where an individual's performance on an IQ test may have been compromised by an associated disorder in cognitive processing, a comorbid mental disorder or general medical condition, or the individual's ethnic or cultural background. If a sensory deficit is present, the learning difficulties must be in excess of those usually associated with the deficit. Learning Disorders may persist into adulthood.

Associated Features and Disorders (APA, 2000)

Demoralization, low self-esteem, and deficits in social skills may be associated with Learning Disorders. The school drop-out rate for children or adolescents with Learning Disorders is reported at nearly 40% (or approximately 1.5 times the average). Adults with Learning Disorders may have significant difficulties in employment or social adjustment. Many individuals (10%–25%) with Conduct Disorder, Oppositional Defiant Disorder, Attention-Deficit/Hyperactivity Disorder, Major Depressive Disorder, or Dysthymic Disorder also have Learning Disorders. There is evidence that developmental delays in language may occur in association with Learning Disorders (particularly Reading Disorder), although these delays may not be sufficiently severe to warrant the separate diagnosis of a Communication Disorder. Learning Disorders may also be associated with a higher rate of Developmental Coordination Disorder.

There may be underlying abnormalities in cognitive processing (e.g., deficits in visual perception, linguistic processes, attention, or memory, or a combination of these) that often precede or are associated with Learning Disorders. Standardized tests to measure these processes are generally less reliable and valid than other psychoeducational tests. Although genetic predisposition, perinatal injury, and various neurological or other general medical conditions may be associated with the development of Learning Disorders, the presence of such conditions does not invariably predict an eventual Learning Disorder, and there are many individuals with Learning Disorders who have no such history. Learning Disorders are, however, frequently found in association with a variety of general medical conditions (e.g., lead poisoning, fetal alcohol syndrome, or fragile X syndrome).

Learning Disorder Not Otherwise Specified (315.9) (APA, 2000)

This category is for disorders in learning that do not meet criteria for any specific Learning Disorder. This category might include problems in all three areas (reading, mathematics, written expression) that together significantly interfere with academic achievement even though performance on tests measuring each individual skill is not substantially below that expected given the person's chronological age, measured intelligence, and age-appropriate education.

Reprinted with permission from the *Diagnostic and Statistical Manual of Mental Disorders, Fourth Edition, Text Revision.* Copyright 2000 American Psychiatric Association.

THE FIVE-PART KUNDALINI YOGA MEDITATION PROTOCOL FOR TREATING LEARNING DISORDERS*

This protocol is a "catch-all" approach for those who have dyslexia or any other learning disorder. However, if a person has dyslexia *only*, Techniques 1 and 2 are sufficient. For others, the sequence provided in the protocol can only be enhanced by including the dyslexia technique, but it can also be left out. The individual's degree of learning difficulties should in part determine the practice times for each technique and for whether all of the protocol is required. The complete protocol can only enhance the rate of recovery and the ultimate level of learning excellence achieved. Also, even if a person has no learning disorders, the practice of this protocol will take him or her to new levels of mental excellence and competence with accelerated learning skills.

*Copyright © David Shannahoff-Khalsa, 2010. No portion of this protocol may be reproduced without the express written permission of the author.

1. Technique to Induce a Meditative State: "Tuning In"

Sit with a straight spine and with the feet flat on the floor if sitting in a chair (see Figure 2.1). Put the hands together at the chest in "prayer pose"—the palms are pressed together with 10–15 pounds of pressure (a mild to medium pressure, nothing too intense). The area where the sides of the thumbs touch rests on the sternum with the thumbs pointing up (along the sternum), and the fingers are together and point up and out at a 60-degree angle to the ground. The eyes are closed and focused on the third eye (imagine a sun rising on the horizon, or the equivalent of the point between the eyebrows at the origin of the nose). This mantra is chanted out loud in a 1½-breath cycle:

"Ong Namo Guru Dev Namo"

Inhale first through the nose and chant "Ong Namo" with an equal emphasis on the *Ong* and the *Namo*. Then immediately follow with a half-breath inhalation through the mouth and chant "Guru Dev Namo" with approximately equal emphasis on each word. (The *o* in *Ong* and *Namo* is a long-*o* sound; *Dev* sounds like *Dave*, with a long-*a* sound.)

- *Ong Namo* means I bow with reverence to that infinite energy that is the basis of all creation.
- *Guru* means teacher or wisdom.
- *Dev* means divine or of God.

The practitioner should focus on the experience of the vibrations these sounds create on the upper palate and throughout the cranium, while letting the mind be carried by the sounds into a new and pleasant mental space. This sequence should be repeated a minimum of three times. We employed it in our group about 10–12 times. This technique helps to create a meditative state of mind and is always used as a precursor to the other techniques. There is no upper time limit for this technique—the longer the better.

2. Meditation Technique for Dyslexia

This previously published technique (Shannahoff-Khalsa, 2004, 2006) is also included in Chapter 8 (Treating the Abused and Battered Psyche) because from the yogic point of view, dyslexia and other learning disabilities are thought to develop occasionally as a result of abuse. According to Yogi Bhajan (personal communication), "Dyslexia is the result of a parental hurt block." This meditation was known to be effective in the treatment of dyslexia, which is understood by yogis to be a problem of information processing in general, not simply of letters or words or mathematical symbols. The retarded processing of emotions is also included in this more general view of dyslexia.

Sit in an easy pose (see Figure 8.3). The eyes are opened and focused on the tip of the nose. The arms are in front of the body and extended slightly out toward the sides with the palms up, the hands at the level of the solar plexus. The fingertips touch the thumb tip in the following order with a light but definite touch:

- First touch the little fingertip (the Mercury finger) to the thumb tip and mentally chant "Sa."
- Then touch the index fingertip (the Jupiter finger) to the thumb tip and mentally chant "Ta."
- Touch the ring fingertip (the Sun finger) to the thumb tip and mentally chant "Na."
- Again touch the Jupiter fingertip to the thumb tip and mentally chant "Ma."
- Touch the middle fingertip (the Saturn finger) to the thumb tip and mentally chant "Wha."
- Again touch the Mercury fingertip to the thumb tip and mentally chant "Hay."
- Open the hands completely (palms are almost flat and no fingers touch) and mentally chant "Guru."

During the entire exercise the tongue tip is held touching the upper palate in the top center, where the palate is hard and smooth; the tongue does not move. The breath has a six-part broken-breath inhale and 1-part exhale, all through the nose only. The six parts of the broken breath of the inhale correspond to the six mental sounds of "Sa," "Ta," "Na," "Ma," "Wha," and "Hay," and the exhale corresponds to the mental sound "Guru." You mentally hear these sounds with each corresponding segment of the breath. End the meditation by closing the eyes, inhaling deeply, and stretching the hands up in the air above the head. Shake the arms and hands and fingers vigorously for about 30–60 seconds.

The rate of thumb–finger tapping can increase to one complete round (going through the whole series of thumb tip to fingertips) in 2 seconds. It takes some time to reach this rate, which is achieved once the practice becomes second nature—that is, when it happens automatically without thinking about the sequence. The time for this extremely powerful technique can be anywhere from 11 to 31 minutes, maximum. It is acceptable to start with less than 11 minutes, and most people may have to do so in the beginning. Slowly build the time up to 31 minutes. Eventually, try to complete 40–120 days at 31 minutes per sitting and marvel at the extraordinary effects. Individuals vary in dyslexic severity, and thus each may vary in the time required to attain all benefits. At 120 days of perfected practice, virtually all of one's processing skills are said to be very much healed, with the brain attaining a near-perfect balance.

3. Meditation to Balance the Jupiter and Saturn Energies: A Technique for Treating Depression, Focusing the Mind, and Eliminating Self-Destructive Behavior

Sit with a straight spine either in a chair or on the floor (see Figure 7.1). The hands are facing forward with the ends of the Jupiter (index) and Saturn (middle) fingers pointing straight up near the sides of the body at the level of the chin. The elbows are relaxed down by the sides and the hands are near the shoulders. Close the ring and little fingers down into the palm, using the thumbs, and keep them there against the palm during the meditation. The Jupiter (index) finger and the Saturn (middle) finger are spread open in a *V* shape (or closed). The eyes are closed.

For 8 minutes open and close the Jupiter and Saturn fingers about once or twice per second. Make sure the two fingers open completely and close completely during the exercise. Simultaneously imagine the planets of Jupiter and Saturn coming together in front of you and then again going apart in synch with the finger movement—the planets should appear to go back and forth along a straight line, in and out to the sides in front of you. It does not matter whether you visualize Jupiter or Saturn on the left or right side.

In the beginning, the visualizatin part may be difficult to do, but this should not slow down the pace of the fingers, which play a more important role here. After 8 minutes, while continuing the same exercise, begin to inhale and exhale through the nose only with this movement: Inhale as the fingers open, exhale as the fingers close. Continue visualizing the planets for 2 additional minutes. Note during the first 8 minutes the breath is not consciously regulated.

Then, for the last minute, spread the two fingers and hold them wide apart (now they do not open and close, they remain in the fixed *V* shape), keeping them very stiff (which requires considerable effort) while also keeping the mouth in an O, or ring, shape. Breathe in and out of the mouth using only the diaphragm (not the wall of the upper chest) with a rate of one to three breaths per second. After 1 minute, inhale, hold the breath in, and tense every muscle tightly (including the hands and fingers, with the *V* shape kept rigid, arms, back, stomach) in the body for 10 seconds. Exhale and repeat two more times for 10 seconds. Then relax.

As previously noted in Chapter 9, Yogi Bhajan explained the effects of this meditation:

> This meditation will help increase a person's ability to focus and concentrate and also increase the IQ of an individual over several months of practice. The mind becomes very focused and clear, the brain becomes very energized. This technique will also help eliminate depression. This technique can also enhance math skills for those who have difficulties with math. The Jupiter and Saturn energies become balanced (the brain is balanced) and this allows one to overcome any challenge, including mastery of the self. This technique also helps to eliminate self-destructive behavior and undesirable (acting out) behavior toward others. In addition, during the beginning of the technique, around the 4 to 8 minute mark, a person can feel very irritable and sometimes it can bring out deep-seated anger. (Bhajan, 1995)

Note: If a person feels dizzy during the meditation, he or she should stop and try it again on another occasion.

4. *Meditation for Learning Disabilities, ADD, and ADHD*

Sit with a straight spine, either in a chair or on the floor, with the lower spine pushed forward, as if "standing at attention." The eyes are closed and focused at the third eye, the point where the nose emerges from the forehead. Use the thumb tip of the right hand (or a nasal plug) to block the right nostril and begin breathing only through the left nostril. The pattern of the breath is as follows: Inhale slowly for the count of 10, hold the breath for the count of 10, and exhale slowly for the count of 10. The "count of 10" can approximate 10 seconds once the practitioner has had some experience with this meditation, and eventually can reach 20 seconds. The time should be increased to a maximum time of 31 minutes, with a good beginning time of 11 minutes. Eventually build the practice to do it perfectly for 31 minutes for 120 days in a row. However, when combined here with the other techniques, 11–15 minutes is adequate.

When the ability to do this technique for the full time of 31 minutes is developed, the person should begin to notice that his or her receptive qualities (the ability to listen, the ability to retain what is heard, and the ability not to be reactive to what is heard and seen) are much improved. This technique is also excellent for the condition wherein things "go in one ear and out the other." The effects of this technique can help relax an individual both physically and mentally. When practicing this technique, always do it for at least 3–5 minutes; doing it for a minute or 2 can actually make the person slightly more active for a few minutes.

5. Meditation to Balance and Synchronize the Cerebral Hemispheres

Sit with a straight spine. The eyes are opened and focused on the tip of the nose (the very end, which is not visible to the practitioner). Both hands are at the shoulder level with palms facing forward and upward with the hands loosely open, the fingers spread pointing up and not straight, as if holding a heavy ball in each hand (see Figure 15.1). Chant out loud

"Har Har Gur Gur"

and with each sound ("Har" or "Gur"), rotate the hands so that the palms face toward the back (see Figure 15.2) and then quickly return them to face the more forward–upward position. The left palm rotates in the clockwise direction and the right hand rotates in the counterclockwise direction (the only natural direction for rotation of each hand when starting with the palms facing upward). Make sure that the tongue quickly touches (flicks) the upper palate on "Har" and the lower palate on "Gur." Also pump the navel point out lightly with each "Har" or "Gur." Chanting for the mantra and rotating the hands takes about 2 seconds per round. The time for practice is 11 minutes. The frontal lobes and other paired regions of the hemispheres are synchronized by this practice to bring clarity, peace, vitality, and intuition.

SEVENTEEN

Treating Schizophrenia and the Other Psychotic Disorders

The American Psychiatric Association's (2000) DSM-IV-TR includes the following nine disorders in a chapter called "Schizophrenia and Other Psychotic Disorders": Schizophrenia, Schizophreniform Disorder, Schizoaffective Disorder, Delusional Disorder, Brief Psychotic Disorder, Shared Psychotic Disorder, Psychotic Disorder Due to a General Medical Condition, Substance-Induced Psychotic Disorder, and Psychotic Disorder Not Otherwise Specified. These disorders all include psychotic symptoms as a primary characteristic. The DSM-IV-TR also describes disorders with psychotic symptoms and "associated features" that include Dementia of the Alzheimer's Type, Substance-Induced Delirium, and Major Depressive Disorder With Psychotic Features.

We are not covering the treatment of the remaining psychotic disorders: "Psychotic Disorder Due to a General Medical Condition," wherein the psychotic symptoms are judged to be "a direct physiological consequence of a general medical condition," or a "Substance-Induced Psychotic Disorder," wherein the psychotic symptoms are judged to be "a direct physiological consequence of a drug of abuse, a medication, or toxin exposure" (APA, 2000). However, the final type "Psychotic Disorder Not Otherwise Specified (298.9)" is included for classifying psychotic presentations that "do not meet the criteria for any of the specific psychotic disorders defined above or psychotic symptomatology about which there is inadequate or contradictory information" (APA, 2000).

DSM DISORDERS

1) Schizophrenia is a disorder that lasts for at least 6 months and includes at least 1 month of active-phase symptoms (i.e., two [or more] of the following: delusions, hallucinations, disorganized speech, grossly disorganized or catatonic behavior, negative symptoms). Definitions for the Schizophrenia subtypes (Paranoid, Disorganized, Catatonic, Undifferentiated, and Residual) are also included in this section.

2) Schizophreniform Disorder is characterized by a symptomatic presentation that is equivalent to Schizophrenia except for its duration (i.e., the disturbance lasts from 1 to 6 months) and the absence of a requirement that there be a decline in functioning.

3) Schizoaffective Disorder is a disorder in which a mood episode and the active-phase symptoms of Schizophrenia occur together and were preceded or are followed by at least 2 weeks of delusions or hallucinations without prominent mood symptoms.

4) Delusional Disorder is characterized by at least 1 month of nonbizarre delusions without other active-phase symptoms of Schizophrenia.

5) Brief Psychotic Disorder is a disorder that lasts more than 1 day and remits by 1 month.

6) Shared Psychotic Disorder is characterized by the presence of a delusion in an individual who is influenced by someone else who has a longer-standing delusion with similar content.

7) In **Psychotic Disorder Due to a General Medical Condition,** the psychotic symptoms are judged to be a direct physiological consequence of a general medical condition.

8) In **Substance-Induced Psychotic Disorder,** the psychotic symptoms are judged to be a direct physiological consequence of a drug of abuse, a medication, or toxin exposure.

9) Psychotic Disorder Not Otherwise Specified is included for classifying psychotic presentations that do not meet the criteria for any of the specific Psychotic Disorders defined in this section or psychotic symptomatology about which there is inadequate or contradictory information.

[Following are the diagnostic criteria for schizophrenia and the four subtypes with their respective coding numbers: Paranoid Type (295.30), Disorganized Type (295.10), Catatonic Type (295.20), and Undifferentiated Type (295.90).]

Diagnostic Criteria for Schizophrenia (APA, 2000)

A. *Characteristic symptoms:* Two (or more) of the following, each present for a significant portion of time during a 1-month period (or less if successfully treated):
1. delusions
2. hallucinations
3. disorganized speech (e.g., frequent derailment or incoherence)
4. grossly disorganized or catatonic behavior
5. negative symptoms, i.e., affective flattening, alogia, or avolition

Note: Only one Criterion A symptom is required if delusions are bizarre or hallucinations consist of a voice keeping up a running commentary on the person's behavior or thoughts, or two or more voices conversing with each other.

B. *Social/occupational dysfunction:* For a significant portion of the time since the onset of the disturbance, one or more major areas of functioning such as work, interpersonal relations, or self-care are markedly below the level achieved prior to the onset (or when the onset is in childhood or adolescence, failure to achieve expected level of interpersonal, academic, or occupational achievement).

C. *Duration:* Continuous signs of the disturbance persist for at least 6 months. This 6-month period must include at least 1 month of symptoms (or less if successfully treated) that meet Criterion A (i.e., active-phase symptoms) and may include periods of prodromal or residual symptoms. During these prodromal or residual periods, the signs of the disturbance may be manifested by only negative symptoms or two or more symptoms listed in Criterion A present in an attenuated form (e.g., odd beliefs, unusual perceptual experiences).

D. *Schizoaffective and Mood Disorder exclusion:* Schizoaffective Disorder and Mood Disorder With Psychotic Features have been ruled out because either (1) no Major Depressive, Manic, or Mixed Episodes have occurred concurrently with the active-phase symptoms; or (2) if mood episodes have occurred during active-phase symptoms, their total duration has been brief relative to the duration of the active and residual periods.

E. *Substance/general medical condition exclusion:* The disturbance is not due to the direct physiological effects of a substance (e.g., a drug of abuse, a medication) or a general medical condition.

F. *Relationship to a Pervasive Developmental Disorder:* If there is a history of Autistic Disorder or another Pervasive Developmental Disorder, the additional diagnosis of Schizophrenia is made only if prominent delusions or hallucinations are also present for at least a month (or less if successfully treated).

[The DSM IV-TR also provides the following six classifications for the longitudinal course that can be applied only after at least 1 year has elapsed since the initial onset of active-phase symptoms:]

1) **Episodic With Interepisode Residual Symptoms** (episodes are defined by the reemergence of prominent psychotic symptoms); *also specify if:* **With Prominent Negative Symptoms**
2) **Episodic With No Interepisode Residual Symptoms**
3) **Continuous** (prominent psychotic symptoms are present throughout the period of observation); *also specify if:* **With Prominent Negative Symptoms**
4) **Single Episode In Partial Remission;** *also specify if:* **With Prominent Negative Symptoms**
5) **Single Episode In Full Remission**
6) **Other or Unspecified Pattern**

[The DSM IV-TR (APA, 2000) also states the following about the diagnostic features (in addition to other information not listed here due to length and some redundancy)]

The characteristic symptoms of Schizophrenia involve a range of cognitive and emotional dysfunctions that include perception, inferential thinking, language and communication, behavioral monitoring, affect, fluency and productivity of thought and speech, hedonic capacity, volition and drive, and attention. No single symptom is pathognomonic of Schizophrenia; the diagnosis involves the recognition of a constellation of signs and symptoms associated with impaired occupational or social functioning.

Delusions (Criterion A1) are erroneous beliefs that usually involve a misinterpretation of perceptions or experiences. Their content may include a variety of themes (e.g., persecutory, referential, somatic, religious, or grandiose). Persecutory delusions are most common; the person believes he or she is being tormented, followed, tricked, spied on, or ridiculed.

Referential delusions are also common; the person believes that certain gestures, comments, passages from books, newspapers, song lyrics, or other environmental cues are specifically directed at him or her. The distinction between a delusion and a strongly held idea is sometimes difficult to make and depends in part on the degree of conviction with which the belief is held despite clear contradictory evidence regarding its veracity.

Although bizarre delusions are considered to be especially characteristic of Schizophrenia, "bizarreness" may be difficult to judge, especially across different cultures. Delusions are deemed bizarre if they are clearly implausible and not understandable and do not derive from ordinary life experiences. An example of a bizarre delusion is a person's belief that a stranger has removed his or her internal organs and has replaced them with someone else's organs without leaving any wounds or scars. An example of a nonbizarre delusion is a person's false belief that he or she is under surveillance by the police. Delusions that express a loss of control over mind or body are generally considered to be bizarre; these include a person's belief that his or her thoughts have been taken away by some outside force ("thought withdrawal"), that alien thoughts have been put into his or her mind ("thought insertion"), or that his or her body or actions are being acted on or manipulated by some outside force ("delusions of control"). If the delusions are judged to be bizarre, only this single symptom is needed to satisfy Criterion A for Schizophrenia.

Hallucinations (Criterion A2) may occur in any sensory modality (e.g., auditory, visual, olfactory, gustatory, and tactile), but auditory hallucinations are by far the most common. Auditory hallucinations are usually experienced as voices, whether familiar or unfamiliar, that are perceived as distinct from the person's own thoughts. The hallucinations must occur in the context of a clear sensorium; those that occur while falling asleep (hypnagogic) or waking up (hypnopompic) are considered to be within the range of normal experience. Isolated experiences of hearing one's name called or experiences that lack the quality of an external percept (e.g., a humming in one's head) should also not be considered as symptomatic of Schizophrenia or any other Psychotic Disorder. Hallucinations may be a normal part of religious experience in certain cultural contexts. Certain types of auditory hallucinations (i.e., two or more voices conversing with one another or voices maintaining a running commentary on the person's thoughts or behavior) have been considered to be particularly characteristic of Schizophrenia. If these types of hallucinations are present, then only this single symptom is needed to satisfy Criterion A.

Disorganized thinking ("formal thought disorder") has been argued by some to be the single most important feature of Schizophrenia. Because of the difficulty inherent in developing an objective definition of "thought disorder," and because in a clinical setting inferences about thought are based primarily on the individual's speech, the concept of disorganized speech (Criterion A3) has been emphasized in the definition for Schizophrenia used in this manual. The speech of individuals with Schizophrenia may be disorganized in a variety of ways. The person may "slip off the track" from one topic to another ("derailment" or "loose associations"); answers to questions may be obliquely related or completely unrelated ("tangentiality"); and, rarely, speech may be so severely disorganized that it is nearly incomprehensible and resembles receptive aphasia in its linguistic disorganization ("incoherence" or "word salad"). Because mildly disorganized speech is common and nonspecific, the symptom must be severe enough to substantially impair effective communication. Less severe disorganized thinking or speech may occur during the prodromal and residual periods of Schizophrenia (see Criterion C).

Grossly disorganized behavior (Criterion A4) may manifest itself in a variety of ways, ranging from childlike silliness to unpredictable agitation. Problems may be noted in any form of goal-directed behavior, leading to difficulties in performing activities of daily living such as preparing a meal or maintaining hygiene. The person may appear markedly disheveled, may dress in an unusual manner (e.g., wearing multiple overcoats, scarves, and gloves on a hot day), or may display clearly inappropriate sexual behavior (e.g., public masturbation) or unpredictable and untriggered agitation (e.g., shouting or swearing). Care should be taken not to apply this criterion too broadly. For example, a few instances of restless, angry, or agitated behavior should not be considered to be evidence of Schizophrenia, especially if the motivation is understandable.

Catatonic motor behaviors (Criterion A4) include a marked decrease in reactivity to the environment, sometimes reaching an extreme degree of complete unawareness (catatonic stupor), maintaining a rigid posture and resisting efforts to be moved (catatonic rigidity), active resistance to instructions or attempts to be moved (catatonic negativism), the assumption of inappropriate or bizarre postures (catatonic posturing), or purposeless and unstimulated excessive motor activity (catatonic excitement). Although catatonia has historically been associated with Schizophrenia, the clinician should keep in mind that catatonic symptoms are nonspecific and may occur in other mental disorders (see Mood Disorders With Catatonic Features, Catatonic Features Specifier), in general medical conditions (see Catatonic Disorder Due to a General Medical Condition, 293.89 Catatonic Disorder Due to a General Medical Condition), and Medication-Induced Movement Disorders (see Neuroleptic-Induced Parkinsonism, 332.1 Neuroleptic-Induced Parkinsonism).

The negative symptoms of Schizophrenia (Criterion A5) account for a substantial degree of the morbidity associated with the disorder. Three negative symptoms—affective flattening, alogia, and avolition—are included in the definition of Schizophrenia; other negative symptoms (e.g., anhedonia) are noted in the "Associated Features and Disorders" section below. Affective flattening is especially common and is characterized by the person's face appearing immobile and unresponsive, with poor eye contact and reduced body language. Although a person with affective flattening may smile and warm up occasionally, his or her range of emotional expressiveness is clearly diminished most of the time. It may be useful to observe the person interacting with peers to determine whether affective flattening is sufficiently persistent to meet the criterion. Alogia (poverty of speech) is manifested by brief, laconic, empty replies. The individual with alogia appears to have a diminution of thoughts that is reflected in decreased fluency and productivity of speech. This must be differentiated from an unwillingness to speak, a clinical judgment that may require observation over time and in a variety of situations. Avolition is characterized by an inability to initiate and persist in goal-directed activities. The person may sit for long periods of time and show little interest in participating in work or social activities.

Subtypes and Course Specifiers (APA, 2000)

The diagnosis of a particular subtype is based on the clinical picture that occasioned the most recent evaluation or admission to clinical care and may therefore change over time. Separate text and criteria are provided for each of the following subtypes:

Diagnostic Criteria for 295.30 Paranoid Type (APA, 2000)

A type of Schizophrenia in which the following criteria are met:

A. Preoccupation with one or more delusions or frequent auditory hallucinations.
B. None of the following is prominent: disorganized speech, disorganized or catatonic behavior, or flat or inappropriate affect.

Diagnostic Criteria for 295.10 Disorganized Type (APA, 2000)

A type of Schizophrenia in which the following criteria are met:

A. All of the following are prominent:
   1. disorganized speech
   2. disorganized behavior
   3. flat or inappropriate affect
B. The criteria are not met for Catatonic Type.

Diagnostic Criteria for 295.20 Catatonic Type (APA, 2000)

A type of Schizophrenia in which the clinical picture is dominated by at least two of the following:

1. motoric immobility as evidenced by catalepsy (including waxy flexibility) or stupor
2. excessive motor activity (that is apparently purposeless and not influenced by external stimuli)
3. extreme negativism (an apparently motiveless resistance to all instructions or maintenance of a rigid posture against attempts to be moved) or mutism
4. peculiarities of voluntary movement as evidenced by posturing (voluntary assumption of inappropriate or bizarre postures), stereotyped movements, prominent mannerisms, or prominent grimacing
5. echolalia or echopraxia

Diagnostic Criteria for 295.90 Undifferentiated Type (APA, 2000)

A type of Schizophrenia in which symptoms that meet Criterion A are present, but the criteria are not met for the Paranoid, Disorganized, or Catatonic Type.

Diagnostic Criteria for 295.60 Residual Type (APA, 2000)

A type of Schizophrenia in which the following criteria are met:

A. Absence of prominent delusions, hallucinations, disorganized speech, and grossly disorganized or catatonic behavior.
B. There is continuing evidence of the disturbance, as indicated by the presence of negative symptoms or two or more symptoms listed in Criterion A for Schizophrenia, present in an attenuated form (e.g., odd beliefs, unusual perceptual experiences).

Reprinted with permission from the *Diagnostic and Statistical Manual of Mental Disorders, Fourth Edition, Text Revision.* Copyright 2000 American Psychiatric Association.

Other Associated Features and Disorders (APA, 2000)

The individual with Schizophrenia may display inappropriate affect (e.g., smiling, laughing, or a silly facial expression in the absence of an appropriate stimulus), which is one of the defining features of the Disorganized Type. Anhedonia is common and is manifested by a loss of interest or pleasure. Dysphoric mood may take the form of depression, anxiety, or anger. There may be disturbances in sleep pattern (e.g., sleeping during the day and nighttime activity or restlessness). The individual may show a lack of interest in eating or may refuse food as a consequence of delusional beliefs. Often there are abnormalities of psychomotor activity (e.g., pacing, rocking, or apathetic immobility). Difficulty in concentration, attention, and memory is frequently evident.

A majority of individuals with Schizophrenia have poor insight regarding the fact that they have a psychotic illness. Evidence suggests that poor insight is a manifestation of the illness itself rather than a coping strategy. It may be comparable to the lack of awareness of neurological deficits seen in stroke, termed *anosognosia*. This symptom predisposes the individual to noncompliance with treatment and has been found to be predictive of higher relapse rates, increased number of involuntary hospital admissions, poorer psychosocial functioning, and a poorer course of illness.

Depersonalization, derealization, and somatic concerns may occur and sometimes reach delusional proportions. Anxiety and phobias are common in Schizophrenia. Motor abnormalities (e.g., grimacing, posturing, odd mannerisms, ritualistic or stereotyped behavior) are sometimes present. The life expectancy of individuals with Schizophrenia is shorter than that of the general population for a variety of reasons. Suicide is an important factor, because approximately 10% of individuals with Schizophrenia commit suicide—and between 20% and 40% make at least one attempt over the course of the illness. Although the risk remains high over the whole lifespan, specific risk factors for suicide include male gender, being under 45 years of age, depressive symptoms, feelings of hopelessness, unemployment, and recent hospital discharge. Suicide risk is also elevated during postpsychotic periods. Males successfully complete suicide more often than females, but both groups are at increased risk relative to the general population.

Many studies have reported that subgroups of individuals diagnosed with Schizophrenia have a higher incidence of assaultive and violent behavior. The major predictors of violent behavior are male gender, younger age, past history of violence, noncompliance with antipsychotic medication, and excessive substance use. However, it should be noted that most individuals with Schizophrenia are not more dangerous to others than those in the general population.

Rates of comorbidity with Substance-Related Disorders are high. Nicotine Dependence is especially high, with estimates ranging from 80% to 90% of individuals with Schizophrenia being regular cigarette smokers. Furthermore, these individuals tend to smoke heavily and to choose cigarettes with high nicotine content. Comorbidity with Anxiety Disorders has also been increasingly recognized in Schizophrenia. In particular, rates of Obsessive–Compulsive Disorder and Panic Disorder are elevated in individuals with Schizophrenia relative to the general population. Schizotypal, Schizoid, or Paranoid Personality Disorder may sometimes precede the onset of Schizophrenia. Whether these Personality Disorders are simply prodromal to Schizophrenia or whether they constitute a separate earlier disorder is not clear.

Diagnostic Criteria for 295.40 Schizophreniform Disorder (APA, 2000)

A. Criteria A, D, and E of Schizophrenia are met.
B. An episode of the disorder (including prodromal, active, and residual phases) lasts at least 1 month but less than 6 months. (When the diagnosis must be made without waiting for recovery, it should be qualified as "Provisional.")

Associated Features and Disorders (APA, 2000)

Also see the discussion in the Associated Features and Disorders section for Schizophrenia, Associated Features and Disorders. Unlike Schizophrenia, impairment in social or occupational functioning is not required for a diagnosis of Schizophreniform Disorder. However, most individuals do experience dysfunction in various areas of daily functioning (e.g., work or school, interpersonal relationships, and self-care).

Reprinted with permission from the *Diagnostic and Statistical Manual of Mental Disorders, Fourth Edition, Text Revision.* Copyright 2000 American Psychiatric Association.

Diagnostic Criteria for 295.70 Schizoaffective Disorder (APA, 2000)

A. An uninterrupted period of illness during which, at some time, there is either a Major Depressive Episode, a Manic Episode, or a Mixed Episode concurrent with symptoms that meet Criterion A for Schizophrenia. **Note:** The Major Depressive Episode must include Criterion A1: depressed mood.
B. During the same period of illness, there have been delusions or hallucinations for at least 2 weeks in the absence of prominent mood symptoms.
C. Symptoms that meet criteria for a mood episode are present for a substantial portion of the total duration of the active and residual periods of the illness.
D. The disturbance is not due to the direct physiological effects of a substance (e.g., a drug of abuse, a medication) or a general medical condition.

Diagnostic Features (APA, 2000)

To meet criteria for Schizoaffective Disorder, the essential features must occur within a single uninterrupted period of illness. The phrase "period of illness" as used here refers to a time period during which the individual continues to display active or residual symptoms of psychotic illness. For some individuals, this period of illness may last for years or even decades. A period of illness is considered to have ended when the individual has completely recovered for a significant interval of time and no longer demonstrates any significant symptoms of the disorder.

The phase of the illness with concurrent mood and psychotic symptoms is characterized by the full criteria being met for both the active phase of Schizophrenia (i.e., Criterion A) (see Schizophrenia) and for a Major Depressive Episode (Major Depressive Episode), a Manic Episode (Manic Episode), or a Mixed Episode (Mixed Episode). The duration of the Major Depressive Episode must be at least 2 weeks; the duration of the Manic or Mixed Episode must be at least 1 week. Because the psychotic symptoms must have a total duration of at least 1 month to meet Criterion A for Schizophrenia, the minimum duration of a schizoaffective episode is also 1 month. An essential feature of a Major Depressive Episode is the presence of either depressed mood or markedly diminished interest or pleasure. Because loss of interest or pleasure is so common in nonaffective Psychotic Disorders, to meet Criterion A for Schizoaffective Disorder the Major Depressive Episode must include pervasive depressed mood (i.e., the presence of markedly diminished interest or pleasure is not sufficient). The phase of the illness with psychotic symptoms alone is characterized by delusions or hallucinations that last at least 2 weeks. Although some mood symptoms may be present during this phase, they are not prominent. This determination can be difficult and may require longitudinal observation and multiple sources of information.

Associated Features and Disorders (APA, 2000)

There may be poor occupational functioning, a restricted range of social contact, difficulties with self-care, and increased risk of suicide associated with Schizoaffective Disorder. Residual and negative symptoms are usually less severe and less chronic than those seen in Schizophrenia. Anosognosia (i.e., poor insight) is also common in Schizoaffective Disorder, but the deficits in insight may be less severe and pervasive than in Schizophrenia. Individuals with Schizoaffective Disorder may be at increased risk for later developing episodes of pure Mood Disorder (e.g., Major Depressive or Bipolar Disorder) or of Schizophrenia or Schizophreniform Disorder. There may be associated Alcohol and other Substance-Related Disorders. Limited clinical evidence suggests that Schizoaffective Disorder may be preceded by Schizoid, Schizotypal, Borderline, or Paranoid Personality Disorder.

Diagnostic Criteria for 297.1 Delusional Disorder (APA, 2000)

A. Nonbizarre delusions (i.e., involving situations that occur in real life, such as being followed, poisoned, infected, loved at a distance, or deceived by spouse or lover, or having a disease) of at least 1 month's duration.
B. Criterion A for Schizophrenia has never been met. **Note:** Tactile and olfactory hallucinations may be present in Delusional Disorder if they are related to the delusional theme.
C. Apart from the impact of the delusion(s) or its ramifications, functioning is not markedly impaired and behavior is not obviously odd or bizarre.
D. If mood episodes have occurred concurrently with delusions, their total duration has been brief relative to the duration of the delusional periods.
E. The disturbance is not due to the direct physiological effects of a substance (e.g., a drug of abuse, a medication) or a general medical condition.

[The DSM-IV-TR provides seven examples of delusional types (APA, 2000):]

Erotomanic Type: delusions that another person, usually of higher status, is in love with the individual
Grandiose Type: delusions of inflated worth, power, knowledge, identity, or special relationship to a deity or famous person
Jealous Type: delusions that the individual's sexual partner is unfaithful
Persecutory Type: delusions that the person (or someone to whom the person is close) is being malevolently treated in some way
Somatic Type: delusions that the person has some physical defect or general medical condition
Mixed Type: delusions characteristic of more than one of the above types but no one theme predominates
Unspecified Type: This subtype applies when the dominant delusional belief cannot be clearly determined or is not described in the specific types (e.g., referential delusions without a prominent persecutory or grandiose component).

Associated Features and Disorders (APA, 2000)

Social, marital, or work problems can result from the delusional beliefs of Delusional Disorder. Ideas of reference (e.g., that random events are of special significance) are common in individuals with this disorder. Their interpretation of these events is usually consistent with the content of their delusional beliefs. Many individuals with Delusional Disorder develop irritable or dysphoric mood, which can usually be understood as a reaction to their delusional beliefs. Especially with the Persecutory and Jealous Types, marked anger and violent behavior can occur. The individual may engage in litigious behavior, sometimes leading to hundreds of letters of protest to government and judicial officials and many court appearances. Legal difficulties can occur in Delusional Disorder, Jealous Type and Erotomanic Type. Individuals with Delusional Disorder, Somatic Type, may be subject to unnecessary medical tests and procedures. Hearing deficiency, severe psychosocial stressors (e.g., immigration), and low socioeconomic status may predispose an individual to the development of certain types of Delusional Disorder (e.g., Paranoid Type). Major Depressive Episodes probably occur in individuals with Delusional Disorder more frequently than in the general population. Delusional Disorder may be associated with Obsessive–Compulsive Disorder, Body Dysmorphic Disorder, and Paranoid, Schizoid, or Avoidant Personality Disorders.

It can be difficult to differentiate **Mood Disorders With Psychotic Features** from Delusional Disorder, because the psychotic features associated with Mood Disorders usually involve nonbizarre delusions without prominent hallucinations, and Delusional Disorder frequently has associated mood symptoms. The distinction depends on the temporal relationship between the mood disturbance and the delusions and on the severity of the mood symptoms. If delusions occur exclusively during mood episodes, the diagnosis is Mood Disorder With Psychotic Features. Although depressive symptoms are common in Delusional Disorder, they are usually mild, remit while the delusional symptoms persist, and do not warrant a separate Mood Disorder diagnosis. Occasionally, mood symptoms that meet full criteria for a mood episode are superimposed on the delusional disturbance. Delusional Disorder can be diagnosed only if the total duration of all mood episodes remains brief relative to the total duration of the delusional disturbance. If symptoms that meet criteria for a mood episode are present for a substantial portion of the delusional disturbance (i.e., the delusional equivalent of Schizoaffective Disorder), then a diagnosis of **Psychotic Disorder**

Not Otherwise Specified accompanied by either **Depressive Disorder Not Otherwise Specified** or **Bipolar Disorder Not Otherwise Specified** is appropriate.

Reprinted with permission from the *Diagnostic and Statistical Manual of Mental Disorders, Fourth Edition, Text Revision.* Copyright 2000 American Psychiatric Association.

Diagnostic Criteria for 298.8 Brief Psychotic Disorder (APA, 2000)

A. Presence of one (or more) of the following symptoms:
    1. delusions
    2. hallucinations
    3. disorganized speech (e.g., frequent derailment or incoherence)
    4. grossly disorganized or catatonic behavior
    Note: Do not include a symptom if it is a culturally sanctioned response pattern.
B. Duration of an episode of the disturbance is at least 1 day but less than 1 month, with eventual full return to premorbid level of functioning.
C. The disturbance is not better accounted for by a Mood Disorder With Psychotic Features, Schizoaffective Disorder, or Schizophrenia and is not due to the direct physiological effects of a substance (e.g., a drug of abuse, a medication) or a general medical condition.

Associated Features and Disorders (APA, 2000)

Individuals with Brief Psychotic Disorder typically experience emotional turmoil or overwhelming confusion. They may have rapid shifts from one intense affect to another. Although brief, the level of impairment may be severe, and supervision may be required to ensure that nutritional and hygienic needs are met and that the individual is protected from the consequences of poor judgment, cognitive impairment, or acting on the basis of delusions. There appears to be an increased risk of mortality (with a particularly high risk for suicide), especially among younger individuals. Preexisting Personality Disorders (e.g., Paranoid, Histrionic, Narcissistic, Schizotypal, or Borderline Personality Disorder) may predispose the individual to the development of the disorder.

Reprinted with permission from the *Diagnostic and Statistical Manual of Mental Disorders, Fourth Edition, Text Revision.* Copyright 2000 American Psychiatric Association.

Diagnostic Criteria for 297.3 Shared Psychotic Disorder (APA, 2000)

A. A delusion develops in an individual in the context of a close relationship with another person(s), who has an already-established delusion.
B. The delusion is similar in content to that of the person who already has the established delusion.

The disturbance is not better accounted for by another Psychotic Disorder (e.g., Schizophrenia) or a Mood Disorder With Psychotic Features and is not due to the direct physiological effects of a substance (e.g., a drug of abuse, a medication) or a general medical condition.

Associated Features and Disorders (APA, 2000)

Aside from the delusional beliefs, behavior is usually not otherwise odd or unusual in Shared Psychotic Disorder. Impairment is often less severe in the individual with Shared Psychotic Disorder than in the primary case.

Reprinted with permission from the *Diagnostic and Statistical Manual of Mental Disorders, Fourth Edition, Text Revision.* Copyright 2000 American Psychiatric Association.

Diagnostic Criteria for 298.9 Psychotic Disorder Not Otherwise Specified

This category includes psychotic symptomatology (i.e., delusions, hallucinations, disorganized speech, grossly disorganized or catatonic behavior) about which there is inadequate information to make a specific diagnosis or about which there is contradictory information, or disorders with psychotic symptoms that do not meet the criteria for any specific Psychotic Disorder.
Examples include

1. Postpartum psychosis that does not meet criteria for Mood Disorder With Psychotic Features, Brief Psychotic Disorder, Psychotic Disorder Due to a General Medical Condition, or Substance-Induced Psychotic Disorder

2. Psychotic symptoms that have lasted for less than 1 month but that have not yet remit-ted, so that the criteria for Brief Psychotic Disorder are not met
3. Persistent auditory hallucinations in the absence of any other features
4. Persistent nonbizarre delusions with periods of overlapping mood episodes that have been present for a substantial portion of the delusional disturbance
5. Situations in which the clinician has concluded that a Psychotic Disorder is present, but is unable to determine whether it is primary, due to a general medical condition, or sub-stance induced

Reprinted with permission from the *Diagnostic and Statistical Manual of Mental Disorders, Fourth Edition, Text Revision.* Copyright 2000 American Psychiatric Association.

A PROTOCOL FOR TREATING THE VARIANTS OF SCHIZOPHRENIA*

The psychotic disorders are the most nuanced and complex category of the disorders de-scribed in this book. More often then not, the afflicted person may be a patient under the care of others who may be responsible for his or her therapy and who will help facilitate the practice of the respective protocol by participating along with them. Therefore, the ap-proach to therapy here is one that requires the assistance of a therapist skilled with the protocol.

People with psychotic disorders have a deep sense of self and a variety of fears that tends to increase as the day progresses. Often these fears accumulate and create a sort of "critical mass" during the waking hours. Compounding this source of stress, the real events that trigger these fears tend to increase over the course of the day. In an effort to combat this strong tendency toward accumulated fear, people will make the best progress if they practice some exercises at least three times per day or even five times per day when neces-sary. This treatment frequency is also dependent on the individuals's ability to self-adminis-

*Copyright © David Shannahoff-Khalsa, 2008. No portion of this protocol may be reproduced without the ex-press written permission of the author.

ter the techniques and the availability of someone, a "coordinator," to help practice the techniques with the patient and then guide him or her in the daily "administration" of the practice.

However, the first step in therapy with these patients is to investigate whether they have the desire to self-heal. Not all do. If they have the desire, then patients are either directly taught the techniques, as one would teach any yoga student, or it may be necessary for the coordinator to first model and practice the techniques so that he or she can observe and then agree to experiment either immediately or at some mutually acceptable time later. Since these patients have a reverence for their own deep selves, which they believe is not honored by others, it is very important and a key to therapy for these patients to be joined in practice by the coordinator. This shared mutual experience is recognized by patients as a tribute to and recognition of their own deep selves. This approach thereby helps convey a holy respect for self that patients are missing and it also helps to provide a greater level of comfort for them when they face their fears. With time, the mutual practice of breathing and chanting together can continue for protracted periods. Typically the practice plateaus with a defined level of achievement, and then it can become more intense as the patient progresses. This increasing intensity and the depth of experience directly honor the patient's deep self. All of the exercises, whether combined as in the multipart protocol presented below or not, must end with the patient inhaling deeply and extending his or her arms up at a 60-degree angle while stretching back behind the body with a full expansion of the chest. This movement must be repeated at least three times. While this step may sound unremarkable, it is critical for the patient's progress in therapy because this movement symbolizes the extension of the deep self that is now reaching out into the world and welcoming and grasping life itself with a much greater capacity.

This protocol has four major components: (1) the essential practice called tuning in; (2) a 10-part exercise set specific for people with schizophrenia, called "True Glue," which helps to realign the spiritual bodies for treating and preventing psychotic episodes, followed by a 10-minute rest; (3) a meditation technique that has appeared in prior protocols—Gan Puttee Kriya; and (4) a meditation technique to help combat delusions and to stabilize a healthy sense of self-identity.

The practice of all four parts in this sequence represents the ideal regimen and protocol for patients with psychosis, as a whole. However, much depends on each patient's initial abilities and will to progress. Some patients have youth, vitality, and a marked enthusiasm to overcome their disorder, whereas others may be older, less capable, and less enthusiastic about experimenting. Some patients are initially willing only to attempt the tuning-in technique, and this may be an excellent starting point for them. When this is the case, the technique can be practiced for much longer times with the participation of the coordinator, even for periods of 11–15 minutes. Every patient is different, and each patient must be respected according to his or her own ability and desire to experiment and to heal. Patients' progress is also often determined by the feeling of love and respect that they receive from their coordinator. This feeling is often a key component to their willingness to proceed and to progress. They must feel an affinity with the coordinator and know that the coordinator feels an affinity with them.

The ideal scenario is that a patient wants to practice the entire protocol. The bottom line: Facilitating compliance of most patients over time is their new sense of clarity, stability, inner peace, rejuvenation, reduced fears, and the reduced length and frequency of their hallucinations. They quickly learn that this work is not easy, but it is much preferred to living with their suffering, fear, dread, confusion, depression, and anxiety.

1. Technique to Induce a Meditative State: Tuning In

Sit with a straight spine and with the feet flat on the floor if sitting in a chair (see Figure 2.1). Put the hands together at the chest in "prayer pose"—the palms are pressed together with 10–15 pounds of pressure (a mild to medium pressure, nothing too intense). The area where the sides of the thumbs touch rests on the sternum with the thumbs pointing up (along the sternum), and the fingers are together and point up and out at a 60-degree angle to the ground. The eyes are closed and focused on the third eye (imagine a sun rising on the horizon, or the equivalent of the point between the eyebrows at the origin of the nose). This mantra is chanted out loud in a 1½-breath cycle:

"Ong Namo Guru Dev Namo"

Inhale first through the nose and chant "Ong Namo" with an equal emphasis on the *Ong* and the *Namo*. Then immediately follow with a half-breath inhalation through the mouth and chant "Guru Dev Namo" with approximately equal emphasis on each word. (The *o* in *Ong* and *Namo* is a long-*o* sound; *Dev* sounds like *Dave*, with a long-*a* sound.)

- *Ong Namo* means I bow with reverence to that infinite energy that is the basis of all creation.
- *Guru* means teacher or wisdom.
- *Dev* means divine or of God.

The practitioner should focus on the experience of the vibrations these sounds create on the upper palate and throughout the cranium, while letting the mind be carried by the sounds into a new and pleasant mental space. This sequence should be repeated a minimum of three times. We employed it in our group about 10–12 times. This technique helps to create a meditative state of mind and is always used as a precursor to the other techniques.

2. True Glue: An Exercise Set Specific for People with Schizophrenia to Realign the Spiritual Bodies for Treating and Preventing Psychotic Episodes

All of the exercises below include a 1-minute relaxation period between each exercise.

- *Exercise A.* Flex the spine as in the elementary spine-flexing exercise, which is also taught in Chapter 2 for anxiety disorders and in several other chapters, but here the arms are extended straight up over the head with the hands facing forward and with the fingers spread wide for 2 minutes (see Figures 17.1 and 17.2). This technique can be practiced while sitting either in a chair or on the floor in a cross-legged position. If you are in a chair, sit with both feet flat on the ground. Begin by raising the chest up and leaning slightly forward, inhaling deeply at the same time. Then exhale as you relax the spine down into a slouching position. Keep the head up straight, as if you were looking forward, without allowing it to move much with the flexing action of the spine. This will help prevent a whip action of the cervical vertebrae.

All breathing should occur through the nose for both the inhalation and exhalation. The eyes are closed, as if you were looking at a central point on the horizon, the third eye. Your mental focus is kept on the sound of the breath while listening to the fluid movement of the inhalation and exhalation. Begin the technique slowly while loosening up the spine. Eventually, a very rapid movement can be achieved with practice, reaching a rate of one or two times per second for the entire movement. Two minutes here is the maximum time. Food should be avoided for several hours, if possible, prior to this exercise set. When finished,

Figures 17.1 and 17.2.
Spine-Flexing Exercise in a Slouch Position and with a Straight Spine

inhale and hold the breath while stretching the arms straight over the head and stretching up the spine, then slowly exhale. Then repeat the inhale, hold and stretch, and exhale procedure two more times.

■ *Exercise B.* The hands are held in the posture called "*gyan* mudra," wherein the tip of the index finger and the tip of the thumb are touching, the other fingers are held straight up from the hand, and the arms are up with the elbows and forearms forming 90-degree angles. The spine, torso, and arms are twisted to the left with the inhalation and to the right with the exhalation. This movement is continued for 2 minutes (see Figure 17.3).

Figure 17.3.
Spine Twist Exercise with Hands in *Gyan* Mudra

■ *Exercise* C. Lay flat on the ground and extend the arms out straight above the head, on the floor, and the legs are out straight on the floor. Inhale through the nose and simultaneously raise the arms and legs up 90 degrees and perpendicular to the floor. Exhale and then lower both the arms and legs to their original position. Continue for 1 minute (see Figure 17.4).

■ *Exercise* D. Inhale through the nose and rise up on the knees with the arms extended above the head (see Figure 17.5), then exhale through the nose and squat on the heels and the knees with the arms extended straight out in front of the body with the palms down. Continue this movement for 2 minutes (see Figure 17.6).

Figure 17.4.
Leg and Arm Raise Exercise With Legs and Arms up at 90 Degrees

Figures 17.5 and 17.6.
Exercise up on Knees with Arms Over Head
and with Arms Extended
Straight Sitting on the Heels

■ *Exercise E.* Inhale through the nose and come up into camel pose with the head hanging back (see Figure 17.7), then exhale and lower the body into baby pose (see Figure 17.8). Continue for 2 minutes.

■ *Exercise F.* Stand up straight and inhale through the nose while twisting to the left with the left arm extended out and swinging around toward the back as far as possible, with the right arm then crossing in front of the chest (see Figure 17.9). Then exhale through the nose while reversing the posture and twisting around to the right, with the right arm then extended back and out toward the back as far as possible and the left arm then coming across the chest. The head also turns with the torso. Keep the hands in lightly closed fists, and continue the movement for 2 minutes.

■ *Exercise G.* Get down on the hands and knees and extend the left arm directly out in front of the body. The right leg is then also extended out straight back behind the body (see Figure 17.10). Flex the wrist to make a right angle with the extended hand so that you appear to be pushing against the wall, and also maintain a right angle at the ankle with the extended foot. The head is raised up and the eyes are open. Visually focus on a point off in the "infinite horizon." Either do Breath of Fire through the nose (see explanation below), or do long, slow, deep breathing through the nose. Maintain the posture perfectly without

Figures 17.7 and 17.8.
Camel Pose and Baby Pose

Figure 17.9.
Side Twisting Exercise

Figure 17.10.
Exercise with Opposite Leg and Arm Extended

bending either limb or losing balance, and continue holding this posture with the breathing for 2 minutes. Rest briefly (1 minute or less) and then reverse sides and continue everything for 2 additional minutes. Note that the opposite arms and legs are extended in the first part and then they are reversed for the second part.

Breath of Fire is practiced where the air is pulled in and pumped out very quickly and rhythmically through the nose, at a rate of about two or three times per second, just like pumping a bellows at the navel point. Make an effort to avoid holding any tension in the muscles of the chest, rib cage, or shoulders, which remain relaxed throughout the breath. The only tension felt is a mild effort by the abdominal muscles when the breath is quickly forced out. Every effort is made so that the sound of the inhale and exhale become nearly equal and indistinguishable and where very little work is being done. The easiest way to understand how to do Breath of Fire is to imagine that you have dirt in your nose and you make the effort to rapidly exhale through the nose to push the dirt out using the breath. When doing this, you need to briefly tighten the abdominal muscles at the navel and force the breath out through the nose. Then the inhalation happens naturally. So this can be one way to help develop the rhythm correctly.

- *Exercise H.* Sit in a chair or on the floor with a straight spine and inhale only through the nose while extending the arms directly out to the sides, parallel to the ground, while maintaining a lock at the elbows. The hands are maintained with the fingers spread wide and loose. In this position the eyes are closed (see Figure 17.11). Then quickly bring the hands toward each other, meeting about 6 inches apart directly in front of the body, without letting the hands touch. This movement is made while exhaling through the nose. Open the eyes when the hands come close together (4–6 inches apart) (see Figure 17.12). Continue to rapidly repeat the movement for 2 minutes, making sure that the eyes and breathing phases are correctly synchronized with the movement of the arms. The pace of the complete movement can approach one cycle every 1 to 2 seconds. This is a brain exercise that mimics the opening and closing of a camera shutter, and it helps to coordinate brain processes and increase the mental focus.
- *Exercise I.* Stand up with the arms extended and raised directly above the head as if reaching for the sky, and inhale when coming up. Then slowly bend forward at the waist without bending the knees and with the head coming toward the ground in front of the body. When the head comes down, the arms swing up behind the body as if reaching up

Figures 17.11 and 17.12.
Exercise with Arms Extended Out to Sides and with Arms 6 Inches Apart in Front

toward the sky. The exhalation through the nose is produced in this phase of the exercise. Start slowly and eventually speed up the pace. Continue for 2 minutes.

■ *Exercise J.* Sat Kriya is the final exercise in this set. It is practiced by sitting on the heels with the knees brought together in front, the tops of the feet flat on the ground and the soles of the feet under the buttocks (see Figure 17.13). It is also possible to do Sat Kriya sitting in a chair. The arms are positioned straight up over the head with the upper arms pressed lightly against the sides of the head. The elbows are locked in an effort to keep the arms straight, and the hands are brought together. The fingers of both hands are interlocked with only the two index fingers pointing straight up. For males, the right thumb crosses over the left thumb in the interlacing of the fingers and the left little finger is the last finger on the outside with this interlock. For females, the interlacing is reversed, with the right little finger on the outside and the left thumb dominating over the right thumb.

The eyes are closed and focused at the third eye point, where the eyebrows meet at the root of the nose. The *bij* mantra "Sat Nam" is chanted out loud with this exercise. While maintaining this position, the navel point is pulled in toward the back of the spine and si-

Figure 17.13.
Sat Kriya

multaneously the muscle between the rectum and sex organ is tightened in what is called root lock. When the navel point is pulled in, the effort will also lead to a diaphragm lock. During the simultaneous pulling of the navel point and tightening of the lower muscle, the sound *Sat* is chanted quickly, almost like a cracking sound, and then the abdominal muscles and the muscle between the sex organ and rectum are briefly relaxed while the sound *Nam* is chanted quickly. Yogi Bhajan helped to clarify the fine details of this practice by explaining:

> Often when you try to do Sat Kriya from the navel point, you incorrectly try to apply one of the locks instead of starting with the navel. If you do Sat Kriya and just apply the root

lock you temporarily raise your blood pressure. If you do Sat Kriya just with the diaphragm lock, you temporarily lower the blood pressure. Actually in Sat Kriya the locks come from an automatic involvement. (personal communication, date unknown)

So the corrective guiding statement is this: "Do Sat Kriya only from the navel point and the two locks should become little helpers automatically in balance." When chanting *Sat*, the mantra sounds more like *Sut*. When the sound *Sat (Sut)* is chanted, mentally visualize healing energy and light coming in through the navel point and traveling up the spine to the center of the head. While chanting *Nam*, visualize the energy and light traveling out from the center of the head and out through the third eye point.

This entire exercise is fairly rapid and rhythmic and is repeated eight times in 10 seconds. It should not be chanted faster or slower—and there can be a tendency to either chant too fast or too slowly. Be careful not to flex the spine during the exercise, although sometimes the shoulders will rise up slightly during the practice. The practice time here is 2 minutes.

Frequently a student will ask about when to inhale and exhale. The best answer here is that the breath regulates itself, and it is not necessary to focus on it. By pulling and releasing the navel rhythmically, the breath will join in to support the process. Trying to focus on the breath only leads to confusion as to how to practice this exercise. Also, it is important to note that the spine stays still and straight. The rhythmic contraction and relaxation produces waves of energy that circulate, energize, and heal the body. This is neither a spinal flex nor a pelvic thrust. The practitioner should remain firmly seated on the heels throughout the motions of this exercise.

To end the practice at 2 minutes, inhale and gently squeeze the muscles from the buttocks all the way up along the spine. Hold the muscles tight for 5–10 seconds as you concentrate on the top of the head. Then exhale completely. Inhale, exhale totally, and hold the breath out as you contract the lower pelvis, lift the diaphragm, lock the chin to straighten the cervical vertebrae, and squeeze all the muscles from the buttocks up to the neck. Hold the breath out for 5–20 seconds according to your comfort and capacity. Then inhale and relax, and immediately proceed to Exercise K. If this technique is practiced by itself, then one should also rest by relaxing on the back for two times the practice time. For those suffering with some form of psychoses, Sat Kriya should be limited to 2 minutes until the person has the ability to perform all the exercises in True Glue and the two meditation techniques that follow in this protocol for their full times, respectively. After that, the times with Sat Kriya can be slowly increased as described below for healthy people. However, 2 minutes is adequate.

Sat Kriya can be practiced for longer times—11, 31, or 62 minutes, or the maximum time of 2 hours and 31 minutes. When there is an effort to practice for longer times, focus your attention on perfecting the form, rhythm, and the visual and mental concentration efforts. When building up the time, start with rotation cycles of 3 minutes of Sat Kriya with 2 minutes of relaxation. This 3 minute–2 minute cycle can be repeated three to five times and then the cycle can be increased to 5 minutes of Sat Kriya and 5 minutes of rest. Then times of 3–5 minutes can more easily be added, depending on the practitioner's ability.

Sat Kriya is the master exercise in Kundalini yoga. It works to heal the nervous and glandular systems, and it helps to correct, open, and balance all eight chakras. The ultimate result of this technique is that it can lead to "a nervous system that is as strong as steel and steady as stone" (Yogi Bhajan) when practiced consistently for the 31 minute and longer times. This is also an excellent technique for people who are trying to recover from the ravaging effects of substance abuse and addiction, which have a destructive effect on the nervous system and the chakras.

- *Exercise K.* When finished with Sat Kriya, relax on the back while maintaining the arms relaxed by the sides with the palms facing up and both legs straight out in front of the body with the heels kept together. This posture is called corpse pose or *shavasana.* Deeply relax in this posture for 10 minutes.

3. Gan Puttee Kriya: A Technique to Help Eliminate Negativity from the Past, Present, and the Future

Gan Puttee Kriya has also been called the "Kriya to Make the Impossible Possible." Yogi Bhajan originally taught this meditation technique on November 2, 1988 (Bhajan, 1998). Yogis disovered this technique as a tool for eliminating the blocks that form in the subconscious mind and stifle growth, frequently leading to destructive, neurotic, and self-defeating patterns of mental activity.

Sit with a straight spine, either on the floor or in a chair. The backs of your hands are resting on your knees with the palms facing upward. The eyes are nine-tenths closed (one-tenth open, but looking straight ahead into the darkness, not the light below), focused on the third eye. Chant from your heart in a natural, relaxed manner, or chant in a steady, relaxed monotone:

"Sa Ta Na Ma Ra Ma Da Sa Sa Say So Hung"

More specifically:

Chant out loud the sound "Sa" (the *a* sounds like *ahhh*), and touch your thumb tips and index fingertips together quickly and simultaneously with about 2 pounds of pressure.
Chant "Ta" and touch the thumb tips to the middle fingertips.
Chant "Na" and touch the thumb tips to the ring fingertips.
Chant "Ma" and touch the thumb tips to the little fingertips.
Chant "Ra" and touch your thumb tips and index fingertips.
Chant "Ma" and touch the thumb tips to the middle fingertips.
Chant "Da" and touch the thumb tips to the ring fingertips.
Chant "Sa" and touch the thumb tips to the little fingertips.
Chant "Sa" and touch your thumb tips and index fingertips.
Chant "Say" (sounds like the word *say* with a long-*a*) and touch the thumb tips to the middle fingertips.
Chant "So" and touch the thumb tips to the ring fingertips.
Chant "Hung" and touch the thumb tips to the little-finger tips.

Chant at a rate of one sound per second. The thumb tip and fingertips touch with a very light (2–3 pounds) pressure with each connection. This light touch helps to consolidate the circuit created by each thumb–finger link. Start with 11 minutes and slowly work up to 31 minutes of practice. To finish, remain in the sitting posture and inhale, holding the breath for 20–30 seconds while you shake and move every part of your body (like a dog shaking off water). Exhale and repeat this shaking motion two more times to circulate the energy and to break the pattern of tapping the thumb and fingertips, which affects the brain. Then immediately proceed with focusing the eyes on the tip of the nose (the end you cannot see) and breathe slowly and deeply through the nose for 1 minute.

Each sound used in this meditation is unique, and they all have a powerful effect on both the conscious and subconscious minds:

"Sa" gives the mind the ability to expand to the infinite.

"Ta" gives the mind the ability to experience the totality of life.

"Na" gives the mind the ability to conquer death.

"Ma" gives the mind the ability to resurrect.

"Ra" gives the mind the ability to expand in radiance (this sound purifies and energizes).

"Da" gives the mind the ability to establish security on the earth plane, providing a ground for action.

"Say" gives the totality of experience.

"So" is the personal sense of identity.

"Hung" is the infinite as a vibrating and real force. Together, *So Hung* means "I am Thou."

The unique qualities of this 12-syllable mantra help cleanse and restructure the subconscious mind and help heal the conscious mind to ultimately experience the *super*conscious mind. All the blocks that result from traumatic or troubling events are eliminated over time with the practice of Gan Puttee Kriya. When doing the whole protocol, 11 minutes for this technique is often adequate; however, 31 minutes is even better, and the maximum time: *Do not go beyond 31 minutes.*

4. A Meditation to Help Combat Delusions and to Help Stabilize a Healthy Sense of Self-Identity

This meditation was first taught by Yogi Bhajan on April 19, 2000, in Espanola, New Mexico, and is identified as #NM0342 in the video series. Yogi Bhajan taught this technique for those who have an overloaded subconscious mind and for those who get stuck in their neuroses and psychoses, where one result is that a haunting thought remains in the conscious mind. He said that this technique is useful when "fantasy overextends to the point that you start believing it, and finally you become that. When reality, earth and the heavenly fantasies do not meet together, we get in trouble." In that condition, he said, "What is keeping you bound down to your lower self? It is your neurosis. You are stuck in your neuroses. You are trapped. You love your ego more than your identity. In God I trust, is what you have to learn."

This is a perfect meditation technique for people who are lost in their neurosis and psychosis and with their sense of self and identity—the condition that manifests when a person becomes delusional. This technique helps to establish a healthy state of mental stability and is most appropriate for the person with schizophrenia who has a weakened identity and is questioning the deep self.

This technique can be practiced while sitting in a chair and maintaining a straight spine, or while sitting on the floor and maintaining a straight spine. Both arms are raised out to the sides (see Figure 17.14) and the elbows are bent at 90 degree angles so that the forearms are pointing straight up. The hands face forward. The eyes are opened and focused at the tip of the nose (the end point that you cannot see). The mantra

"Humee Hum Brahm Hum"

is chanted. The mantra is most effective when it is chanted to the rhythm of a CD (Humee Hum and Peace and Tranquillity, Kaur, Nirinian. Available at http://www.spiritvoyage .com/). In rhythm with the mantra, touch the top of your head with the left hand (see Figure 17.15) while chanting *Humee Hum* and blessing yourself. Then return to the original position while chanting *Brahm Hum*. The meditation is continued for 11 minutes.

To end the technique, inhale through the nose, hold the breath, tighten the spine, and stiffen only the left hand. Pull the energy of the spine into the left hand. Then exhale and repeat the breath, holding and tightening two more times, and then relax. In part, the intention with this technique is to a learn to become kind, humble, helpful, and compassionate.

Additional Meditation Techniques for People with Schizophrenia

Other meditation techniques in this book would also be most useful for helping to treat patients with the nine variants of the psychoses.

■ There are two techniques in Chapter 18 for treating the personality disorders that would be appropriate: (1) the multipart meditation to release pressure from the subconscious mind and overcome compulsive behavior patterns (pp. 277–278, and (2) a meditation technique to help overcome all psychological weaknesses (pp. 284–285).

Figures 17.14 and 17.15.
Meditation to Help Combat Delusions and to Help Stabilize a Healthy Sense of Self-Identity

■ Five techniques in Chapter 19 for treating the pervasive developmental disorders would also be most beneficial, including (1) the meditation to balance and synchronize the cerebral hemispheres (pp. 311–312); (2) the meditation for balancing the brain hemispheres (pp. 314–315); (3) a meditation to balance the western hemisphere of the brain with the base of the eastern hemisphere (pp. 315–317); (4) the meditation to balance the two brain hemispheres and to correct any spiritual, mental, and physical imbalance (pp. 317–318); and (5) a meditation to correct language and communication disorders ("Ad Nad Kriya") (pp. 319–320).

These seven meditation techniques would be best as single additions to the protocol for treating the variants of schizophrenia presented above. To date, that protocol—including the True Glue exercise set, Gan Puttee Kriya, and the meditation to help combat delusions and to help stabilize a healthy sense of self-identity—has been the most widely tested, and it has always been successful for treating patients with schizophrenia. It is also a very balanced and comprehensive protocol and should be appropriate for all patients with any of the nine variants of the psychoses. In some cases, it may also be more beneficial to add one of these seven additional meditation techniques. All seven are completely balanced as individual techniques, and they will only add to the positive and more rapid treatment for this patient population. They are not overstimulating, nor are they likely to take the patient too far into the etheric realms if they are practiced with the initial suggested treatment times.

One caution must be taken with patients who have schizophrenia: They should not practice techniques that are too powerful and specifically meant to exclusively and directly open chakras five through eight. However, none of the techniques described in this chapter, or referred to as possible substitutions in the other chapters, is too powerful for the patient with a psychosis when it is practiced for the specified length of time.

A FOUR-PART MINIPROTOCOL FOR HELPING TO TERMINATE HALLUCINATIONS*

This protocol is best applied as soon as the patient begins to experience any hallucinations or has any prodromal symptoms of onset that he or she can detect based on past experience. The evidence to date suggests that the best and quickest results are achieved if the patient can begin the practice within the first 10 minutes or earlier. Although the intent here is to have the patient sit down and practice the entire protocol, the first two steps can be started if the patient is not in a place where this is possible, and it is not possible for the patient to close his or her eyes or openly practice any meditation techniques. The four-part protocol is as follows.

1. Technique to Induce a Meditative State: Tuning In

Use the tuning in technique (see Figure 2.1 and the description in the Protocol for Treating the Variants of Schizophrenia, pp. 214–215).

---

2. Technique for Meeting Mental Challenges: The Vic-tor-y Breath

This technique can be used at any time (Shannahoff-Khalsa, 1997, 2003, 2005, 2006, 2010); it does not require a sitting position. It can be employed while driving a car, while participating in a conversation, or while taking a test. The eyes can be open or closed, depending on the situation. Take a near-full breath through the nose. Hold this breath without straining or tensing the stomach muscles for exactly 3–4 seconds and only during this holding phase mentally say to yourself the three separate sounds *vic–tor–y*. Then exhale. Mentally creating the three separated sounds should take 3–4 seconds, no longer or less. The entire time of each repetition should take about 8–10 seconds. The breath should not be exaggerated to the extent that anyone would even notice that you are taking a deep breath. Although it can be employed multiple times until you achieve the desired relief, when it is being practiced in the four-part protocol, the practice times here for the protocol are 5–11 minutes. Sitting with a straight spine with the eyes closed will help to maximize the benefits. There is no upper time limit for its practice.

3. The Right Nostril Four-Part Breath Using the Mantra Sa Ta Na Ma

Sit in a chair with the feet flat on the ground or in an easy, cross-legged pose and maintain a straight spine. The left hand is raised up in front of the face and the left thumb tip is used to block the end of the left nostril. The remaining fingers point straight up and the palm faces toward the right. The elbow of the left hand is relaxed by the side to help avoid producing tension in the left arm and shoulder. The right hand is relaxed in the lap with the palm facing up, and the tip of the right index finger is touching the tip of the right thumb, forming *gyan* mudra. The eyes are closed.

The breath pattern is exclusively practiced through the right nostril even if it is slightly congested or feels completely blocked. It is still possible to breathe through a congested nostril, and with a little practice the congestion usually reduces. The inhalation and exhalation phases are both broken into four approximately equal steps: The first step involves inhaling to fill the lungs approximately to one-fourth volume, then the second part fills the lungs to approximately one-half lung volume, the third step to approximately three-fourths capacity, and the final step to full capacity. However, in practice the lungs are never stretched to full capacity. The above description is meant to clarify the point that each inhalation of the breath is about one-fourth of the lung volume. No strain is required here, and it is not mandatory to fill the lungs to full capacity. However, the breath should be somewhat force-ful—it is definitely not a light, timid, or weak breath effort.

The same pattern is repeated in four parts when emptying the lungs with equal force. The full breath cycle to complete the inhalation and exhalation phases should take about 5 seconds. This pattern is called a four-part breath.

Instead of counting the four parts using numbers, the mantra

"Sa Ta Na Ma"

is mentally recited, with each of the four sounds paired to each of the four breath parts on both the inhalation and exhalation phases. This then includes two cycles of the *Sa Ta Na Ma* mantra per breath cycle. The mantra is repeated once on the inhalation and once on the exhalation.

This mantra is called the *Panj Shabd*, which means the five primal sounds of the universe:

"Sa" gives the mind the ability to expand to the infinite.
"Ta" gives the mind the ability to experience the totality of life.
"Na" gives the mind the ability to conquer death.
"Ma" gives the mind the ability to resurrect.

A fifth sound is the *ah* sound that is common to all four sounds. This technique is practiced for 11 minutes.

4. The Silent L-Form Meditation Technique Using the Mantra Sa Ta Na Ma

This technique is practiced immediately after doing the preceding meditation. The spine remains straight and the person now sits with both hands resting on the knees, palms facing up and the tips of the index fingers are touching the tips of the thumbs (*gyan* mudra) on the respective hands. The eyes are kept closed with this technique and the person mentally vi-sualizes the four separate syllables of the "Sa Ta Na Ma" mantra in what is called the L-form meditation:

- The patient visualizes a white or gold light and healing energy coming in through the top center of the head

232

- ◼ . . . while mentally hearing the sound of *S* as it comes down to the middle of the head
- ◼ . . . and then the *ah* sound is heard as it exits out through the third eye region (the point where the eyebrows meet and where the nose has its origin).

This is the use of the sound *Sa* more clearly differentiated with the two parts. Note that the mantra is heard silently, not chanted out loud. The healing light is visualized as the light comes in and goes out.

The same process is practiced for the three remaining sounds of *Ta*, *Na*, and *Ma*, whereby each sound is slightly broken into its respective two components. The entire cycle for the four-part mantra takes about 3–5 seconds. This is practiced for 11 minutes. The breath is not regulated here.

EIGHTEEN

Treating the Personality Disorders

(Paranoid, Schizoid, Schizotypal, Antisocial, Borderline, Histrionic, Narcissistic, Avoidant, Dependent, and Obsessive–Compulsive Personality Disorders)

The American Psychiatric Association's (2000) DSM-IV-TR describes 10 Personality Disorders. A very brief definition is given below for each, followed by more extensive diagnostic criteria, diagnostic features, and associated features and disorders. The following material is presented with permission from the (APA, 2000).

DSM DISORDERS

A Personality Disorder is an enduring pattern of inner experience and behavior that deviates markedly from the expectations of the individual's culture, is pervasive and inflexible, has an onset in adolescence or early adulthood, is stable over time, and leads to distress or impairment. The Personality Disorders included in this section are listed below.

Paranoid Personality Disorder is a pattern of distrust and suspiciousness such that others' motives are interpreted as malevolent.

Schizoid Personality Disorder is a pattern of detachment from social relationships and a restricted range of emotional expression.

Schizotypal Personality Disorder is a pattern of acute discomfort in close relationships, cognitive or perceptual distortions, and eccentricities of behavior.

Antisocial Personality Disorder is a pattern of disregard for, and violation of, the rights of others.

Borderline Personality Disorder is a pattern of instability in interpersonal relationships, self-image, and affects, and marked impulsivity.

Histrionic Personality Disorder is a pattern of excessive emotionality and attention seeking.

Narcissistic Personality Disorder is a pattern of grandiosity, need for admiration, and lack of empathy.

Avoidant Personality Disorder is a pattern of social inhibition, feelings of inadequacy, and hypersensitivity to negative evaluation.

Dependent Personality Disorder is a pattern of submissive and clinging behavior related to an excessive need to be taken care of.

Obsessive–Compulsive Personality Disorder is a pattern of preoccupation with orderliness, perfectionism, and control.

Personality Disorder Not Otherwise Specified (301.9) is a category provided for two situations: 1) the individual's personality pattern meets the general criteria for a Personality Disorder and traits of several different Personality Disorders are present, but the criteria for any specific Personality Disorder are not met; or 2) the individual's personality pattern meets the general criteria for a Personality Disorder, but the individual is considered to have a Personality Disorder that is not included in the Classification (e.g., passive–aggressive personality disorder).

The Personality Disorders are grouped into three clusters based on descriptive similarities. Cluster A includes the Paranoid, Schizoid, and Schizotypal Personality Disorders. Individuals with these disorders often appear odd or eccentric. Cluster B includes the Antisocial, Borderline, Histrionic, and Narcissistic Personality Disorders. Individuals with these disorders often appear dramatic, emotional, or erratic. Cluster C includes the Avoidant, Dependent, and Obsessive–Compulsive Personality Disorders. Individuals with these disorders often appear anxious or fearful. It should be noted that this clustering system, although useful in some research and educational situations, has serious limitations and has not been consistently validated. Moreover, individuals frequently present with co-occurring Personality Disorders from different clusters.

Diagnostic Criteria for Personality Disorders in General (APA, 2000)

A. An enduring pattern of inner experience and behavior that deviates markedly from the expectations of the individual's culture. This pattern is manifested in two (or more) of the following areas:
   1. cognition (i.e., ways of perceiving and interpreting self, other people, and events)
   2. affectivity (i.e., the range, intensity, lability, and appropriateness of emotional response)
   3. interpersonal functioning
   4. impulse control
B. The enduring pattern is inflexible and pervasive across a broad range of personal and social situations.
C. The enduring pattern leads to clinically significant distress or impairment in social, occupational, or other important areas of functioning.
D. The pattern is stable and of long duration, and its onset can be traced back at least to adolescence or early adulthood.
E. The enduring pattern is not better accounted for as a manifestation or consequence of another mental disorder.
F. The enduring pattern is not due to the direct physiological effects of a substance (e.g., a drug of abuse, a medication) or a general medical condition (e.g., head trauma).

More on Diagnostic Features (APA, 2000)

Personality traits are enduring patterns of perceiving, relating to, and thinking about the environment and oneself that are exhibited in a wide range of social and personal contexts. Only when personality traits are inflexible and maladaptive and cause significant functional impairment or subjective distress do they constitute Personality Disorders.

The items in the criteria sets for each of the specific Personality Disorders are listed in order of decreasing diagnostic importance as measured by relevant data on diagnostic efficiency (when available). The diagnosis of Personality Disorders requires an evaluation of the individual's long-term patterns of functioning, and the particular personality features must be evident by early adulthood. The personality traits that define these disorders must also be distinguished from characteristics that emerge in response to specific situational stressors or more transient mental states (e.g., Mood or Anxiety Disorders, Substance Intoxication). The clinician should assess the stability of personality traits over time and across different situations. Although a single interview with the person is sometimes sufficient for making the diagnosis, it is often necessary to conduct more than one interview and to space these over time. Assessment can also be complicated by the fact that the characteristics that define a Personality Disorder may not be considered problematic by the individual (i.e., the traits are often ego-syntonic). To help overcome this difficulty, supplementary information from other informants may be helpful.

Personality Disorders must be distinguished from **personality traits that do not reach the threshold for a Personality Disorder.** Personality traits are diagnosed as a Personality Disorder only when they are inflexible, maladaptive, and persisting and cause significant functional impairment or subjective distress.

Reprinted with permission from the *Diagnostic and Statistical Manual of Mental Disorders, Fourth Edition, Text Revision.* Copyright 2000 American Psychiatric Association.

Diagnostic Criteria for 301.0 Paranoid Personality Disorder (APA, 2000)

A. A pervasive distrust and suspiciousness of others such that their motives are interpreted as malevolent, beginning by early adulthood and present in a variety of contexts, as indicated by four (or more) of the following:
 1. suspects, without sufficient basis, that others are exploiting, harming, or deceiving him or her
 2. is preoccupied with unjustified doubts about the loyalty or trustworthiness of friends or associates
 3. is reluctant to confide in others because of unwarranted fear that the information will be used maliciously against him or her
 4. reads hidden demeaning or threatening meanings into benign remarks or events
 5. persistently bears grudges, i.e., is unforgiving of insults, injuries, or slights

6. perceives attacks on his or her character or reputation that are not apparent to others and is quick to react angrily or to counterattack
7. has recurrent suspicions, without justification, regarding fidelity of spouse or sexual partner

B. Does not occur exclusively during the course of Schizophrenia, a Mood Disorder With Psychotic Features, or another Psychotic Disorder and is not due to the direct physiological effects of a general medical condition.

Associated Features and Disorders (APA, 2000)

Individuals with Paranoid Personality Disorder are generally difficult to get along with and often have problems with close relationships. Their excessive suspiciousness and hostility may be expressed in overt argumentativeness, in recurrent complaining, or by quiet, apparently hostile aloofness. Because they are hypervigilant for potential threats, they may act in a guarded, secretive, or devious manner and appear to be "cold" and lacking in tender feelings. Although they may appear to be objective, rational, and unemotional, they more often display a labile range of affect, with hostile, stubborn, and sarcastic expressions predominating. Their combative and suspicious nature may elicit a hostile response in others, which then serves to confirm their original expectations.

Because individuals with Paranoid Personality Disorder lack trust in others, they have an excessive need to be self-sufficient and a strong sense of autonomy. They also need to have a high degree of control over those around them. They are often rigid, critical of others, and unable to collaborate, although they have great difficulty accepting criticism themselves. They may blame others for their own shortcomings. Because of their quickness to counterattack in response to the threats they perceive around them, they may be litigious and frequently become involved in legal disputes. Individuals with this disorder seek to confirm their preconceived negative notions regarding people or situations they encounter, attributing malevolent motivations to others that are projections of their own fears. They may exhibit thinly hidden, unrealistic grandiose fantasies, are often attuned to issues of power and rank, and tend to develop negative stereotypes of others, particularly those from population groups distinct from their own. Attracted by simplistic formulations of the world, they are often wary of ambiguous situations. They may be perceived as "fanatics" and form tightly knit "cults" or groups with others who share their paranoid belief systems.

Particularly in response to stress, individuals with this disorder may experience very brief psychotic episodes (lasting minutes to hours). In some instances, Paranoid Personality Disorder may appear as the premorbid antecedent of Delusional Disorder or Schizophrenia. Individuals with this disorder may develop Major Depressive Disorder and may be at increased risk for Agoraphobia and Obsessive–Compulsive Disorder. Alcohol and other Substance Abuse or Dependence frequently occur. The most common co-occurring Personality Disorders appear to be Schizotypal, Schizoid, Narcissistic, Avoidant, and Borderline.

Other Personality Disorders may be confused with Paranoid Personality Disorder because they have certain features in common. It is, therefore, important to distinguish among these disorders based on differences in their characteristic features. However, if an individual has personality features that meet criteria for one or more Personality Disorders in addition to Paranoid Personality Disorder, all can be diagnosed. Paranoid Personality Disorder and Schizotypal Personality Disorder share the traits of suspiciousness, interpersonal aloofness, and paranoid ideation, but Schizotypal Personality Disorder also includes symptoms such as magical thinking, unusual perceptual experiences, and odd thinking and speech. Individuals with behaviors that meet criteria for Schizoid Personality Disorder are often perceived as strange, eccentric, cold, and aloof, but they do not usually have prominent paranoid ideation. The tendency of individuals with Paranoid Personality Disorder to react to minor stimuli with anger is also seen in Borderline and Histrionic Personality Disorders. However, these disorders are not necessarily associated with pervasive suspiciousness. People with Avoidant Personality Disorder may also be reluctant to confide in others, but more because of a fear of being embarrassed or found inadequate than from fear of others' malicious intent. Although antisocial behavior may be present in some individuals with Paranoid Personality Disorder, it is not usually motivated by a desire for personal gain or to exploit others as in Antisocial Personality Disorder, but rather is more often due to a desire for revenge. Individuals with Narcissistic Personality Disorder may occasionally display suspiciousness, social withdrawal, or alienation, but this derives primarily from fears of having their imperfections or flaws revealed.

Paranoid traits may be adaptive, particularly in threatening environments. Paranoid Personality Disorder should be diagnosed only when these traits are inflexible, maladaptive, and persisting and cause significant functional impairment or subjective distress.

Diagnostic Criteria for 301.20 Schizoid Personality Disorder (APA, 2000)

A. A pervasive pattern of detachment from social relationships and a restricted range of expression of emotions in interpersonal settings, beginning by early adulthood and present in a variety of contexts, as indicated by four (or more) of the following:
   1. neither desires nor enjoys close relationships, including being part of a family
   2. almost always chooses solitary activities
   3. has little, if any, interest in having sexual experiences with another person
   4. takes pleasure in few, if any, activities
   5. lacks close friends or confidants other than first-degree relatives
   6. appears indifferent to the praise or criticism of others
   7. shows emotional coldness, detachment, or flattened affectivity
B. Does not occur exclusively during the course of Schizophrenia, a Mood Disorder With Psychotic Features, another Psychotic Disorder, or a Pervasive Developmental Disorder and is not due to the direct physiological effects of a general medical condition.

Associated Features and Disorders (APA, 2000)

Individuals with Schizoid Personality Disorder may have particular difficulty expressing anger, even in response to direct provocation, which contributes to the impression that they lack emotion. Their lives sometimes seem directionless, and they may appear to "drift" in their goals. Such individuals often react passively to adverse circumstances and have difficulty responding appropriately to important life events. Because of their lack of social skills and lack of desire for sexual experiences, individuals with this disorder have few friendships, date infrequently, and often do not marry. Occupational functioning may be impaired, particularly if interpersonal involvement is required, but individuals with this disorder may do well when they work under conditions of social isolation. Particularly in response to stress, individuals with this disorder may experience very brief psychotic episodes (lasting minutes to hours). In some instances, Schizoid Personality Disorder may appear as the premorbid antecedent of Delusional Disorder or Schizophrenia. Individuals with this disorder may sometimes develop Major Depressive Disorder. Schizoid Personality Disorder most often co-occurs with Schizotypal, Paranoid, and Avoidant Personality Disorders.

Diagnostic Criteria for 301.22 Schizotypal Personality Disorder

A. A pervasive pattern of social and interpersonal deficits marked by acute discomfort with, and reduced capacity for, close relationships as well as by cognitive or perceptual distortions and eccentricities of behavior, beginning by early adulthood and present in a variety of contexts, as indicated by five (or more) of the following:
   1. ideas of reference (excluding delusions of reference)
   2. odd beliefs or magical thinking that influences behavior and is inconsistent with sub-cultural norms (e.g., superstitiousness, belief in clairvoyance, telepathy, or "sixth sense"; in children and adolescents, bizarre fantasies or preoccupations)
   3. unusual perceptual experiences, including bodily illusions
   4. odd thinking and speech (e.g., vague, circumstantial, metaphorical, overelaborate, or stereotyped)
   5. suspiciousness or paranoid ideation
   6. inappropriate or constricted affect
   7. behavior or appearance that is odd, eccentric, or peculiar
   8. lack of close friends or confidants other than first-degree relatives
   9. excessive social anxiety that does not diminish with familiarity and tends to be associated with paranoid fears rather than negative judgments about self
B. Does not occur exclusively during the course of Schizophrenia, a Mood Disorder With Psychotic Features, another Psychotic Disorder, or a Pervasive Developmental Disorder.

Associated Features and Disorders (APA, 2000)

Individuals with Schizotypal Personality Disorder often seek treatment for the associated symptoms of anxiety, depression, or other dysphoric affects rather than for the personality disorder features per se. Particularly in response to stress, individuals with this disorder may experience transient psychotic episodes (lasting minutes to hours), although they usually are insufficient in duration to warrant an additional diagnosis such as Brief Psychotic Disorder or Schizophreniform Disorder. In some cases, clinically significant psychotic symptoms may develop that meet criteria for Brief Psychotic Disorder, Schizophreniform Disorder, Delusional Disorder, or Schizophrenia. Over half may have a history of at least one Major Depressive Episode. From 30% to 50% of individuals diagnosed with this disorder have a concurrent diagnosis of Major Depressive Disorder when admitted to a clinical setting. There is considerable co-occurrence with Schizoid, Paranoid, Avoidant, and Borderline Personality Disorders.

Reprinted with permission from the *Diagnostic and Statistical Manual of Mental Disorders, Fourth Edition, Text Revision.* Copyright 2000 American Psychiatric Association.

Diagnostic Criteria for 301.7 Antisocial Personality Disorder (APA, 2000)

A. There is a pervasive pattern of disregard for and violation of the rights of others occurring since age 15 years, as indicated by three (or more) of the following:
1. failure to conform to social norms with respect to lawful behaviors as indicated by repeatedly performing acts that are grounds for arrest
2. deceitfulness, as indicated by repeated lying, use of aliases, or conning others for personal profit or pleasure
3. impulsivity or failure to plan ahead
4. irritability and aggressiveness, as indicated by repeated physical fights or assaults
5. reckless disregard for safety of self or others
6. consistent irresponsibility, as indicated by repeated failure to sustain consistent work behavior or honor financial obligations
7. lack of remorse, as indicated by being indifferent to or rationalizing having hurt, mistreated, or stolen from another
B. The individual is at least age 18 years.
C. There is evidence of Conduct Disorder (see Diagnostic criteria for Conduct Disorder) with onset before age 15 years.
D. The occurrence of antisocial behavior is not exclusively during the course of Schizophrenia or a Manic Episode.

Associated Features and Disorders (APA, 2000)

Individuals with Antisocial Personality Disorder frequently lack empathy and tend to be callous, cynical, and contemptuous of the feelings, rights, and sufferings of others. They may have an inflated and arrogant self-appraisal (e.g., feel that ordinary work is beneath them or lack a realistic concern about their current problems or their future) and may be excessively opinionated, self-assured, or cocky. They may display a glib, superficial charm and can be quite voluble and verbally facile (e.g., using technical terms or jargon that might impress someone who is unfamiliar with the topic). Lack of empathy, inflated self-appraisal, and superficial charm are features that have been commonly included in traditional conceptions of psychopathy that may be particularly distinguishing of the disorder and more predictive of recidivism in prison or forensic settings where criminal, delinquent, or aggressive acts are likely to be nonspecific. These individuals may also be irresponsible and exploitative in their sexual relationships. They may have a history of many sexual partners and may never have sustained a monogamous relationship. They may be irresponsible as parents, as evidenced by malnutrition of a child, an illness in the child resulting from a lack of minimal hygiene, a child's dependence on neighbors or nonresident relatives for food or shelter, a failure to arrange for a caretaker for a young child when the individual is away from home, or repeated squandering of money required for household necessities. These individuals may receive dishonorable discharges from the armed services, may fail to be self-supporting, may become impoverished or even homeless, or may spend many years in penal institutions. Individuals with Antisocial Personality Disorder are more likely than people in the general population to die prematurely by violent means (e.g., suicide, accidents, and homicides).

Individuals with this disorder may also experience dysphoria, including complaints of tension, inability to tolerate boredom, and depressed mood. They may have associated Anxiety Disorders, Depressive Disorders, Substance-Related Disorders, Somatization Disorder, Pathological Gambling, and other disorders of impulse control. Individuals with Antisocial Personality Disorder also often have personality features that meet criteria for other Personality Disorders, particularly Borderline, Histrionic, and Narcissistic Personality Disorders. The likelihood of developing Antisocial Personality Disorder in adult life is increased if the individual experienced an early onset of Conduct Disorder (before age 10 years) and accompanying Attention-Deficit/Hyperactivity Disorder. Child abuse or neglect, unstable or erratic parenting, or inconsistent parental discipline may increase the likelihood that Conduct Disorder will evolve into Antisocial Personality Disorder.

Diagnostic Criteria for 301.83 Borderline Personality Disorder (APA, 2000)

A pervasive pattern of instability of interpersonal relationships, self-image, and affects, and marked impulsivity beginning by early adulthood and present in a variety of contexts, as indicated by five (or more) of the following:

1. frantic efforts to avoid real or imagined abandonment. **Note:** Do not include suicidal or self-mutilating behavior covered in Criterion 5.
2. a pattern of unstable and intense interpersonal relationships characterized by alternating between extremes of idealization and devaluation
3. identity disturbance: markedly and persistently unstable self-image or sense of self
4. impulsivity in at least two areas that are potentially self-damaging (e.g., spending, sex, substance abuse, reckless driving, binge eating). **Note:** Do not include suicidal or self-mutilating behavior covered in Criterion 5.
5. recurrent suicidal behavior, gestures, or threats, or self-mutilating behavior
6. affective instability due to a marked reactivity of mood (e.g., intense episodic dysphoria, irritability, or anxiety usually lasting a few hours and only rarely more than a few days)
7. chronic feelings of emptiness
8. inappropriate, intense anger or difficulty controlling anger (e.g., frequent displays of temper, constant anger, recurrent physical fights)
9. transient, stress-related paranoid ideation or severe dissociative symptoms

Associated Features and Disorders (APA, 2000)

Individuals with Borderline Personality Disorder may have a pattern of undermining themselves at the moment a goal is about to be realized (e.g., dropping out of school just before graduation; regressing severely after a discussion of how well therapy is going; destroying a good relationship just when it is clear that the relationship could last). Some individuals develop psychotic-like symptoms (e.g., hallucinations, body-image distortions, ideas of reference, and hypnagogic phenomena) during times of stress. Individuals with this disorder may feel more secure with transitional objects (i.e., a pet or inanimate possession) than in interpersonal relationships. Premature death from suicide may occur in individuals with this disorder, especially in those with co-occurring Mood Disorders or Substance-Related Disorders. Physical handicaps may result from self-inflicted abuse behaviors or failed suicide attempts. Recurrent job losses, interrupted education, and broken marriages are common. Physical and sexual abuse, neglect, hostile conflict, and early parental loss or separation are more common in the childhood histories of those with Borderline Personality Disorder. Common co-occurring Axis I disorders include Mood Disorders, Substance-Related Disorders, Eating Disorders (notably Bulimia), Posttraumatic Stress Disorder, and Attention-Deficit/Hyperactivity Disorder. Borderline Personality Disorder also frequently co-occurs with the other Personality Disorders.

Reprinted with permission from the *Diagnostic and Statistical Manual of Mental Disorders, Fourth Edition, Text Revision.* Copyright 2000 American Psychiatric Association.

Diagnostic Criteria for 301.50 Histrionic Personality Disorder (APA, 2000)

A pervasive pattern of excessive emotionality and attention seeking, beginning by early adulthood and present in a variety of contexts, as indicated by five (or more) of the following:

1. is uncomfortable in situations in which he or she is not the center of attention
2. interaction with others is often characterized by inappropriate sexually seductive or provocative behavior
3. displays rapidly shifting and shallow expression of emotions
4. consistently uses physical appearance to draw attention to self
5. has a style of speech that is excessively impressionistic and lacking in detail
6. shows self-dramatization, theatricality, and exaggerated expression of emotion
7. is suggestible, i.e., easily influenced by others or circumstances
8. considers relationships to be more intimate than they actually are

Associated Features and Disorders (APA, 2000)

Individuals with Histrionic Personality Disorder may have difficulty achieving emotional intimacy in romantic or sexual relationships. Without being aware of it, they often act out a role (e.g., "victim" or "princess") in their relationships to others. They may seek to control their partner through emotional manipulation or seductiveness on one level, whereas displaying a marked dependency on them at another level. Individuals with this disorder often have impaired relationships with same-sex friends because their sexually provocative interpersonal style may seem a threat to their friends' relationships. These individuals may also alienate friends with demands for constant attention. They often become depressed and upset when they are not the center of attention. They may crave novelty, stimulation, and excitement and have a tendency to become bored with their usual routine. These individuals are often intolerant of, or frustrated by, situations that involve delayed gratification, and their actions are often directed at obtaining immediate satisfaction. Although they often initiate a job or project with great enthusiasm, their interest may lag quickly. Longer-term relationships may be neglected to make way for the excitement of new relationships.

The actual risk of suicide is not known, but clinical experience suggests that individuals with this disorder are at increased risk for suicidal gestures and threats to get attention and coerce better caregiving. Histrionic Personality Disorder has been associated with higher rates of Somatization Disorder, Conversion Disorder, and Major Depressive Disorder. Borderline, Narcissistic, Antisocial, and Dependent Personality Disorders often co-occur.

Diagnostic Criteria for 301.81 Narcissistic Personality Disorder (APA, 2000)

A pervasive pattern of grandiosity (in fantasy or behavior), need for admiration, and lack of empathy, beginning by early adulthood and present in a variety of contexts, as indicated by five (or more) of the following:

1. has a grandiose sense of self-importance (e.g., exaggerates achievements and talents, expects to be recognized as superior without commensurate achievements)
2. is preoccupied with fantasies of unlimited success, power, brilliance, beauty, or ideal love
3. believes that he or she is "special" and unique and can only be understood by, or should associate with, other special or high-status people (or institutions)
4. requires excessive admiration
5. has a sense of entitlement, i.e., unreasonable expectations of especially favorable treatment or automatic compliance with his or her expectations
6. is interpersonally exploitative, i.e., takes advantage of others to achieve his or her own ends
7. lacks empathy: is unwilling to recognize or identify with the feelings and needs of others
8. is often envious of others or believes that others are envious of him or her
9. shows arrogant, haughty behaviors or attitudes

Associated Features and Disorders (APA, 2000)

Vulnerability in self-esteem makes individuals with Narcissistic Personality Disorder very sensitive to "injury" from criticism or defeat. Although they may not show it outwardly, criticism may haunt these individuals and may leave them feeling humiliated, degraded, hollow, and empty. They may react with disdain, rage, or defiant counterattack. Such experiences often lead to social withdrawal or an appearance of humility that may mask and protect the grandiosity. Interpersonal relations are typically impaired due to problems derived from entitlement, the need for admiration, and the relative disregard for the sensitivities of others. Though overweening ambition and confidence may lead to high achievement, performance may be disrupted due to intolerance of criticism or defeat. Sometimes vocational functioning can be very low, reflecting an unwillingness to take a risk in competitive or other situations in which defeat is possible. Sustained feelings of shame or humiliation and the attendant self-criticism may be associated with social withdrawal, depressed mood, and Dysthymic or Major Depressive Disorder. In contrast, sustained periods of grandiosity may be associated with a hypomanic mood. Narcissistic Personality Disorder is also associated with Anorexia Nervosa and Substance-Related Disorders (especially related to cocaine). Histrionic, Borderline, Antisocial, and Paranoid Personality Disorders may be associated with Narcissistic Personality Disorder.

Diagnostic Criteria for 301.82 Avoidant Personality Disorder (APA, 2000)

A pervasive pattern of social inhibition, feelings of inadequacy, and hypersensitivity to negative evaluation, beginning by early adulthood and present in a variety of contexts, as indicated by four (or more) of the following:

1. avoids occupational activities that involve significant interpersonal contact, because of fears of criticism, disapproval, or rejection
2. is unwilling to get involved with people unless certain of being liked
3. shows restraint within intimate relationships because of the fear of being shamed or ridiculed
4. is preoccupied with being criticized or rejected in social situations
5. is inhibited in new interpersonal situations because of feelings of inadequacy
6. views self as socially inept, personally unappealing, or inferior to others
7. is unusually reluctant to take personal risks or to engage in any new activities because they may prove embarrassing

Associated Features and Disorders (APA, 2000)

Individuals with Avoidant Personality Disorder often vigilantly appraise the movements and expressions of those with whom they come into contact. Their fearful and tense demeanor may elicit ridicule and derision from others, which in turn confirms their self-doubts. They are very anxious about the possibility that they will react to criticism with blushing or crying. They are described by others as being "shy," "timid," "lonely," and "isolated." The major problems associated with this disorder occur in social and occupational functioning. The low self-esteem and hypersensitivity to rejection are associated with restricted interpersonal contacts. These individuals may become relatively isolated and usually do not have a large social support network that can help them weather crises. They desire affection and acceptance and may fantasize about idealized relationships with others. The avoidant behaviors can also adversely affect occupational functioning because these individuals try to avoid the types of social situations that may be important for meeting the basic demands of the job or for advancement.

Other disorders that are commonly diagnosed with Avoidant Personality Disorder include Mood and Anxiety Disorders (especially Social Phobia of the Generalized Type). Avoidant Personality Disorder is often diagnosed with Dependent Personality Disorder, because individuals with Avoidant Personality Disorder become very attached to and dependent on those few other people with whom they are friends. Avoidant Personality Disorder also tends to be diagnosed with Borderline Personality Disorder and with the Cluster A Personality Disorders (i.e., Paranoid, Schizoid, or Schizotypal Personality Disorders).

Diagnostic Criteria for 301.6 Dependent Personality Disorder (APA, 2000)

A pervasive and excessive need to be taken care of that leads to submissive and clinging behavior and fears of separation, beginning by early adulthood and present in a variety of contexts, as indicated by five (or more) of the following:

1. has difficulty making everyday decisions without an excessive amount of advice and reassurance from others
2. needs others to assume responsibility for most major areas of his or her life
3. has difficulty expressing disagreement with others because of fear of loss of support or approval. **Note:** Do not include realistic fears of retribution.
4. has difficulty initiating projects or doing things on his or her own (because of a lack of self-confidence in judgment or abilities rather than a lack of motivation or energy)
5. goes to excessive lengths to obtain nurturance and support from others, to the point of volunteering to do things that are unpleasant

6. feels uncomfortable or helpless when alone because of exaggerated fears of being unable to care for himself or herself
7. urgently seeks another relationship as a source of care and support when a close relationship ends
8. is unrealistically preoccupied with fears of being left to take care of himself or herself

Associated Features and Disorders (APA, 2000)

Individuals with Dependent Personality Disorder are often characterized by pessimism and self-doubt, tend to belittle their abilities and assets, and may constantly refer to themselves as "stupid." They take criticism and disapproval as proof of their worthlessness and lose faith in themselves. They may seek overprotection and dominance from others. Occupational functioning may be impaired if independent initiative is required. They may avoid positions of responsibility and become anxious when faced with decisions. Social relations tend to be limited to those few people on whom the individual is dependent. There may be an increased risk of Mood Disorders, Anxiety Disorders, and Adjustment Disorder. Dependent Personality Disorder often co-occurs with other Personality Disorders, especially Borderline, Avoidant, and Histrionic Personality Disorders. Chronic physical illness or Separation Anxiety Disorder in childhood or adolescence may predispose the individual to the development of this disorder.

Reprinted with permission from the *Diagnostic and Statistical Manual of Mental Disorders, Fourth Edition, Text Revision.* Copyright 2000 American Psychiatric Association.

Diagnostic Criteria for 301.4 Obsessive–Compulsive Personality Disorder (APA, 2000)

A pervasive pattern of preoccupation with orderliness, perfectionism, and mental and interpersonal control, at the expense of flexibility, openness, and efficiency, beginning by early adulthood and present in a variety of contexts, as indicated by four (or more) of the following:

1. is preoccupied with details, rules, lists, order, organization, or schedules to the extent that the major point of the activity is lost

2. shows perfectionism that interferes with task completion (e.g., is unable to complete a project because his or her own overly strict standards are not met)
3. is excessively devoted to work and productivity to the exclusion of leisure activities and friendships (not accounted for by obvious economic necessity)
4. is overconscientious, scrupulous, and inflexible about matters of morality, ethics, or values (not accounted for by cultural or religious identification)
5. is unable to discard worn-out or worthless objects even when they have no sentimental value
6. is reluctant to delegate tasks or to work with others unless they submit to exactly his or her way of doing things
7. adopts a miserly spending style toward both self and others; money is viewed as something to be hoarded for future catastrophes shows rigidity and stubbornness

Associated Features and Disorders (APA, 2000)

When rules and established procedures do not dictate the correct answer, decision making may become a time-consuming, often painful process. Individuals with Obsessive–Compulsive Personality Disorder may have such difficulty deciding which tasks take priority or what is the best way of doing some particular task that they may never get started on anything. They are prone to become upset or angry in situations in which they are not able to maintain control of their physical or interpersonal environment, although the anger is typically not expressed directly. For example, a person may be angry when service in a restaurant is poor, but instead of complaining to the management, the individual ruminates about how much to leave as a tip. On other occasions, anger may be expressed with righteous indignation over a seemingly minor matter. People with this disorder may be especially attentive to their relative status in dominance–submission relationships and may display excessive deference to an authority they respect and excessive resistance to authority that they do not respect.

Individuals with this disorder usually express affection in a highly controlled or stilted fashion and may be very uncomfortable in the presence of others who are emotionally expressive. Their everyday relationships have a formal and serious quality, and they may be stiff in situations in which others would smile and be happy (e.g., greeting a lover at the airport). They carefully hold themselves back until they are sure that whatever they say will be perfect. They may be preoccupied with logic and intellect, and intolerant of affective behavior in others. They often have difficulty expressing tender feelings, rarely paying compliments. Individuals with this disorder may experience occupational difficulties and distress, particularly when confronted with new situations that demand flexibility and compromise.

Individuals with Anxiety Disorders, including Generalized Anxiety Disorder, Obsessive–Compulsive Disorder, Social Phobia, and Specific Phobias, have an increased likelihood of having a personality disturbance that meets criteria for Obsessive–Compulsive Personality Disorder. Even so, it appears that the majority of individuals with Obsessive–Compulsive Disorder do not have a pattern of behavior that meets criteria for this Personality Disorder. Many of the features of Obsessive–Compulsive Personality Disorder overlap with "type A" personality characteristics (e.g., preoccupation with work, competitiveness, and time urgency), and these features may be present in people at risk for myocardial infarction. There may be an association between Obsessive–Compulsive Personality Disorder and Mood and Eating Disorders.

Reprinted with permission from the *Diagnostic and Statistical Manual of Mental Disorders, Fourth Edition, Text Revision.* Copyright 2000 American Psychiatric Association.

TREATING THE PERSONALITY DISORDERS WITH KUNDALINI YOGA MEDITATION TECHNIQUES

The American Psychiatric Association groups the 10 personality disorders into three separate groups or clusters with their respective major differentiating factors and shared characteristics. To review:

- Cluster A disorders are termed "odd-eccentric" and include the paranoid, schizoid, and schizotypal personality disorders.
- Cluster B disorders are termed "dramatic, emotional, or erratic" and include the antisocial, borderline, histrionic, and narcissistic personality disorders.
- Cluster C disorders are termed "anxious-fearful" and include the avoidant, dependent, and obsessive–compulsive personality disorders.

The 10 yogic protocols for treating the 10 respective personality disorders all include a technique that is specifically related to a concrete symbol in nature that is itself characteristic of one of the 10 distinctive personality variants. Each symbol represents a state of being that is inherent and representative of the nature of the respective personality disorder. These 10 symbol-related techniques are then included in a larger protocol that is also specific for one of the three clusters. The 10 symbols, as they relate to the respective personality disorders, are as follows.

Cluster A Personality Disorders

1. *Paranoid*: a cave where the patient dwells in an effort to escape other people due to his or her "pervasive distrust and suspiciousness of others such that their motives are interpreted as malevolent" (American Psychiatric Association, 2000).

2. *Schizoid*: a tall tree that represents the aloof, singular, and isolated nature that patients must overcome due to their characteristic "detachment from social relationships and a restricted range of expression of emotions in interpersonal settings" (American Psychiatric Association, 2000).

3. *Schizotypal*: a low tree that symbolizes patients' separateness and nearly singular and exclusive focus on their own weakly rooted belief systems that represent their source for life, that inadvertently stifles their growth, and that leads to the "social and interpersonal deficits marked by acute discomfort with, and reduced capacity for, close relationships as well as by cognitive or perceptual distortions and eccentricities of behavior" (American Psychiatric Association, 2000).

Cluster B Personality Disorders

1. *Antisocial*: a spiral shell that symbolizes a twisted and self-contained state that needs to become untwisted and opened to the world of others. The spiral shell needs to open up and overcome "the failure to conform to social norms, deceitfulness as indicated by repeated lying, use of aliases, conning others for personal gain; impulsive, irritable, and aggressive behavior, reckless disregard for others, consistent irresponsibility, and lack of remorse" (American Psychiatric Association, 2000).

2. *Borderline*: a stick or branch that easily bends or snaps under pressure in an effort to overcome the "frantic efforts to avoid real or imagined abandonment" (American Psychi-

atric Association, 2000) The bending and snapping also leads "to unstable relationships, unstable self-images that cause impulsivity, which leads to self-damaging, suicidal, and self-mutilating behavior, affective instability (intense episodic dysphoria, irritability, and anxiety), chronic feelings of emptiness and worthlessness, difficulty controlling anger, and transient paranoid ideation, delusions, or dissociative symptoms" (American Psychiatric Association, 2000).

3. *Histrionic*: a waterfall that symbolizes the continuous overflow and flooding of everything in their environment with (excessive emotionality and attention-seeking) behavior (American Psychiatric Association, 2000).

4. *Narcissistic*: a snake that symbolizes the low, slick, and sneaky movements of these individuals in the world and "their persona of a grandiose sense of self-importance; preoccupation with fantasies; special, unique, and high status that requires excessive admiration; and sense of entitlement. They are interpersonally exploitative, lack empathy, and are envious of others or believe others are envious of them, with arrogant, haughty behaviors or attitudes" (American Psychiatric Association, 2000).

Cluster C Personality Disorders

1. *Avoidant*: a stone that symbolizes how these people can become solidly and rigidly fixed in place and set in their ways because they avoid significant interpersonal contact and are "unwilling to get involved with people unless certain of being liked, show restraint initiating intimate relationships because of the fear of being shamed and rejected, view themselves as socially inept, and are unwilling to take personal risks" (American Psychiatric Association, 2000). This stone needs to be turned around in therapy to face the therapist and reality.

2. *Dependent*: a claw that attaches to others with the "pervasive and excessive need to be taken care of that leads to submissive and clinging behavior and fears of separation." In their attachment, "they have difficulty in making everyday decisions, need others to assume responsibility, have difficulty expressing disagreement and initiating projects on their own, go to obsessive lengths to obtain nurturance and support from others, and are helpless when alone because of exaggerated fears of inadequacy" (American Psychiatric Association, 2000).

3. *Obsessive–Compulsive Personality Disorder*: a bird that symbolizes the state where patients are always up in the air with their wings flapping, flying around and unable to land and find a position to rest. These patients are "preoccupied with details, rules, lists, order, or

schedules to the point that the major point of the activity is lost"; they show "perfectionism that interferes with task completion"; they are "excessively devoted to work and productivity to the exclusion of leisure activities and friendships"; they are "over conscientious, scrupulous, and inflexible about matters of morality, ethics, or values"; and they are "unable to discard worn-out or worthless objects, reluctant to delegate tasks, miserly, and show rigidity and stubbornness" (American Psychiatric Association, 2000).

The approach to therapy using the symbols and the techniques described below involves an interactive relationship between the therapist and the patient. The two engage in therapy using a disorder-specific symbol-related yogic technique that is to be included in the cluster-specific protocol. One very important key here for understanding this patient population is that they are wholly or largely not accepting of their own condition; they are rarely aware of their behavior or personality deficits. They do not present in the office or clinic and say, "I have a schizoid personality," or "I have a narcissistic personality disorder," or "I have an antisocial personality disorder." They say, "I have come for treatment. Can you help me?" They present for some other reason, which is often the result of a dysfunctional relationship or an Axis I disorder that they perceive as causing their suffering.

The philosophy here is to modify patients' thinking so that they can relate to themselves using the symbol as a part of nature instead of trying to get them to directly identify with the disorder by name. They have to see how their behavior can affect their life and others around them, and the use of the symbol as descriptive of their condition can be more useful and less threatening. The idea is to help them shift their mood or thought processes when they cannot otherwise diagnose their own negative or troublesome behaviors and how they think. Eight of the ten symbols are fairly neutral and easily conceived without stirring much of a negative reaction. However, the snake in most societies is symbolic of evil, and care must be used here with patients who have narcissistic personality disorder. The claw may also have a negative connotation for some patients, but less so than the snake. But they also usually understand that clingy and clawlike attachments have been part of how they operate that have led to their suffering.

This work proceeds somewhat differently than the yoga protocols to treat most of the Axis I disorders (OCD, anxiety, depression, addictions, impulse control, eating, sleep, chronic fatigue syndrome, ADHD, and PTSD), where patients can more readily identify with their respective conditions and symptoms, and where they can also then easily learn to self-administer the respective protocols independently of the therapist, if they choose (Shannahoff-Khalsa, 2006). Although the yogic approach to treatment for schizophrenia, autism, and the autism spectrum disorders also includes a unique one-to-one therapeutic relationship, the approach here with patients who have a personality disorder will involve a uniquely different interactive therapeutic style. Whereas patients with schizophrenia can be told directly of their diagnosis, you will see in Chapter 19 that patients with autism or Asperger's disorder are not told about their diagnosis and, in fact, the approach to therapy is one that involves only play. Other differences are also apparent when the approaches to treatment are compared.

The treatment of each personality disorder includes a unique personality disorder-specific technique that is related to the symbol, and this technique is then included in a cluster-specific protocol along with what are called "water" exercises. There are three different water exercises, each relating to one of the three natural symbols of the ocean, river, and rain.

- The ocean exercise helps the patient "meet the shore in life" using a waveform-like exercise that is symbolic of the curling and uncurling process of the waves breaking on the shore; this exercise helps the patient push him- or herself forward to meet a new shore—a new life experience.
- The river exercise represents the process of flowing smoothly and stretching out in the world, and it helps the patient feel a greater flow in daily life.
- The rain exercise represents an opening up, blessing, and saturation whereby these aspects are brought into the psyche of the patient.

Each cluster-specific protocol includes an ocean exercise near the start, a river exercise during, and a rain exercise at the end of each protocol. To summarize:

- There are 10 discrete protocols, one for each personality disorder.
- They all include the same water exercises.
- Each disorder is also treated with one of the 10 respective symbol-based exercises or meditations.

These protocols can also include substitutions for some of the core meditation techniques. Although patients can be shown all of the techniques, they must be presented in a manageable sequence that is dependent on multiple factors that vary with each patient. These factors include patients' openness and enthusiasm, physical and mental condition, and why they are presenting for treatment in the first place. Here we are going to ignore the various possibilities for why patients come for therapy, and therefore the protocols are presented as if the patient was a "pure" personality disorder patient seeking therapy for their respective condition. However, the various cluster-specific, symbol-specific, and water exercises all have multiple virtues, and some of these are described with each of these unique meditation techniques. The overall benefits are also useful for treating many of the Axis I disorder symptoms.

It goes without saying that some conditions, like the addictive and substance abuse disorders, are better treated by also including the meditation technique specific for addiction that is described in Chapter 12 and in a prior publication (Shannahoff-Khalsa, 2006). Clearly, the yogic approach to treating complicated psychiatric disorders is also an art wherein the administration of the formulas requires a patient-based use of discretion.

The 10 Symbol-Related Techniques*

1. The Cave

In the cave the patient feels contained, closed off, and withdrawn, and the treatment here includes both an exercise that is symbolic of the contained state and the complement that helps strengthen and open the patient to the world. These complementary states are achieved by teaching the patient the classic movements that include the camel pose and baby pose exercises, which are also presented in Chapter 17 (p. 219) as Exercise E in the series called True Glue. The therapist explains the need for the patient to emerge from the cave (baby pose) and to extend up and out into the world in camel pose.

This practice starts with the patient facing the therapist. The patient inhales through the nose and then comes up into camel pose with the head hanging back and the arms extended down and back with the hands holding the ankles (see Figure 17.7); then the patient exhales and lowers the body into baby pose (see Figure 17.8). This dynamic movement is continued for 2 minutes. In time, once the patient understands how the basic cavelike condition is symbolized by baby pose and how the end goal is the perfected posture in camel pose, he or she can then choose to practice only the camel pose exercise with either slow deep breathing or preferably with Breath of Fire and slowly extend the practice time up to a maximum of 15 minutes. However, even 3–5 minutes of camel pose with Breath of Fire (also called Kapalabhati) will yield a most satisfactory result. But in the beginning, a maximum practice time of 2 minutes of going back and forth from baby pose to camel pose is sufficient.

2. The Tall Tree

As a tall tree, this patient feels aloof, singular, and isolated, and is detached from any meaningful social relationships. In addition, patients with this personality disorder have a restricted range of emotions in any interpersonal setting. The remedy here is to help patients increase their awareness of their inflexible and "planted" condition, their limited desire for reaching out to form new social connections, and their stifled emotional sensitivity, which also reduces their opportunity for any healthy emotional contacts. In part, this new awareness can be facilitating by including Exercise F of True Glue (Chapter 17, p. 219). This technique helps patients reach around in life and extend themselves in all directions. The therapist explains this symbolism and how this exercise is a good start at healing the condition.

The patient faces the therapist, standing up straight, and inhales through the nose while twisting to the left with the left arm extended out and swinging toward the back as far as possible, with the right arm then crossing in front of the chest (see Figure 17.9). Then the patient exhales through the nose while reversing the posture and twisting around to the right, with the right arm then extended towards the back as far as possible, with the left arm then coming across the chest. The head also turns with the torso. Keep the hands in lightly closed fists and continue the movement for 2 minutes.

3. The Low Tree

This little tree, which is too attached and grounded in its own root system, without space for additional growth and expansion, needs to reenergize, emerge, and reach up into the fresh air. Here it will find a new realm for its nourishment—the kindlier realms of the heavens that are far beyond the superficial and surface-only root system (patients' faulty, limited, and stifling belief systems) that has led to inadequate nourishment.

The therapist explains the virtues of this technique, and the patient experiences the virtues of the two postures, whereby he or she clearly feels a greater comfort in the standing position. The patient faces the therapist. In the starting position the patient stands up straight with the arms extended above the head and hands interlocked, with the index fingers extended straight up. This is the inhalation posture. The patient exhales while maintaining the arms and hands up as straight as possible and then squats into a low position where the buttocks come close to the floor in what is called crow pose. The feet are shoulder width apart to help provide stability, and the eyes are kept open throughout the movement. Once in the squat position, the patient then inhales through the nose and straightens up, with the arms and hands extended up to the heavens. The feet are kept flat in this exercise without the heels coming off the ground. The exercise should begin slowly, and 2 minutes is a good practice time here. One great virtue of this exercise is that it will increase the vital energy of the body through the use of the lower body, and it will also help change the thought processes of the patient once it has been completed. These patients need a renewed energy and will so that they can reach up and extend toward a higher and more inclusive goal and realm in life.

4. The Spiral Shell

Antisocial patients live in a twisted relationship with almost all of the individuals whom they encounter in their lives, and this leads to substantial pain for everyone. They require the experience of the pain of the twisted state compared to the straightforward, open, honest, and untwisted state. This can be taught by having patients first sit in a twisted posture in one direction and then return to the untwisted state, and next twist in the opposite direction, and then again twist to the straightforward posture.

Patients first sit facing the therapist. They close their eyes and place their hands on their shoulders with the fingers in the front and the thumbs placed toward the back. Then they inhale and twist toward the left with the head, shoulders, and torso. This exercise is similar to the exercise in the True Glue set (see Figure 17.4), except that the hands are on the shoulders instead of up straight. Patients hold this posture and then exhale as they return to the forward-facing posture. Then repeat this motion while inhaling and twisting to the right. The first 2 minutes should be done slowly while holding the twisted positions for as long as possible. Then in the final minute, the movement should be rapid, inhaling to the left and exhaling to the right. The therapist times the two phases of the exercise. At the end the patient sits facing forward and takes several slow deep breaths. The first phase of the exercise gives the patient the painful experience of the twisted condition and how the forward-facing posture is so much more pleasant, and the final minute also helps to rapidly change the thought patterns of the patient to a new and more positive state of mind.

5. The Stick or Branch

The marked instability of the stick or branch and the impulsive nature of the borderline patient are both taught through example here. The condition is also corrected in part by the following exercise, which is Exercise G in Chapter 17 (p. 219) in the True Glue series.

The patient faces the therapist while the therapist explains the virtues and symbolism of this exercise. The patient gets down on the hands and knees and starts by extending the left arm directly out in front of the body. The right leg is then also extended straight back like a rigid stick behind the body (see Figure 17.10). The patient makes a right angle with the extended left hand by flexing the wrist, so that it looks like the patient is pushing against the wall, and the patient also maintains a right angle at the ankle with the extended right foot. The head is raised up, the eyes are open, and the patient visually focuses on a point directly out in front of the body and off in an infinite horizon.

The patient can hold this position while either doing Breath of Fire only through the nose, or by doing long, slow, deep breathing only through the nose. The patient must maintain this posture perfectly without bending either limb or losing balance, and continue with the breathing for 2 minutes. Next the patient lowers the opposing arm and leg and balances on both hands and knees, resting briefly (1 minute or less), and then reverses sides and continues everything for 2 additional minutes. Note that the opposite arms and legs are extended in the first part and then they are reversed for the second part.

The difficulty of this exercise will help convey to patients how unstable the "stick" is and in time they learn through experience the virtues of not bending, how rewarding this can be, and how it leads to an inner strength and balance that helps them overcome their impulsive nature.

6. The Waterfall

Histrionic patients have to learn the virtues of *not* overflowing, flooding, or making waves in their environments by the constant release and sharing of their emotions. They have to understand how disturbing this affective flooding can be for others, and how it can damage their own life when they are always making the effort to become the center of attention. They can begin to learn the negative repercussions of this disturbing hand-waving-like behavior, how much better they can feel by remaining still and silent, and the positive experience that comes from this uninterrupted silence.

The following technique is a shortened version of a meditation technique that Yogi Bhajan taught in Los Angeles on October 11, 1996, for developing and strengthening the subtle body. This technique is invaluable for those who want to become healers as it also helps build and strengthen the subtle body, the immortal body, the working body of the healer and saint. This technique also helps build an incredible aura and arcline, which is ultimately what histrionic patients desire in their efforts to attract attention, and the immediate results can produce marvelous benefits when practiced longer or for the maximum times.

Things come to us from the universe through the subtle body. The effects of this technique therefore help bring prosperity in all of the positive ways, but they must be earned through the virtues of this practice. It is claimed that the radiance of the practitioner can be increased so much that people really no longer focus on the physical features of their face; they only see the brightness, the glow.

The patient sits facing the therapist. While the eyes can be open or closed, here it is best to keep the eyes open so that patients are more easily aware of their own arms and hands in this dramatic motion. The patient inhales and exhales only through the mouth, shaped like an O, and the lips are slightly pursed, and the sound of the breath is like a hiss. The arms are down by the sides, and the hands are held with the fingers loose (see Figure 18.1). As the patient inhales, he or she lifts both hands rapidly up to the top of the head, forming an arc-like structure whereby the left hand comes over the top of the right hand, and the right hand is closer to the top of the head (see Figure 18.2). At this point, both palms are over the crown but do not touch each other or the top of the head. On the exhale, both hands come down, in a reverse arc-like movement, all the way toward the legs but do not touch the legs or the body.

Once the hands are down at the sides again, the backs of the hands are near, but not touching the floor if the person is sitting on the ground. The key here is to make an arc-like shape as the hands and arms ascend and descend. The hands and fingers remain relaxed, but the movement is rapid as they are moving up and down with each powerful breath, approaching one cycle every 1 to 2 seconds. To complete the technique, the patient interlocks the hands straight over the head while inhaling, holding the breath, and then tightening all

Figures 18.1 and 18.2.
Meditation for Developing and Strengthening the Subtle Body

of the muscles in the body. Next the patient exhales and relaxes but maintains the posture, then repeats the sequence of inhaling, holding the breath, and tightening the muscles two more times. The patient then sits quietly and enjoys the benefits of stillness and the incredible joy that comes from within.

A good practice time here is 2–5 minutes. This is enough time to help patients understand that the rapid and disruptive movement of their emotional "arms" in life are not only disruptive to others but will ultimately bring them pain. But they also learn that a correct practice of this technique can quickly lead to a much improved state of mind and the true radiance and attractive qualities that they are seeking in life.

A normal and healthy starting time for this technique, when it is practiced as a single therapy for developing the remarkable healing qualities of the subtle body, would be 11 minutes, building slowly up to 20 or 22 minutes, and finally with a maximum practice time of 33 minutes. When 33 minutes are reached and the technique is finished correctly, the immediate benefits are indescribably magnificent. This may appeal to the histrionic patient, at least in theory.

7. *The Snake*

The slithering and low behavior of the narcissist can be mimicked by the patient facing the therapist in cobra pose (see Figure 18.3). Patients start by lying prone, on their bellies, with their legs stretched back and the tops of their feet flat on the floor, keeping the heels together. The hands are positioned flat on the floor near their shoulders, as if they were going to do a push-up. The pelvis remains flat on the ground. Then patients begin to inhale and straighten their arms while lifting the chest off the floor until the head is held up as high as possible with the eyes opened and focused toward a point on the ceiling. In this posture the spine is stretched as much as possible while working to distribute the effort equally throughout the spine. The entire body is kept as relaxed as possible, and the posture is held for up to 2 minutes as patients do Breath of Fire or slow, long, deep breathing. To finish, patients relax back down with their head turned toward the side and the arms relaxed along the sides of the body.

Figure 18.3.
Cobra Pose

While holding cobra pose, patients realize the pain of maintaining a snake-like posture and how snakes look to the world when their chest is protruding and their head is held too high. But patients also gain the benefits of having changed their own mental patterns and thought processes through a productive and healthy practice wherein they stretch themselves out instead of stretching others out in the world. They learn in time that working on themselves, rather than manifesting their grandiose importance, leads to a better internal and more meaningful result.

8. The Stone

The stone symbolizes the avoidant personality, which manifests with a "pervasive pattern of social inhibition, feelings of inadequacy, and hypersensitivity to negative evaluation" (APA, 2000) . The stone does not like to change or to be moved from its safe space, or to be confronted by anything that represents a potential challenge, difficulty, or threat. Its tendency is to not move—stones do not move by themselves.

Patients sit either on the floor or in a swivel chair (the easier of the two) and maintain a straight spine throughout the practice. In either position (on the floor or in a chair), patients begin by facing away from the therapist. Then while practicing the breathing technique described below, they slowly rotate counterclockwise (to their left), bit by bit to face the therapist. This can be accomplished by using the hands to lift and reposition the body on the ground a few inches at a time—or if they are on a swivel chair or stool, the feet can be used to help them reposition themselves. Then they return to the original position facing away from the therapist and continue with the breathing meditation, slowly rotating clockwise (toward their right), bit by bit. This bit-by-bit movement slowly forces patients to face the therapist, who encourages and guides the process, as needed, if patients are reluctant to turn. The therapist also becomes a mirror to patients and their advocate for change.

The eyes can be either opened or closed in the beginning, depending on the choice of the patient. However, in time patients can also practice the technique with their eyes open so that they are acutely aware of what they are doing, how they look to the world, and how they are not harmed by the slow process of change. There will also be significant and pleasant rewards on mental and physical levels when the following breath technique is practiced.

The eight-part breath pattern helps patients experience their expansion, increased awareness, and the integration of their mental processes. If the eyes are closed, they are focused on the third eye, where the root of the nose meets the eyebrows. If patients choose to keep the eyes open, they should be encouraged to focus straight ahead on a fixed point on the horizon that will slowly change as they rotate. The hands are relaxed in the lap.

The breathing pattern begins by first inhaling through the mouth; the tongue is curled, creating a *U*-shaped appearance, and extended slightly out of the mouth. The inhalation is broken into eight equal parts. Then the tongue is brought back into the mouth, and the mouth is closed. Likewise, the exhalation through the nose is broken into eight equal parts. There is no pause after completing the full inhalation or full exhalation phases of the breath cycle. The pattern is continued with the cycle of eight parts in through the curled tongue and eight parts out through the nose. This cycle takes about 10 seconds for one complete round.

The benefits of this technique can be magnified by using the mantra

Sa Ta Na Ma

with two silent repetitions of the complete mantra on the inhalation, and two repetitions on the exhalation. Here each of the four syllables is sequentially paired with one part of the inhalation or exhalation, such that the mantra is mentally repeated twice through on the inhalation and twice through on the exhalation. This is preferable to counting 1–8 for each part of the breath cycle. Patients who are unwilling to use the mantra can mentally focus only on the sounds of the breath.

The ability to curl the tongue is a genetic trait, and patients who cannot curl their tongue into the *U* shape must inhale only through the nose in eight parts, keeping the mouth closed, and exhale only out the nose in eight parts. Curling the tongue in the *U* shape helps stimulate the thyroid and parathyroid glands.

The patient can start with 3–5 minutes while slowly rotating first to the left, and then 3–5 minutes while slowly rotating to the right. The final end position is facing the therapist. Equal times should be practiced in both directions. Upon finally completing this technique, the patient should take at least three long, slow, deep breaths (unbroken) through the nose and then relax.

This is a relatively easy technique and can bring considerable comfort to the patient when practiced correctly. There is no need to make an effort to completely fill the lungs on the inhalation or to completely empty the lungs on the exhalation. This is not a pattern that should strain the patient. This eight-part breath technique can also be practiced while sitting straight for 11–31 minutes. But used here as a technique for helping the avoidant personality, the slow turning is critical to the patient's benefit.

9. *The Claw*

The claw symbolizes the approach to life of patients with dependent personality disorder. These individuals latch onto people in their life and are rarely willing to disengage. Other people tend to experience them as thorns or like a cat with claws that insistently tears at and scratches them. Patients must have a direct experience with the therapist wherein they attach, *but also let go*, and where there is a give and take that is balanced and mutual. Their claw-like attachment and the process of changing it into a fulfilling relationship are magnified in the following practice of a Venus Kriya. In this practice, patients learn the positive benefits of mutual relationship based on fair and balanced give and take.

This Venus Kriya, also called Pushing Palms, was previously published (Shannahoff-Khalsa, 2006). There are two standard versions of this technique, depending on the mantra employed. The patient and therapist sit facing each other in a cross-legged position on the floor, with a straight spine. The right knee touches the left knee of the partner. (Sitting in chairs is acceptable, but the knees must still touch.) The eyes are open looking directly into the partner's eyes. This technique is practiced with the hands at shoulder level, open and facing forward and up, with the palms held flat as if they are going to push something. Here, the patient and therapist touch hands, palm to palm, with the left palm of each partner touching the right palm of the other. Start with the hands at an equal distance from each other (the line where the knees meet). Then the right hands push forward and the left hands come back toward the shoulder, and the reverse, with the left hands pushing forward and the right hands moving back toward the shoulders.

With this alternating movement, the words are chanted, one by the woman, who can be either the patient or the therapist if they are of opposite gender, followed by one by the man. (If the therapist and patient are both males, or both females, the therapist should take the male role in this meditation technique and the patient, the female role.) To restate this point another way, the patient and the therapist do not chant together, but alternate the use of the eight sounds. One word of one mantra is chanted with each movement sequence (i.e., two hands pushing forward, two hands moving back toward shoulders). Only the woman chants the words

"Gobinday, Udaray, Harying, Nirnamay"

and only the man chants the words

"Mukanday, Aparay, Karying, Akamay."

Note that the woman chants *when the right hands go forward*, the man chants when *the left hands go forward*, and the respective mantra is chanted only once with each push. So, back to the beginning:

- Right hands of each partner push forward: The woman chants the word *Gobinday* (means "sustainer").
- Left hands push forward and the right hands come back toward the shoulder: The man chants *Mukanday* (sounds like *mookunday*) (means "liberator").
- Right hands move forward and left hands move back: The woman chants *Udaray* (sounds like *oohdaray*) (means "enlightener").
- Left hands push forward: The man chants *Aparay* (the initial *A* sounds like *ah*) (means "infinite").

These alternating pushing movements continue:

- Right hands forward: The woman chants *Harying* (sounds like *hareeing* but with the sound of har as in hard) (means "destroyer").
- Left hands forward: The man chants *Karying* (sounds like *kareeing*) (means "creator").
- Right hands forward: The woman chants *Nirnamay* (sounds like *nearnamay*) (means "nameless").
- Left hands forward: The man chants *Akamay* (sounds like *aahkamay*) (means "desireless").

Then the entire mantra is repeated, again with the woman only chanting "Gobinday" and the man only chanting "Mukanday," and so on. The rate of chanting and moving the arms in the pushing movement is about one sound per movement per second. The total time limit for practice is 3 minutes and must not go beyond 3 minutes. When finished, the patient and therapist sit for a moment with their hands separated and relaxed in their laps, and the patient reflects on the need for a mutual give-and-take interaction if there is a "clawed" interlock in a relationship.

This eight-part mantra is the first version of Pushing Palms. There is also another version that is easier for beginners using the mantra

"Sa Ta Na Ma."

- Right hands forward: The woman chants *Sa* (the *a* sounds as in *father* for each word).
- Left hands forward: The man chants *Ta*.
- Right hands forward: The woman chants *Na*.
- Left hands forward: The man chants "Ma."

This four-part mantra is repeated with the same sequence for a maximum time of 3 minutes. All other aspects of the practice are the same as the first version with the eight-part mantra. Note also that this is chanting out loud; it is not a silent chant. Each sound used in this meditation is unique, and they all have a powerful effect on both the conscious and subconscious minds:

"Sa" gives the mind the ability to expand to the infinite.
"Ta" gives the mind the ability to experience the totality of life.
"Na" gives the mind the ability to conquer death.
"Ma" gives the mind the ability to resurrect and also means "rebirth."

In short, the mantra can translate to mean "infinity, life, death, and rebirth." This is a very powerful mantra for cleansing and restructuring the subconscious mind and helping to set a mental framework in the conscious mind to experience higher states of consciousness (Shannahoff-Khalsa & Bhajan, 1988; Shannahoff-Khalsa & Bhajan, 1991). Both mantras here help awaken the individual beyond a finite identity to live in higher states of consciousness. The first version has been my favorite Venus Kriya.

10. The Bird

A bird is best symbolized by the constant flapping of its wings to keep afloat in the air. This is how we see a bird in action. But there is a need for the bird to come back down to earth, to keep things in perspective, and to finish a task. This is an ability that is lost by patients with an obsessive–compulsive personality disorder.

This technique, called *Hast Kriya*, helps patients understand how they look to the world (with the constant flapping of the wings) and also helps them achieve a balance between their earth activities and the heavens (Bhajan, 2002). The patient sits in an easy, cross-legged pose or in a chair, facing the therapist, to practice a shorter version of this meditation technique. Maintaining a straight spine with a light neck lock, the patient pulls in the chin slightly toward the chest to help straighten the cervical vertebrae. When this lock is in place, the practitioner immediately feels how straight the neck can become. (The lock is called *Jalandhar Bandh*.) The eyes are kept closed and focused on the third eye point. There is no specific breath pattern, and in time the breath comes naturally.

Alternatively, the practitioner can inhale as the arms are lifted over the head and exhale as the arms come down and the fingers touch the floor. The patient extends the index fingers on both hands and locks down the other fingers into a fist with the thumbs coming across the middle and ring fingers. The timing of the movements here is best practiced by listening to a tape (Singh, 1996) with the mantra

"Sat Nam Wha-Hay Guru."

- Touch the index fingers to the floor on both sides near the body (see Figure 18.4) when the musician chants *Sat*.
- Then, lifting the arms, touch the index fingers together over the top of the head when the musician chants *Nam* (see Figure 18.5).
- Lower the arms and touch the index fingers to the floor on both sides when the musician chants "*Wha-Hay*"
- Lift the arms and touch the index fingers together again over the top of the head when the musician chants "*Guru*."

However, there are 2 *Sat Nam*s followed by 2 *Wha-Hay Guru*s in the sequence here, instead of the more common singular sequence of *Sat Nam Wha-Hay Guru*. To end the tech-

269

Figures 18.4 and 18.5.
Hast Kriya Meditation

nique patients inhale deeply, hold the breath for 10 seconds, then exhale and relax for a few minutes before going on to the next part of the protocol for obsessive–compulsive personality disorder. This practice, resembling wings flapping up and down, can continue for 3–5 minutes or longer; the maximum and preferred time is 22 minutes when Hast Kriya is practiced perfectly as an independent technique.

This procedure helps patients with obsessive–compulsive disorder heal and gain a new perspective and the balance that is so profoundly missing in their lives. When Yogi Bhajan taught this technique as a method to help develop a balance of the earth and the heavens, he commented: "This kriya renews the nervous system and can heal nerve pain and sciatica. It is so powerful it can hold the Hand of God; so powerful, it can hold the hand of death. 'Sat Nam Wahe Guru' is a <u>Jupiter mantra</u>" (Bhajan, 2002) . The term *Jupiter* here refers to the effects that this technique has via the use of the index finger, which is also called the Jupiter finger. In addition, Yogi Bhajan (2002) said the following:

The most graceful power and knowledge comes from Jupiter. Jupiter controls the medulla oblongata, the neurological center of the brain and the three rings of the brain stem. If you do this kriya for 22 minutes a day, you will totally change your personality. Power will descend from above and clean you out. Anger and obnoxiousness will disappear from your personality.

Three Water-Related Exercises

1. The Ocean

The choice here, "spine flexing for vitality," is for an exercise that contains the wave-like actions that help propel the patient forward to meet the shore in life. This technique is one of the most elementary exercises in Kundalini yoga, and when it is practiced sitting on the ground, it is also called *camel ride*. This technique follows the tuning in meditation for each of the three cluster-specific protocols (below) for personality disorders. Frequently, even when patients have the right formula, they hesitate to go forward, and the consequence is that they sit in a doldrum-like state. This simple spine-flexing exercise is an easy way to help patients propel themselves forward and overcome their inertia and resistance to engaging in the full protocol. The complete details for practice are provided in Technique 2 of the Cluster A protocol (p. 273).

2. The River

This exercise helps the patient flow and stretch out in life. When the flow of energy in the body is blocked through the major meridians that are related to the spine, the patient will not progress easily. This technique will help expedite the entire growth process and it is also healing for the sex meridians, sciatic nerves, and lower back. This is the life nerve-stretching exercise with the legs spread wide. See the complete description of the technique in The Eight-Part Kundalini Yoga Meditation Protocol for Treating the Cluster A Personality Disorders (p. 274) .

3. The Rain

This exercise helps the patient experience an opening up, blessing, and saturation of the psyche with a healing light and energy. This technique, the "Meditation with the Magic

Mantra" is described as Technique 8 below in the Cluster A protocol (pp. 278–282). This technique is always the last exercise for the specific protocols for Clusters A, B, and C.

THE THREE CLUSTER-SPECIFIC PROTOCOLS FOR THE PERSONALITY DISORDERS

Three yoga treatment protocols are described here for the personality disorders, and each protocol is specific for one of the Clusters, A, B, or C as defined by the American Psychiatric Association.

The Eight-Part Kundalini Yoga Meditation Protocol Specific for Treating the Cluster A Personality Disorders: Paranoid, Schizoid, and Schizotypal*

1. Technique to Induce a Meditative State: Tuning In

Sit with a straight spine and with the feet flat on the floor if sitting in a chair (see Figure 2.1). Put the hands together at the chest in "prayer pose"—the palms are pressed together with 10–15 pounds of pressure (a mild to medium pressure, nothing too intense). The area where the sides of the thumbs touch rests on the sternum with the thumbs pointing up (along the sternum), and the fingers are together and point up and out at a 60-degree angle to the ground. The eyes are closed and focused on the third eye (imagine a sun rising on the horizon, or the equivalent of the point between the eyebrows at the origin of the nose). This mantra is chanted out loud in a 1½-breath cycle:

"Ong Namo Guru Dev Namo"

Inhale first through the nose and chant "Ong Namo" with an equal emphasis on the *Ong* and the *Namo*. Then immediately follow with a half-breath inhalation through the mouth and chant "Guru Dev Namo" with approximately equal emphasis on each word. (The *o* in *Ong* and *Namo* is a long-*o* sound; *Dev* sounds like *Dave*, with a long-*a* sound.)

- *Ong Namo* means I bow with reverence to that infinite energy that is the basis of all creation.
- *Guru* means teacher or wisdom.
- *Dev* means divine or of God.

The practitioner should focus on the experience of the vibrations these sounds create on the upper palate and throughout the cranium, while letting the mind be carried by the sounds into a new and pleasant mental space. This sequence should be repeated a minimum of three times. We employed it in our group about 10–12 times. This technique helps to create a meditative state of mind and is *always* used as a precursor to the other techniques.

2. The Ocean Exercise: Spine-Flexing Technique for Vitality

See the comments under "Three Water-Related Exercises" above. This technique can be practiced while sitting either in a chair or on the floor in a cross-legged position. If you are in a chair, hold the knees with both hands for support and leverage. If you are sitting cross-legged, grasp the ankles in front with both hands. Begin by pulling the chest up and slightly forward, inhaling deeply through the nose at the same time. Then exhale as you relax the spine down into a slouching position. Keep the head up straight, as if you were looking forward, without allowing it to move much while flexing the spine. This position will help prevent a whip effect in the cervical vertebrae. Breathe only through the nose for both the inhalation and exhalation. The eyes are closed, as if you were looking at a central point on the horizon, the third eye. Your mental focus is kept on the sound of the breath while listening to the fluid movement of the inhalation and exhalation. Begin the technique slowly while loosening up the spine. Eventually, a very rapid movement can be achieved with practice, reaching a rate of one to two times per second for the entire movement. A few minutes are adequate in the beginning. Later, there is no upper time limit. Food should be avoided just prior to this exercise. Be careful to flex the spine *slowly* in the beginning. Relax for 1 minute when finished.

3. Ganesha Meditation for Focus and Clarity

Sit with a straight spine, the eyes closed (see Figure 2.2). The left thumb and little finger are sticking out from the hand. The other fingers are curled into a fist with fingertips on the moon mound (the root of the thumb area that extends down to the wrist). The left hand and elbow are parallel to the floor, with the pad of the tip of the left thumb pressing on the curved notch of the nose between the eyes. The little finger is sticking out. With right hand and elbow parallel to the floor, grasp the left little finger with the right hand and close the right hand into a fist around it, so that both hands now extend straight out from your head. Push the notch with the tip of the left thumb to the extent that you feel some soreness as you breathe long and deep. (This soreness lessens with continued practice.) Do this for no longer than 3 minutes. To finish, inhale as you maintain the posture with eyes closed. Push a little more and pull the naval point in by tightening the abdominal muscles for 10 seconds, then exhale powerfully through the mouth. Repeat the inhale, hold, press, tighten, and exhale one more time for 10 seconds.

4. The River Exercise

See the comments under "Three Water-Related Exercises," above. Here the choice is to sit on the ground and spread the legs out to the sides as far as possible. The patient grabs around the back of the big toe of each foot with the index and middle fingers of the respective hand and the thumbs hold against the front of the big toes to help secure the grip. Patients who cannot stretch out this far should attempt to take hold of the ankles or as close as possible to the ends of the lower legs, around the calf muscle area. From this position a stretch-and-release routine is performed following a pattern of right leg, center, left leg, right, center, left. Specifically, from this stretched position and with the head in line with the spine, on the exhalation patients twist the torso gently a bit to the right and pull themselves down slowly, stretching out toward the right foot. Then they inhale as they release that stretch, while maintaining the grips on the toes (or wherever), and follow by exhaling down toward the center between both legs. Inhale on the straightening portion, then exhale while pulling back down over the left leg, and inhale back up. Repeat the sequence of right, center, left, right, center, left, etc.

This stretching routine will help energize patients further, adding to the flow in their life, while helping to change the mental patterns that are blocking them. With practice, moving through the right, center, and left positions takes about 2 seconds. A good practice time is 1 to 2 minutes.

5. The Respective Exercise from the 10 Symbol-Related Techniques

See the detailed description for the pertinent disorder-specific exercise in the section "The 10 Symbol-Related Techniques" (pp. 257–271). The techniques for the cave, tall tree, and low tree are all described in detail.

6. Gan Puttee Kriya: A Technique to Help Eliminate Negativity from the Past, Present, and Future

Gan Puttee Kriya has also been called the "Kriya to Make the Impossible Possible." Yogi Bhajan originally taught this meditation technique on November 2, 1988 (Bhajan, 1998). Yogis disovered this technique as a tool for eliminating the blocks that form in the subconscious mind and stifle growth, frequently leading to destructive, neurotic, and self-defeating patterns of mental activity.

Sit with a straight spine, either on the floor or in a chair. The backs of your hands are resting on your knees with the palms facing upward. The eyes are nine-tenths closed (one-tenth open, but looking straight ahead into the darkness, not the light below), focused on the third eye. Chant from your heart in a natural, relaxed manner, or chant in a steady, relaxed monotone:

"Sa Ta Na Ma Ra Ma Da Sa Sa Say So Hung"

More specifically:

Chant out loud the sound "Sa" (the *a* sounds like *ah*), and touch your thumb tips and index fingertips together quickly and simultaneously with about 2 pounds of pressure.
Chant "Ta" and touch the thumb tips to the middle fingertips.
Chant "Na" and touch the thumb tips to the ring fingertips.
Chant "Ma" and touch the thumb tips to the little fingertips.
Chant "Ra" and touch your thumb tips and index fingertips.
Chant "Ma" and touch the thumb tips to the middle fingertips.
Chant "Da" and touch the thumb tips to the ring fingertips.
Chant "Sa" and touch the thumb tips to the little fingertips.
Chant "Sa" and touch your thumb tips and index fingertips.

Chant "Say" (sounds like the word *say* with a long-*a*) and touch the thumb tips to the middle fingertips.
Chant "So" and touch the thumb tips to the ring fingertips.
Chant "Hung" and touch the thumb tips to the little-finger tips.

Chant at a rate of one sound per second. The thumb tip and fingertips touch with a very light (2–3 pounds) pressure with each connection. This light touch helps to consolidate the circuit created by each thumb–finger link. Start with 11 minutes and slowly work up to 31 minutes of practice. To finish, remain in the sitting posture and inhale, holding the breath for 20–30 seconds while you shake and move every part of your body (like a dog shaking off water). Exhale and repeat this shaking motion two more times to circulate the energy and to break the pattern of tapping the thumb and fingertips, which affects the brain. Then immediately proceed with focusing the eyes on the tip of the nose (the end you cannot see) and breathe slowly and deeply through the nose for 1 minute.

Each sound used in this meditation is unique, and they all have a powerful effect on both the conscious and subconscious minds:

"Sa" gives the mind the ability to expand to the infinite.
"Ta" gives the mind the ability to experience the totality of life.
"Na" gives the mind the ability to conquer death.
"Ma" gives the mind the ability to resurrect.
"Ra" gives the mind the ability to expand in radiance (this sound purifies and energizes).
"Da" gives the mind the ability to establish security on the earth plane, providing a ground for action.
"Say" gives the totality of experience.
"So" is the personal sense of identity.
"Hung" is the infinite as a vibrating and real force. Together, *So Hung* means "I am Thou."

The unique qualities of this 12-syllable mantra help cleanse and restructure the subconscious mind and help heal the conscious mind to ultimately experience the *super*conscious mind. All the blocks that result from traumatic or troubling events are eliminated over time with the practice of Gan Puttee Kriya. When doing the whole protocol, 11 minutes for this technique is often adequate; however, 31 minutes is even better, and the maximum time: *Do not go beyond 31 minutes.*

7. Multipart Meditation to Release Pressure from the Subconscious Mind and Overcome Compulsive Behavior Patterns

This technique was first taught by Yogi Bhajan in Los Angeles on March 11, 1997. Sit with a straight spine, either in a chair with both feet flat on the ground or on the floor with the legs crossed. There are four parts to this meditation, with a total practice time of about 26 minutes. This meditation is useful for people who are tortured by their compulsive behavior and reactions that result from the intense pressures coming from the subconscious mind.

Part A. The arms are bent and the upper arms are drawn against the front of the chest with the elbows against the ribcage (see Figure 18.6). The palms are open and flat and face up toward the heavens; they are kept flat, as if to hold something that may fall into the hands. The fingers are together and the thumbs are next to the fingers. The fingers of the right hand are facing out to the right side and the fingers of the left hand are facing out to the left side. The fingers are thus facing in opposite directions. This posture produces a slight pressure on the back of the forearms and forces a stretch on the hands. While maintaining this posture, keep the eyes opened and focused on the tip of the nose. This focus point is called *ajna band*, which means "mind lock," and it helps to normalize the activity of the frontal lobes. The mouth is made into a tight O shape, which stimulates the vagus nerves. The breath pattern is slow and deep only through the O-shaped mouth for 13 minutes.

Part B. Keep the same hand–arm–eye–mouth posture as in Part A. Now for 6 minutes chant out loud through the O-shaped mouth the mantra "Har" with a rate of about one *Har* per second. Each time that you chant "Har," pump–push the navel point out in phase with the mantra. The navel relaxes on its own after it is pumped out. You can either listen to the Tantric Har recording while chanting the mantra if you do not know the rhythm of the mantra (Khalsa, 2000).

Part C. Maintain the same hand–arm–eye posture as in Parts A and B, but now whistle out loud to the "Ardas Bhaee" recording for 3 minutes (Anahata, 2001). It is also permissible not to use the recording if you know the beat and rhythm of the mantra.

Figure 18.6.
Meditation to Release Pressure from the Subconscious Mind and Overcome
Compulsive Behavior Patterns, Part A

Part D. Now close the eyes and focus on the third eye, extending the arms out straight in front of the body parallel to each other with the palms facing up. Do slow, deep breathing through the nose for 3 minutes without moving any muscles (see Figure 18.7). To end Part D, maintain the arm–hand–eye postures and inhale, hold the breath, and tighten all the muscles in the arms and shoulders. Also tighten the muscles in the back as if to lift the spine up from its base. Hold for 10 seconds, and then exhale powerfully. Repeat the entire inhalation and muscle-tightening routine two more times for a total of three times.

Figure 18.7.
Meditation to Release Pressure from the Subconscious Mind and
Overcome Compulsive Behavior Patterns, Part D

8. The Rain Exercise to Open Up, Bless, and Saturate the Psyche with Divine Healing Energy

The mantra for this technique was taught earlier in Chapter 3 as the "Technique to Turn Negative Thoughts into Positive Thoughts" as part of the 11-part Kundalini yoga protocol for treating OCD (Shannahoff-Khalsa, 2006). This is the most powerful mantra in the system of Kundalini yoga, as taught by Yogi Bhajan. Here this mantra is taught as part of a full meditation exercise, the "Meditation with the Magic Mantra," that Yogi Bhajan taught on April 26, 1976 (Khalsa, 2006). Patients who can work hard enough to go through the seven previous exercises deserve to be blessed and saturated with the glorious healing energy generated by this meditation technique.

This technique should be employed while sitting with a straight spine. The hands are lifted to the level of the heart center with the palms facing up and the elbows relaxed at the sides. The patient forms a shallow cup with the hands by placing the sides of the hands together along the sides of the little fingers up to where the wrists begin (see Figure 18.8). The fingers are kept together as if the patient is forming a bowl, but the thumbs are spread out to the sides, away from the hands, and without holding tension. The edges of the "bowl" are about a 30-degree angle up from the parallel plane. The important factor here is to keep the line along the sides of the little (Mercury) fingers touching all the way up to where the

Figure 18.8.
The Meditation With the Magic Mantra

wrists begin. Normally, there is no opening whatsoever. However, some people have a gap between their little fingers, and this gap should be kept to a minimum. During the practice the eyes are closed, but the visual focus is looking into the center of the bowl formed by the hands. This technique must be practiced in a peaceful and serene environment, the more sacred the better. The meditation is practiced by chanting the mantra

"Ek Ong Kar Sat Gurprasad Sat Gurprasad Ek Ong Kar"

one time per breath with a rate of 4–5 seconds per cycle of the mantra.

When the mantra is chanted as a single practice in the "Technique to Turn Negative Thoughts into Positive Thoughts," it is chanted rapidly, up to five full repetitions of the entire mantra per breath. However, that is not the case here, where it is chanted only one time per breath cycle at the rate of 4–5 seconds per cycle. The way to chant/prounounce the mantra in this manner:

The "Ek" sound is the same as the *eck* in *neck*.
"Ong" has a long-*o* (not *ung*).
"Kar" sounds like *car* but with an emphasis on the *k* sound.
"Sat" has a short-*a* sound, as in the English *sat* and sounds like the word "sought."
"*Gurprasad*" has short vowel sounds (*u* as in *urgent*; *a* as in *ahhh*.

Eventually, one no longer thinks about the order of the sounds; they come automatically. The mental focus should be on the vibration created against the upper palate and throughout the cranium. If performed correctly, a very peaceful and "healed" state of mind is achieved that can lead to a bliss-like state of being. The maximum practice time for this meditation is 31 minutes. However, even 5–11 minutes can produce very powerful effects when the meditation is practiced correctly. That is usually more than adequate to gain the experience of the opening, blessing, and saturation effect that is desired.

Here are the comments on the "Meditation with the Magic Mantra" that were given by Yogi Bhajan when he first taught the technique:

> Thirty-one minutes of this can keep you very high. A couple of days of practice can give you certain stimulation which is beyond explanation. It is very rare that the Mercury fingers are joined in this way, but that is what makes the difference. Remember to keep the gap between the Mercury fingers as small as possible. Ek Ong Kar Sat Gurprasad Sat Gur-

prasad Ek Ong Kar is the most powerful of all mantras. The entire Siri Guru Granth Sahib is nothing but an explanation of this mantra. It is so strong that it elevates the self beyond duality and establishes the flow of the spirit. This mantra will make the mind so powerful that it will remove all obstacles. We call it the magic mantra because its positive effect happens quickly and lasts a long time. But it has to be chanted with reverence in a place of reverence. You can mock any mantra you like except this one, because this mantra is known to have a backlash. Normally mantras have no backlash. When you chant them well, they give you the benefit, but when you chant them wrong they don't have an ill effect. If they don't do any good, at least they won't hurt you. But, if you chant Ek Ong Kar Sat Gurprasad Sat Gurprasad Ek Ong Kar wrong, it can finish you. I must give you this basic warning. This mantra is not secret, but it is very sacred. So chant it with reverence; write it with reverence and use it with reverence. Normally we chant to God before practicing this mantra. Either chant the Mul Mantra (Ek Ong Kar Sat Nam Karta Purkh Nirbhao Nirvair Akal Moort Ajuni Sai Bhung Gurprasad Jap Ad Sach Jugad Sach Haibhee Sach Nanak Hosee Bhee Sach) or the Mangala Charan Mantra (Ad Gureh Nameh Jugad Gurey Nameh Sat Gurey Nameh Siri Guru Devay Nameh).

If patients practice all of the techniques in their respective cluster protocol, the chanting of the Mul Mantra or Mangala Charan Mantra is unnecessary. However, all of the other cautions must be respected.

Optional Substitutions for Meditation 7 in the Eight-Part Kundalini Yoga Meditation Protocol Specific for Treating the Cluster A Personality Disorders

1. The Ardas Bhaee Mantra

For those individuals who are less inclined to perform the four-part meditation technique in the seventh step of the protocol, because of the physically challenging arm and hand posture, the easiest substitute is a mantra called *Ardas Bhaee*. This mantra can be chanted for 11–31 minutes with the eyes closed and focused on the third eye point, with the hands in the *gyan* mudra (the thumb tip and index fingertip touch) and the palms facing up, resting on the knees.

An alternative and slightly more powerful posture is to relax the upper arms at the sides, but to interlock the hands and hold them in front of the heart center, gripping them a

Figure 18.9.
Meditation with the Mantra "Ardas Bhaee"

little tighter than usual if they were only held loosely (see Figure 18.9). With this posture the eyes are open and focused on the tip of the nose The full mantra is

"Ardas Bhaee, Amardas Guru, Amardas Guru, Ardas Bhaee, Ram Das Guru, Ram Das Guru, Ram Das Guru, Sachee Sahee."

We've encountered most of these words in prior meditations, with the exception of the following:

"Bhaee" sounds like *bah* and long *e*.

"Sachee" sounds like *sah* and *chee* as in cheese
"Sahee" sounds like *sah* and *he* with a long *e*

Yogi Bhajan (2000) described the effects of this mantra, which he taught on January 29, 1986, as follows:

> Normally there is no power in the human but the power of prayer. And to do prayer, you have to put your mind and body together and then pray from the soul. *Ardas Bhaee* is a mantra prayer. If you sing it, your mind, body, and soul automatically combine and without saying what you want, the need of the life is adjusted. That is the beauty of this prayer. (Bhajan, 2000)

2. A Meditation Technique to Help Overcome All Psychological Weaknesses

This meditation was taught by Yogi Bhajan in Los Angeles, California, on October 30, 1978. Regarding the effects of this technique, he commented "This meditation directs your fear toward motivating you to infinity. It will bring a simple polarity of your own magnetic field, and anything which has been neutralized, and is weak with you, it will make strong."

Sit in a chair with the feet flat on the floor or in an easy, cross-legged pose and maintain a straight spine. Bend the neck and lock the chin down against the chest. Relax the arms down, bend the elbows, and raise the forearms up and in toward the chest, until the hands meet in front of the chest at the level of the heart. Extend and join all fingers and the thumb of each hand, placing the right hand above the left hand. Point the palm of the left hand down at the ground and the palm of the right hand up at the sky. The hands should be parallel to each other and to the ground (see Figure 18.10). This is not an easy hand posture, but it is done most easily by keeping the forearms parallel to the ground.

The eyes are opened and focused on the tip of the nose (the end you cannot see). Begin the meditation by deeply inhaling and completely exhaling three times. Then inhale and chant out loud the following mantra three times with each breath as the breath is exhaled:

"Aad Sach, Jugaad Sach, Haibhee Sach, Nanak Hosee Bhee Sach."

Begin with 11 minutes and slowly build the time to 31 minutes. Upon completion of the meditation, deeply inhale, hold the breath for an extended period of time, and completely

Figure 18.10.
Meditation Technique to Help Overcome All Psychological Weaknesses

exhale. Repeat the deep inhaling and holding process two more times. Chant/prounounce this mantra as follows:

"Aad" sounds like *odd*
"Sach" sounds like an *s* before the *atch* in watch
"Jugaad" sounds like *jewgod*
"Haibhee" sounds like *heh* and *bee* but as one word
"Nanak" sounds like *nah* and *knock* but as one word
"Hosee" sounds like *hoe* and the letter *c but as one word*
"Bhee" sounds like the *bee* that stings.

The mantra translates as follows: "He was true in the beginning, true through all the ages, true even now. Nanak shall ever be true." This mantra protects against the darkest fate and rewrites one's destiny by helping to institute a new internal guidance system that will assist the practioner in overcoming the pitfalls of a defective personality that result from the limiting effects of fears, insecurities, and neuroses. This meditation technique helps elevate the human to new heights.

The Nine-Part Kundalini Yoga Meditation Protocol
Specific for Treating Cluster B Personality Disorders: Antisocial, Borderline, Histrionic, and Narcissistic*

1. Technique to Induce a Meditative State: Tuning In

See Figure 2.1 and the description of Technique 1 in the Cluster A protocol (p. 272) .

2. The Ocean Exercise: Spine-Flexing Technique for Vitality

See the description of Technique 2 in the Cluster A protocol (p. 273).

3. Ganesha Meditation for Focus and Clarity

See Figure 2.2 and the description of Technique 3 in the Cluster A protocol (p. 273).

4. The River Exercise

See the comments under The Three Water-Related Exercises and the description of Technique 4 in the Cluster A protocol (p. 274).

5. The Respective Exercise from the 10 Symbol-Related Techniques

See the detailed description for the four disorder-specific exercises in the section "The 10 Symbol-Related Techniques" (pp. 257–271). The techniques for the spiral shell, stick/branch, waterfall, and snake are all described in complete detail.

6. Gan Puttee Kriya: A Technique to Help Eliminate Negativity from the Past, Present, and Future

See the description of Technique 6 in the Cluster A protocol (pp. 275–277).

7. Meditation to Release Pressure from the Subconscious Mind and Overcome Compulsive Behaviors Patterns

See Figures 18.6 and 18.7 and the description of Technique 7 in the Cluster A protocol (pp. 277–279).

8. A Brain-Balancing Technique for Reducing Silliness, Focusing the Mind, and Controlling the Ego

Sit straight with the arms out to the sides and making a 90-degree angle at the forearm and upper arm. The hands, facing forward, open completely and close completely, with the thumbs tucked into the palms and enclosed by the fingers to form a fist. Then the hands open again with all of the fingers straight up and the thumbs are out to the sides, loosely extended. Then alternately the hands close and the thumbs are *not* enclosed in the fists. The thumbs alternate between being enclosed and being outside as the fists open and close. Every effort is made to open and extend the fingers straight up. This is a rapid open and closing movement, in which both hands open and close in synchrony. When the technique is practiced appropriately, the opening and closing of the hands can occur two to three times per second. The best practice times are between 2 and 5 minutes. The eyes are closed during the exercise and focused at the third eye point.

*9. The Rain Exercise to Open Up, Bless, and Saturate the Psyche
with Divine Healing Energy*

See Figure 18.8 and the description of Technique 8 in the Cluster A protocol (p. 279–282).

*Optional Substitutions for Meditation 7 in the Nine-Part Kundalini Yoga
Meditation Protocol for Cluster B Personality Disorders*

1. Homeh Bandana Kriya for Self-Pride and Vanity

This meditation technique is very suited for those diagnosed with a narcissistic personality disorder. Yogi Bhajan taught this technique in Los Angeles on September 1, 1978 . He commented there:

> This is a very sacred, very simple, but very powerful meditation. It takes away a person's self-pride and vanity. If the number of repetitions of the mantra is increased to the maxi-

mum, another person should be present with the meditator. The meditator may be rocketed so far into the ethers that he [or she] may find it hard to come back down.

Sit either in a chair with both feet flat on the ground or in an easy, cross-legged position while maintaining a straight spine. The arms are relaxed down with the elbows bent. Make fists of both hands with the thumbs extended out from the fists. Raise the forearms up and in toward each other until the thumb pads touch. Hold the hand position in front of the chest at the heart-center level. No fingers of the opposite hands touch each other at any time. Apply 25 pounds of pressure per square inch on the thumbs (see Figure 18.11). The eyes are closed and focused at the third eye point. Deeply inhale and completely exhale as the following mantra is chanted in a monotone voice four times:

"Whahay Whahay Whahay Guroo."

Four times is the starting number of repetitions of the mantra; it may be increased up to eight repetitions per breath. For *Whahay*, chant/pronounce:

"Wha" as in the *wa* of *water*
"-hay" as in "*hey!*"

The mental focus is on the sound and vibrations created by the mantra. Upon completion of the meditation, deeply inhale and completely exhale for about 1 minute. Eleven minutes is a good starting time, then slowly build up to the maximum time of 31 minutes.

2. A Meditation for Ego Problems and Mental Disease

This meditation technique is also very suited for use by those diagnosed with narcissistic personality disorder, and of course it will also be especially useful for those diagnosed with borderline personality disorder. Yogi Bhajan taught this technique in Los Angeles on September 18, 1978. He commented there:

The hand position is known as Shiva mudra. It is a very heavy mudra. The more pressure applied on the hands, the stronger will be the reaction in the brain. The mantra is also very heavy. There must be five repetitions of the first line per breath. If it is pronounced prop-

Figure 18.11.
Homeh Bandana Kriya for Self-Pride and Vanity

erly and completely chanted in one breath, on the fifth repetition all the organs in the solar chakra or solar plexus area—the pancreas, gall bladder, spleen, etc.—are stimulated and activated to bring about the heavy changes. If a person dedicates himself to this mantra 31 minutes a day for 90 days, all ego problems and mental diseases are cured.

Sit either in a chair with both feet flat on the ground or in an easy, cross-legged position while maintaining a straight spine. The arms are relaxed down with the elbows bent. Raise the forearms up and in toward the chest until the hands meet at the level of the heart. Then make a very weak fist of the left hand with the thumb pointing up. Wrap the right hand around the outside of the fingers of the left hand (they are not to be extended past the larger knuckles where the fingers meet the hands) with the thumb pointing up. Drop the left thumb down over the two hands on top, where it will touch both the index fingers from both hands. Then place the right thumb on top of the left thumb and apply pressure to the double fists (see Figure 18.12). Continue to hold the hand position at the level of the heart. Either leave the eyes one-tenth open or close them completely. If the eyes are left one-tenth open, focus on the tip of the nose or on the third eye point. If the eyes are completely closed, attempt to focus on the spot that is the very top and center of the head. The latter posture is the more difficult eye position to hold. Deeply inhale and completely exhale as the mantra is chanted five times in one breath cycle:

"Whahay Guru Whahay Guru Whahay Guru Whahay Jeeo."

To chant/pronounce this mantra:

"Wha" is like *wa* in *water*.

Figure 18.12.
Meditation for Ego Problems and Mental Disease

"Hay" sounds just like the food for horses.

"Jeeo" sounds like the two letters, *g* and *o*, run together.

Starting at 11 minutes and building up to a maximum time of 31 minutes is a good way to start.

An Optional Meditation Technique for Tranquilizing an Angry Mind

The following simple meditation, for use as needed, is especially helpful for the Cluster B personality disorders, but it can be useful for anyone, including individuals without any diagnosis.

"Jeeo, Jeeo, Jeeo, Jeeo"

Chant continuously and rapidly for 11 minutes without stopping (pronounced like the names for the letters *g* and *o*). Rapid chanting involves about 8–10 repetitions per 5 seconds. During continuous chanting, you do not stop to take long breaths, but continue with just enough short breaths through the mouth to keep the sound going. Eleven minutes is all that is needed, no more or less. The effect can last for up to 3 days. If necessary, it can be chanted for 11 minutes twice a day. This technique is most suitable for treating a "red-hot" angry mind.

The Eight-Part Kundalini Yoga Meditation Protocol Specific for Treating the Cluster C Personality Disorders: Avoidant, Dependent, and Obsessive-Compulsive Personality Disorder*

1. Technique to Induce a Meditative State: Tuning In

See Figure 2.1 and the description of Technique 1 in the Cluster A protocol (p. 272).

2. The Ocean Exercise: The Spine-Flexing Technique for Vitality

See the description of Technique 2 in the Cluster A protocol (p. 273).

3. Ganesha Meditation for Focus and Clarity

See Figure 2.2 and the description of Technique 3 in the Cluster A protocol (p. 273).

4. The River Exercise

See the comments under The Three Water-Related Exercises and see the description of Technique 4 in the Cluster A protocol (p. 274).

5. The Respective Exercise From the 10 Symbol-Related Techniques

See the detailed description for the three respective Cluster C personality disorder exercises in the section "The 10 Symbol-Related Techniques" (pp. 257–271). The techniques for the stone, claw, and bird are each described in complete detail.

6. Gan Puttee Kriya: A Technique to Help Eliminate Negativity
from the Past, Present, and Future

See the description of Technique 6 in the Cluster A protocol (pp. 275–277).

7. Meditation to Release Pressure From the Subconscious Mind
and Overcome Compulsive Behavior Patterns

See Figures 18.6 and 18.7 and the description of Technique 7 in the Cluster A protocol (pp. 277–279).

8. The Rain Exercise to Open Up, Bless, and Saturate the Psyche
with Divine Healing Energy

See Figure 18.8 and the description of Technique 8 in the Cluster A protocol (pp. 279–282).

Two Optional Substitutes for Meditation 7 in the Eight-Part
Kundalini Yoga Meditation Protocol for Cluster C Personality Disorders

1. Meditation for Overcoming Blocks in the Subconscious and Conscious Mind
and Achieving a Deep Meditative State

Yogi Bhajan taught this technique in Los Angeles on September 28, 1978. He commented there:

This is a very spacey meditation. It is highly recommended that it only be practiced when there is nothing scheduled for 3–4 hours after the meditation. It is a very powerful meditation whose listing of the effects covers several pages in the holy scriptures. It can totally take you to a different frequency of your meditative capacity.

Sit either in a chair with both feet flat on the ground or in an easy, cross-legged position while maintaining a straight spine. The upper arms are relaxed down with the elbows bent. The forearms are raised up and in toward each other until the hands meet in front of the chest at the level of the solar plexus (the region just under where the ribs meet). Press the entire length of the fingers of the opposite hands together, from the mounds where we normally form calluses to the fingertips, but leave the palms spread far apart. Cross the thumbs, with the right thumb over the left thumb (see Figure 18.13).

The patient can choose one of two positions for the fingers. The fingers can point up, which is the position that is traditionally taught, or, as presented in the figure, the fingers can point straight forward (which is much easier and my preference). The eyes are one-tenth open with a little light coming in at the bottom, but the focus is maintained at the third eye point, not on the light.

To start this meditation, take several powerful deep breaths to help open up the lungs before beginning to chant the mantra. This mantra must be chanted for a minimum of two repetitions per breath. The maximum number of repetitions per breath is five. The mantra is the following:

"Aad Sach Jugaad Sach Habhay Sach Nanak Hosee Bhay Sach."

This mantra is similar to the second alternate technique for the Cluster A protocol. However, there are subtle differences, for the words *Habhay* and *Hosee Bhay* are used here rather than *Haibhee* and *Hosee Bhee*. Chant/prounounce this mantra as follows:

"Aad" sounds like *odd*
"Sach" sounds like an *s* before the *atch* in watch
"Jugaad" sounds like *jewgod*
"Habhay" sounds like *heh* and *bay* (the body of water) as one word
"Nanak" sounds like *nah* and *knock* but as one word

Figure 18.13.
Meditation for Overcoming Blocks in the Subconscious and Conscious Mind
and Achieving a Deep Meditative State

"Hosee" sounds like *ho* in hold and *sea*, the body of water but as one word
"Bhay" sounds like *bay* the body of water

The maximum time for practicing this meditation is 31 minutes, although a great starting time is 11 minutes. When completed, it is best to relax without any other demanding responsibilities for several hours.

2. A Meditation to Block Any Negative Approach to Life: Praan Adhaar Kriya

Yogi Bhajan taught this technique in Los Angeles on August 27, 1979. He commented there: "This kriya is very ancient, very sacred, and very secretly given to people. Anyone who can practice it for one hour can intuitively block any negative approach to his life." Sit either in a chair with both feet flat on the ground or in an easy, cross-legged position while maintaining a straight spine. The arms are relaxed down with the elbows bent. Raise the forearms up and in toward each other until they meet in front of the chest at the level of the heart. Interlace the fingers with the palms facing toward the body, and press the pads of the thumbs together (see Figure 18.14). Keep the eyes one-tenth open. Deeply inhale and exhale completely as the following mantra is chanted in a monotone, with four complete repetitions per breath cycle:

"Whahay Guru Whahay Guru Whahay Guru Whahay Jeeo."

Figure 18.14.
Meditation to Block Any Negative Approach to Life: Praan Adhaar Kriya

Chant/pronounce as follows:

"Wha" is like *wa* in *water*.
"Hay" sounds just like the food for horses.
"Jeeo" sounds like the two letters, *g* and *o*, run together.

Start by practicing this meditation technique for 11 minutes and increase gradually, week by week, to 31 minutes. Stay at that time frame for a long time, and then slowly work up to 1 hour. Yogi Bhajan commented on the times for practice: "Don't be a fanatic."

CONCLUDING THOUGHTS

Since Personality Disorder NOS (301.9) is the most common diagnosis for the personality disorders, the therapist must decide which cluster-specific personality disorder protocol and which of the 10 symbol-based techniques is most appropriate for a particular patient. The decision is then based on the array of symptoms. Although the symptoms are usually scattered across the three clusters, it is probably also the case that they are not randomly distributed, such that there are more symptoms in one cluster and for one of the 10 personality disorders than the others. The rule of thumb then is to

- Use that cluster-specific protocol.
- Decide which of the 10 personality disorders is the closest to the patient's condition.
- Choose the most appropriate symbol-related technique.

NINETEEN

Treating Autism and Asperger's Disorder

Autistic and Asperger's Disorders are two of five Pervasive Developmental Disorders (PDDs). The other three are Rett's Disorder, Childhood Disintegrative Disorder, and Pervasive Developmental Disorder Not Otherwise Specified. Only Autistic and Asperger's Disorders are covered here. The PDDs are a subgroup of disorders that are included and often confused with the more inclusive group, Specific Developmental Disorders, which also include communication disorders, learning disorders, and motor skills disorders as defined by the DSM-IV-TR (APA, 2000).

DSM DISORDERS

Diagnostic Criteria for 299.00 Autistic Disorder (APA, 2000)

A. A total of six (or more) items from (1), (2), and (3), with at least two from (1), and one each from (2) and (3):
   1. qualitative impairment in social interaction, as manifested by at least two of the following:
      a. marked impairment in the use of multiple nonverbal behaviors such as eye-to-eye gaze, facial expression, body postures, and gestures to regulate social interaction
      b. failure to develop peer relationships appropriate to developmental level
      c. a lack of spontaneous seeking to share enjoyment, interests, or achievements with

other people (e.g., by a lack of showing, bringing, or pointing out objects of interest)

    d. lack of social or emotional reciprocity

2. qualitative impairments in communication as manifested by at least one of the following:

    a. delay in, or total lack of, the development of spoken language (not accompanied by an attempt to compensate through alternative modes of communication such as gesture or mime)

    b. in individuals with adequate speech, marked impairment in the ability to initiate or sustain a conversation with others

    c. stereotyped and repetitive use of language or idiosyncratic language

    d. lack of varied, spontaneous make-believe play or social imitative play appropriate to developmental level

3. restricted repetitive and stereotyped patterns of behavior, interests, and activities, as manifested by at least one of the following:

    a. encompassing preoccupation with one or more stereotyped and restricted patterns of interest that is abnormal either in intensity or focus

    b. apparently inflexible adherence to specific, nonfunctional routines or rituals

    c. stereotyped and repetitive motor mannerisms (e.g., hand or finger flapping or twisting, or complex whole-body movements)

    d. persistent preoccupation with parts of objects

B. Delays or abnormal functioning in at least one of the following areas, with onset prior to age 3 years: (1) social interaction, (2) language as used in social communication, or (3) symbolic or imaginative play.

C. The disturbance is not better accounted for by Rett's Disorder or Childhood Disintegrative Disorder.

Associated Features and Disorders (APA, 2000)

In most cases, there is an associated diagnosis of Mental Retardation, which can range from mild to profound. There may be abnormalities in the development of cognitive skills. The profile of cognitive skills is usually uneven, regardless of the general level of intelligence, with verbal skills typically weaker than nonverbal skills. Sometimes special skills are present (e.g., a 4½-year-old girl with Autistic Disorder may be able to "decode" written materials with minimal understanding of the meaning of what is read [hyperlexia] or a 10-year-old boy may have prodigious abilities to calculate dates [calendar calculation]). Estimates of single-word (receptive or expressive) vocabulary are not always good estimates of language level (i.e., actual language skills may be at much lower levels).

Individuals with Autistic Disorder may have a range of behavioral symptoms, including hyperactivity, short attention span, impulsivity, aggressiveness, self-injurious behaviors, and, particularly in young children, temper tantrums. There may be odd responses to sensory stimuli (e.g., a high threshold for pain, oversensitivity to sounds or being touched, exaggerated reactions to light or odors, fascination with certain stimuli). There may be abnormalities in eating (e.g., limiting diet to a few foods, Pica) or sleeping (e.g., recurrent awakening at night with rocking). Abnormalities of mood or affect (e.g., giggling or weeping for no apparent reason, an apparent absence of emotional reaction) may be present. There may be a lack of fear in response to real dangers, and excessive fearfulness in response to harmless objects. A variety of self-injurious behaviors may be present (e.g., head banging or finger, hand, or wrist biting). In adolescence or early adult life, individuals with Autistic Disorder who have the intellectual capacity for insight may become depressed in response to the realization of their serious impairment.

Reprinted with permission from the *Diagnostic and Statistical Manual of Mental Disorders, Fourth Edition, Text Revision.* Copyright 2000 American Psychiatric Association.

Diagnostic Criteria for 299.80 Asperger's Disorder (APA, 2000)

A. Qualitative impairment in social interaction, as manifested by at least two of the following:
   1. marked impairment in the use of multiple nonverbal behaviors such as eye-to-eye gaze, facial expression, body postures, and gestures to regulate social interaction
   2. failure to develop peer relationships appropriate to developmental level
   3. a lack of spontaneous seeking to share enjoyment, interests, or achievements with other people (e.g., by a lack of showing, bringing, or pointing out objects of interest to other people)

4. lack of social or emotional reciprocity

B. Restricted repetitive and stereotyped patterns of behavior, interests, and activities, as manifested by at least one of the following:

1. encompassing preoccupation with one or more stereotyped and restricted patterns of interest that is abnormal either in intensity or focus

2. apparently inflexible adherence to specific, nonfunctional routines or rituals

3. stereotyped and repetitive motor mannerisms (e.g., hand or finger flapping or twisting, or complex whole-body movements)

4. persistent preoccupation with parts of objects

C. The disturbance causes clinically significant impairment in social, occupational, or other important areas of functioning.

D. There is no clinically significant general delay in language (e.g., single words used by age 2 years, communicative phrases used by age 3 years).

E. There is no clinically significant delay in cognitive development or in the development of age-appropriate self-help skills, adaptive behavior (other than in social interaction), and curiosity about the environment in childhood.

F. Criteria are not met for another specific Pervasive Developmental Disorder or Schizophrenia.

Associated Features and Disorders (APA, 2000)

In contrast to Autistic Disorder, Mental Retardation is not usually observed in Asperger's Disorder, although occasional cases in which Mild Mental Retardation is present have been noted (e.g., when the Mental Retardation becomes apparent only in the school years, with no apparent cognitive or language delay in the first years of life). Variability of cognitive functioning may be observed, often with strengths in areas of verbal ability (e.g., vocabulary, rote auditory memory) and weaknesses in nonverbal areas (e.g., visual–motor and visual–spatial skills). Motor clumsiness and awkwardness may be present but usually are relatively mild, although motor difficulties may contribute to peer rejection and social isolation (e.g., inability to participate in group sports). Symptoms of overactivity and inattention are frequent in Asperger's Disorder, and indeed many individuals with this condition receive a diagnosis of Attention-Deficit/Hyperactivity Disorder prior to the diagnosis of Asperger's

Disorder. Asperger's Disorder has been reported to be associated with a number of other mental disorders, including Depressive Disorders.

Reprinted with permission from the *Diagnostic and Statistical Manual of Mental Disorders, Fourth Edition, Text Revision.* Copyright 2000 American Psychiatric Association.

YOGIC PROTOCOLS FOR TREATMENT

The intention and direction for treatment here is to help patients develop a lasting experience of wholeness and unity in their conscious awareness. This is a slow process, and it involves different ministages that are often dependent on the age and status of the patient, and the talent and charisma of the individual who helps to coordinate this process.

Dance of the Heart Protocol to Treat Autistic and Asperger's Disorders *

The first step in this protocol is to reach out to the individual in the form of a dance that is perceived as playful. This must be done in such a way that the person does not understand the therapeutic motive for the activity—it must appear to be simply a playful game. This process does not have to be carried out by a psychiatrist, psychotherapist, or parent. It can be coordinated by anyone who has the skills and with whom the patient already has a natural affinity: an older brother or sister, or even a younger brother or sister, if the patient is older and the sibling has the skills; any relative, family friend, or a neighbor.

In principle, this process is not that different from what a therapist or yogi does with anyone who has been traumatized and is seeking help. But the outward steps here are very different. At the start, the coordinator can be either standing or sitting. A standing posture is much preferred, but not all patients may be able or willing to join in a standing posture. The coordinator extends his or her hands, without leaning forward, and coaxes the patient to lean forward and touch hands with the coordinator. The fingers can be interlaced to form a comfortable, secure link between the two. At this point, if standing, the coordinator then

*Copyright © David Shannahoff-Khalsa, 2008. No portion of this protocol may be reproduced without the express written permission of the author.

leads the individual in an unstructured playful dance wherein the patient is being guided while in a receptive mode. It is imperative that the coordinator leads, but the dance can take any playful form.

The second critical part of the protocol includes a breathing technique whereby the coordinator first begins to practice a breathing pattern that is recognized by the patient. Three patterns with increasing complexity are suggested below. The practice of these breathing patterns can happen while the two are still moving or while the two are standing still for a moment. Once the patient recognizes the pattern as part of the game, the coordinator asks the patient to make the same breathing pattern.

After the patient makes the same breathing pattern, the coordinator asks the patient to make and hold eye contact with the coordinator. It is not always necessary to ask the patient to hold the eye contact out loud—it can also happen spontaneously without the verbal input, though it is rare. At first the patient may not want to join in with the breathing pattern or to initiate or maintain eye contact. The most critical component here is that patients *have fun* so that they will be willing to "play" in this way another day.

In the next stage of the process the coordinator begins to chant a mantra out loud, but in phase with the breath pattern. The coordinator then asks the patient to join in with the chanting while maintaining the breathing pattern and eye contact. However, the chanting with breathing can be started either before or after the eye contact is made. But eventually, the regulated breathing, the eye contact, and the chanting must all occur together. This is in fact a meditation practice, but one that is perceived as play, a game. This process of the dance, wherein the patient is being led and is breathing and chanting in a prescribed pattern, continues until a connection is perceived, which is ultimately critical to the final step of the process.

The next step of the process is to be balanced in the standing position without the patient leaning on the coordinator and while the breathing, eye contact, and chanting continue. Ideally, both participants feel centered and stable, and the patient feels like he or she is drawing in a measure of love from the coordinator, consciously identifying and experiencing the heartfelt connection and the flow of love. This final step is why this process is called the *Dance of the Heart*.

This multipart description outlines the ideal sequence and includes all of the essentials. However, the coordinator cannot expect the person to follow through the first time, or even the second, third, or fourth time. It can take months of play and practice to arrive at the final stage of this sequence. Much is dependent on the frequency of the play. It is very important that the coordinator *avoid* going into this process with any expectations and intentions *other than* to enjoy it, to help the patient have immediate fun, and ultimately to help the patient have the experience of creating a personal and loving connection. This healing process is different with each individual; much depends on the extremes of the person's condition, the magnetism and playful nature of the coordinator, and his or her ability to help create a loving, heartfelt connection that touches the soul of the patient.

A variety of options are listed below from which the coordinator can select the breathing patterns and the mantra. The choices here will vary depending on the comfort, familiarity, and ability of the coordinator, but mostly they should be determined by the condition, cooperative nature, and age of the patient. The positions and forms of the dance too can vary. Both the patient and coordinator have to enjoy this playful process. Sometimes the process is best initiated by the coordinator, who first begins to dance alone and then starts chanting along with the dance, so that it is obvious to the patient that the coordinator is having a great deal of fun.

To reiterate: *This process must be repeated over and over and over again.* This is play that comes from the heart, not from the head—this is not an intellectual process. The head has to bow to the heart in this game. In reality, we all seek love, and none of us wants to be told that we are not already normal, united, or whole, or that our world is unreal and that we are not adequate. We all want to live in love and union, but rarely are we willing to reach out for it or acknowledge that our lives are missing this divine quality. The patient with PDD is certainly no different in this regard

The initial position, breathing patterns, chants, and the final balance position are all somewhat variable. The key here is to make it fun and to make the experience of the techniques playful, healing, and rewarding for the patient with PDD. For this to happen, the experience must also be fun for the coordinator. There is a sequence and an end point, but there are no minimum times for each of the respective stages of play. However, the chanting, breathing, and eye contact should not be practiced for longer than 11 minutes, and 3 minutes is usually an adequate time for this part of the protocol. If the child (or adult) can reach 3 minutes in this phase, this is a great achievement.

Patients who make substantial progress may be willing to forgo the earlier stages of the dance and leaning. At this point, the participants can start by locking the hands and looking eye to eye while the breathing and chanting occur in synchrony with the coordinator's. The coordinator and patient can also practice a variety of techniques at this stage, called *Venus Kriyas*, which are published elsewhere (Shannahoff-Khalsa, 2006). However, the best results with any of the Venus Kriyas for the patient with PDD will be achieved by practicing the techniques for which the eyes are open, eye contact with the coordinator is maintained, and the mantra is chanted out loud. For this purpose, I recommend the one called Pushing Palms (pp. 266–268). But the intent must still be playful and loving, a play of the heart and soul.

The final and fine-tuning stages of healing and growth can be achieved by the patient learning to practice a variety of Kundalini yoga meditation techniques that are described below in the sections for "Additional and Elementary Brain-Balancing Techniques for the Patient with PDD" and the Advanced Techniques for the Accomplished Patient with PDD." The latter techniques will help the patient overcome any final symptoms and "residue."

This procedure must begin with the coordinator tuning in using the mantra "Ong Namo Guru Dev Namo." As I've noted throughout this volume, this is the standard and essential practice for any of the protocols or individual techniques that are taught in this book or for any of the techniques, in general, that are part of the system of Kundalini yoga as taught by Yogi Bhajan. The coordinator can chant the mantra out loud or silently, but it must be practiced before entering into the dance relationship with the patient. If the coordinator chooses, he or she can do it silently while in the same room with the patient before starting, or the coordinator can chant it out loud prior to entering the room. This decision is based solely on what is most convenient and comfortable for the patient and the coordinator. The coordinator can also start by doing a meditation in the same room, with the patient only observing, or not observing. Some of my clients use this as a key to help interest the patient in the activity. Most patients with PDD enjoy the mental state of the coordinator once they tune in and begin to practice. They may not show this openly, but on one level they may begin to connect. The world of meditation is more familiar to them than the ordinary world of daily life. They too are living in another world.

Technique to Induce a Meditative State: Tuning In

Sit with a straight spine and with the feet flat on the floor if sitting in a chair (see Figure 2.1). Put the hands together at the chest in "prayer pose"—the palms are pressed together with 10–15 pounds of pressure (a mild to medium pressure, nothing too intense). The area where the sides of the thumbs touch rests on the sternum with the thumbs pointing up (along the sternum), and the fingers are together and point up and out at a 60-degree angle to the ground. The eyes are closed and focused on the third eye (imagine a sun rising on the horizon, or the equivalent of the point between the eyebrows at the origin of the nose). This mantra is chanted out loud in a 1½-breath cycle:

"Ong Namo Guru Dev Namo"

Inhale first through the nose and chant "Ong Namo" with an equal emphasis on the *Ong* and the *Namo*. Then immediately follow with a half-breath inhalation through the mouth and chant "Guru Dev Namo" with approximately equal emphasis on each word. (The *o* in *Ong* and *Namo* is a long-*o* sound; *Dev* sounds like *Dave*, with a long-*a* sound.)

- *Ong Namo* means I bow with reverence to that infinite energy that is the basis of all creation.
- *Guru* means teacher or wisdom.
- *Dev* means divine or of God.

The practitioner should focus on the experience of the vibrations these sounds create on the upper palate and throughout the cranium, while letting the mind be carried by the sounds into a new and pleasant mental space. This sequence should be repeated a minimum of three times. We employed it in our group about 10–12 times. This technique helps to create a meditative state of mind and is always used as a precursor to the other techniques.

Suggested Breathing Patterns

1. The first and most basic pattern is to simply and consciously inhale and exhale through the nose, with a slow and distinguishable breath rate, where it is apparent to the patient that the breathing is being consciously controlled. When it is used with any of the mantras in the following section, the mantra is chanted only on the exhalation phase of the breath cycle. However, remember that the mantra does not have to be added right away. (Note that the inhalation is not done through the mouth, only through the nose.)

2. The second breath pattern can be a four-part breath cycle through the nose, wherein the inhalation phase of the breath cycle is broken into four equal parts. This is also called a *four-part broken breath*, wherein there are four distinct and approximately equal steps for the inhalation phase. After the inhalation phase the breath is exhaled through the nose in a

single breath, without breaking the exhalation into parts. After the patient learns to comply and match the pattern, the coordinator then continues with the four-part inhalation but then chants one of the mantras on the exhalation phase. It is natural to chant out loud only during the exhalation phase.

3. The third permissible pattern here is the eight-part broken breath, which is similar to the four-part broken breath, except that the inhalation through the nose is broken into eight parts. The exhalation is again only through the nose in a continuous, unbroken, and slow expiration of the breath, or later when a mantra is chanted out loud.

Suggested Mantras

These mantras must all be chanted out loud. They are listed in order of increasing complexity, but the practice can include any of the following. The choice here depends on the age, skill, appeal, and willingness of the patient. However, it is obviously much preferred to attempt the simplest mantras first, using either "Ma," "Ra," "Um," "Ee," or "Oooh." The patient is likely to have a greater affinity to one sound than to the others.

1. "Ma" should be chanted as one long word on the exhale. The sound means mother, rebirth, resurrection, and renewal. This sound helps to awaken the primary feminine principle and essence of the psyche. This is a good starting place and may have a high appeal.

2. "Ra" should be chanted as one long word. The sound relates to the primary male principle and essence of the psyche. It is simple and may have a high appeal.

3. "Um," "Ee," and "Oooh" are three individual sounds that must be chanted as single long words. They can be chanted individually in a practice session, or with approximately equal times for all three in the order of *Um*, *Ee*, and *Oooh*. It is also permissible to only chant *Um* for a few minutes followed by *Ee* for a few minutes. But the order should not be altered if they are combined within a few minutes for each (Shannahoff-Khalsa & Bhajan, 1988).

I recommend starting with *Um* for a short time. These are all simple sounds that are very easy to reproduce and very basic to the psyche, and they may already be sounds that are practiced by some children in their repetitive behaviors. They give a very pleasurable sensation when they are vibrated correctly. Patients may find that they like one of these three sounds better than another, or they may show no preference. If they have a preference, they should use that sound until they are willing to have fun chanting any of the other two sounds.

4. "Sat Nam" is a seed or *bij* mantra, and it is one of the most basic mantras in the system of Kundalini yoga. *Sat* translates as truth, and *Nam* is the manifestation of that truth. It is a very simple mantra that helps to merge the infinite and finite identities of the practitioner. When it is used in practice here, it is best chanted in the long version, called *long Sat Nam*, where there is a quick and punchy sound to *Sat* followed immediately by a long extended *Nam*. Here it is meant to be chanted completely through in one breath cycle, all chanted on the exhale.

5. "Sat Nam Sat Nam Sat Nam Sat Nam Sat Nam Sat Nam Whahay Guru" is a powerful healing mantra that helps to awaken and elevate the psyche. *Sat Nam* is repeated six times, followed by *Whahay Guru* once. Eventually the practitioner can learn to chant the entire mantra through quickly on one breath cycle or even to chant it through twice on a single breath cycle. Here *Sat* and *Nam* are of approximately equal length; there is no extension of the sound *Nam* or of the sounds *Whahay* and *Guru*.

6. "Sa Ta Na Ma" is called the *Panj Shabad*, and it is the combination of the five primal sounds of the universe.

"Sa" gives the mind the experience of the infinite.
"Ta" gives the mind the experience of the totality of life.
"Na" gives the mind the ability to conquer death.
"Ma" gives the mind the power of rebirth and resurrection.

(The fifth sound is *ah*, which is common to all four basic sounds; this is why it is called the *Panj Shabad*—the word *Panj* means five.) Here the four syllables can be repeated all in one breath, with approximately equal emphasis on each sound on the exhale. Or it can be practiced whereby *Sa* is chanted on the first breath, *Ta* on the second breath, *Na* on the third breath, and *Ma* on the fourth breath; the cycle is repeated in exactly the same sequence using all four syllables. This is one of the most powerful and frequently used mantras in Kundalini yoga. Although it is not likely that the coordinator and patient would ever reach 11 minutes, this time is technically the longest time that this mantra should ever be chanted out loud as a single mantra, unless specified otherwise with another meditation technique.

7. "Whahay Guru" is called the *Guru Mantra* or the *mantra of ecstasy*. It is not readily translatable, but chanting it elevates the spirit and gives the practitioner a natural high and the experience of the Infinite in its totality. There is equal emphasis on both words.

8. "Whahay Guru, Whahay Guru, Whahay Guru, Whahay Jeeo": The meaning essentially translates to "the ecstasy of consciousness is my beloved." All four segments of the mantra are practiced with equal times and emphasis. With extended practice and capacity, it can be repeated through more than once per breath cycle.

9. "Hum Dum Har Har": This mantra opens the heart chakra and means, "We the universe, God, God." *Dum* sounds like the word *dumb*, and *Hum* rhymes with *Dum*. The four sounds should be chanted with equal times and emphasis, and the entire mantra can be repeated more than once per breath cycle.

10. "Ong Namo Guru Dev Namo" is the Adi Mantra that precedes any Kundalini yoga practice. This mantra tunes us into our higher self. Ong means, "Infinite creative energy in manifestation and activity." (*Om* or *Aum* is God absolute and unmanifested and is not used here.) Namo means "reverent greetings," implying humility; Guru means "teacher or wisdom"; Dev means "divine or of God"; and Namo reaffirms the state of humility and reverence that is experienced when this mantra is mastered. In all it means, "I bow to the infinite creative energy, and I bow to the divine wisdom as it is awakened within me."

11. "Ang Sung Whahay Guru" means, in essence, "Every cell of my body vibrates with the divine wisdom and indescribable happiness that carries me from darkness to light." This mantra eliminates haunting thoughts and gives the experience of the divine within each fiber of the being. Here it should be chanted through in a monotone with equal emphasis on each sound. It can also be chanted through more than once if the lung capacity can support it.

12. "Guru Guru Whahay Guru Guru Ram Das Guru": This mantra is very healing and it gives a feeling of balance, elevation, guidance, and protection. The earth and ether qualities of human existence come into balance; the first four words relate to the etheric realm and the last four words cover the earthly realm of existence. *Guru* means the technique, teacher, or guide that brings one out from the darkness into the light. The sound *Whahay* gives the experience of divine ecstasy. *Ram Das* translate as "servant of God," and is the name of the guru who is the royal yogi and father of the lineage of Kundalini yogi as taught by Yogi Bhajan.

13. "Ra Ra Ra Ra Ma Ma Ma Ma Rama Rama Rama Rama Sa Ta Na Ma" is a healing mantra that helps balance the sun and moon qualities, or left and right brain hemispheres,

respectively. This mantra also helps to eliminate the pain from earlier experiences that are left as residues in the psyche and subconscious mind, and it is a unique aid in the process of development. The 16 syllables of the mantra should be chanted with approximately equal emphasis. The entire mantra can be chanted quickly enough to be completed in one breath cycle.

14. "Sa Ray Sa Sa, Sa Ray Sa Sa, Sa Ray Sa Sa, Sa Rung, Har Ray Har Har, Har Ray Har Har, Har Ray Har Har, Har Rung." This is obviously the most complex and most difficult mantra in this group. The meaning is, "Infinite totality is here, everywhere. The creativity of God is here, everywhere." Chant/prounounce:

"Sa" sounds like *saw*.
"Ray" sounds like the English word *ray* as in sun ray.
When "Har" is chanted, the tongue tip flicks the upper palate to slightly roll the *r* and
    thereby to induce the correct impact on the brain.

The power and effect of this mantra can help set a perfect foundation for the developing psyche and ultimately take the practitioner into the realm of the infinite. The whole mantra is meant to be chanted in one breath cycle. However, it can also be chanted halfway through (ending at *Sa Rung*) on one breath for those with a lesser lung capacity, and completed on the next breath cycle. In a lecture in Los Angeles on July 3, 1989, Yogi Bhajan explained the effects of this mantra:

> It takes away the ugliness of life. It will bring peace to those on whose forehead it is not written. It will bring prosperity to those who do not know how to spell it. It will bring you good luck when you have done nothing good, ever. Because this is the lotus, this is the opening of the lotus and turning the Mother Divine power back to the navel point. It is a path.

Additional and Elementary Brain-Balancing Techniques for Patients with PDD

These simple techniques can be used once the patient is willing to practice Kundalini yoga meditation techniques independently of the essential core practice using the Dance of the Heart protocol. These techniques will further accelerate the patient's healing—however, they are not essential to recovery. Nonetheless, they can help patients develop the excellent neurodevelopmental capacity that is their birthright. Note that practice with these individual techniques must also include the tuning in technique.

1. A Brain-Balancing Technique for Reducing Silliness, Focusing the Mind, and Controlling the Ego

Sit straight with the arms out to the sides and making a 90-degree angle at the forearm and upper arm. The hands, facing forward, open completely and close completely, with the thumbs tucked into the palms and enclosed by the fingers to form a fist. Then the hands open again with all of the fingers straight up and the thumbs are out to the sides, loosely extended. Then alternately the hands close and the thumbs are *not* enclosed in the fists. The thumbs alternate between being enclosed and being outside as the fists open and close. Every effort is made to open and extend the fingers straight up. This is a rapid open and closing movement, in which both hands open and close in synchrony. When the technique is practiced appropriately, the opening and closing of the hands can occur two to three times per second. The best practice times are between 2 and 5 minutes. The eyes are closed during the exercise and focused at the third eye point.

2. Brain Exercise for Normalizing Frontal Lobes and Enhancing Focus, Clarity and the Ability to Communicate (Listen and Articulate)

Sit straight and raise the hands to shoulder level, with the hands facing forward and the elbows by the sides. The first three fingers (index, middle, and ring finger) are kept straight and point up. The thumb tip and the tip of the little finger continuously touch and let go at a very rapid pace at about two to five times per second, the faster the pace the better. The eyes are kept closed. Continue the rapid contact and release of the thumb and little finger for a maximum time of 3 minutes. Effort should be made to move both the thumb and little finger in the movement, not just the thumbs. After 2 minutes, the person begins to create the effect he or she wants, but 3 minutes is ideal. The immediate effects can last up to a maximum of 4 hours. Over time this technique will enhance the development and cooperative nature of the frontal lobes.

3. For Mental Development and Mental Coordination

Sit straight with the arms bent so that the hands face forward at shoulder level, with the elbows relaxed by the sides. Follow the sequence of touching the thumb tip to the respective fingers: Touch the thumb to (1) the little fingertip, (2) the index fingertip, (3) the tip of the ring finger, (4) the tip of the index finger, (5) the tip of the ring finger again, and (6) the tip of the middle finger. Then repeat the entire cycle 1–6, building up the pace until the cycle takes 2–3 seconds, and it becomes a learned exercise that does not require any conscious focus on the pattern—and when the real benefits are achieved. The eyes are closed once the pattern is learned.

Build up the time to 11 minutes with a rapid pace. This is an excellent technique for enhancing mental development and mental excellence. There is a similar pattern with a slightly different finger tapping order that also includes additional elements that has been published and is specific for treating dyslexia and the other learning disorders (See Chapter 16, pp. 191–193).

4. A Technique for Brain Balancing and Mental Development

Sit with a straight spine and, if seated in a chair, keep both feet flat on the floor. Place the arms straight up and over the head, with the upper arms against the ears. Enclose the thumbs with the fingers, then slowly extend and straighten, one at a time:

- The index fingers keeping the other fingers in a fist.
- Then close the index fingers and extend only the middle fingers.
- Now close the middle fingers and extend only the ring fingers (usually the most difficult finger).
- Finally, close the ring fingers and extend only the little fingers.

Then start the full cycle again with index, middle, ring, and little fingers, all the time trying to keep the other fingers down in place. The eyes remain closed throughout. Try to build up the pace with a maximum time of 3 minutes.

Advanced Techniques for Accomplished Patients with PDD

1. Meditation to Balance and Synchronize the Cerebral Hemispheres

This technique was also presented in the multipart protocol for treating ADHD and comorbid disorders (see Chapter 15).

Sit with a straight spine. The eyes are opened and focused on the tip of the nose (the very end, which is not visible to the practitioner). Both hands are at the shoulder level with palms facing forward and upward with the hands loosely open, the fingers spread pointing up and not straight, as if holding a heavy ball in each hand (see Figure 15.1). Chant out loud

"Har Har Gur Gur"

and with each sound ("Har" or "Gur"), rotate the hands so that the palms face toward the back (see Figure 15.2) and then quickly return them to face the more forward–upward position. The left palm rotates in the clockwise direction and the right hand rotates in the counterclockwise direction (the only natural direction for rotation of each hand when starting with the palms facing upward). Make sure that the tongue quickly touches (flicks) the upper palate on "Har" and the lower palate on "Gur." Also pump the navel point out lightly with each "Har" or "Gur." Chanting for the mantra and rotating the hands takes about 2 seconds per round. The time for practice is 11 minutes. The frontal lobes and other paired regions of the hemispheres are synchronized by this practice to bring clarity, peace, vitality, and intuition.

2. Gan Puttee Kriya: A Technique to Help Eliminate Negativity from the Past, Present, and the Future

Gan Puttee Kriya has also been called the "Kriya to Make the Impossible Possible." Yogi Bhajan originally taught this meditation technique on November 2, 1988 (Bhajan, 1998). Yogis disovered this technique as a tool for eliminating the blocks that form in the subconscious mind and stifle growth, frequently leading to destructive, neurotic, and self-defeating patterns of mental activity.

Sit with a straight spine, either on the floor or in a chair. The backs of your hands are resting on your knees with the palms facing upward. The eyes are nine-tenths closed (one-tenth open, but looking straight ahead into the darkness, not the light below), focused on the third eye. Chant from your heart in a natural, relaxed manner, or chant in a steady, relaxed monotone:

"Sa Ta Na Ma Ra Ma Da Sa Sa Say So Hung"

More specifically:

Chant out loud the sound "Sa" (the *a* sounds like *ah*), and touch your thumb tips and
    index fingertips together quickly and simultaneously with about 2 pounds of pressure.
Chant "Ta" and touch the thumb tips to the middle fingertips.
Chant "Na" and touch the thumb tips to the ring fingertips.
Chant "Ma" and touch the thumb tips to the little fingertips.
Chant "Ra" and touch your thumb tips and index fingertips.
Chant "Ma" and touch the thumb tips to the middle fingertips.
Chant "Da" and touch the thumb tips to the ring fingertips.
Chant "Sa" and touch the thumb tips to the little fingertips.
Chant "Sa" and touch your thumb tips and index fingertips.
Chant "Say" (sounds like the word *say* with a long-*a*) and touch the thumb tips to the
    middle fingertips.
Chant "So" and touch the thumb tips to the ring fingertips.
Chant "Hung" and touch the thumb tips to the little-finger tips.

Chant at a rate of one sound per second. The thumb tip and fingertips touch with a very
light (2–3 pounds) pressure with each connection. This light touch helps to consolidate the
circuit created by each thumb–finger link. Start with 11 minutes and slowly work up to 31
minutes of practice. To finish, remain in the sitting posture and inhale, holding the breath
for 20–30 seconds while you shake and move every part of your body (like a dog shaking off
water). Exhale and repeat this shaking motion two more times to circulate the energy and
to break the pattern of tapping the thumb and fingertips, which affects the brain. Then immediately proceed with focusing the eyes on the tip of the nose (the end you cannot see)
and breathe slowly and deeply through the nose for 1 minute.

Each sound used in this meditation is unique, and they all have a powerful effect on
both the conscious and subconscious minds:

"Sa" gives the mind the ability to expand to the infinite.
"Ta" gives the mind the ability to experience the totality of life.
"Na" gives the mind the ability to conquer death.
"Ma" gives the mind the ability to resurrect.
"Ra" gives the mind the ability to expand in radiance (this sound purifies and energizes).
"Da" gives the mind the ability to establish security on the earth plane, providing a
    ground for action.

"Say" gives the totality of experience.

"So" is the personal sense of identity.

"Hung" is the infinite as a vibrating and real force. Together, *So Hung* means "I am Thou."

The unique qualities of this 12-syllable mantra help cleanse and restructure the subconscious mind and help heal the conscious mind to ultimately experience the *super*conscious mind. All the blocks that result from traumatic or troubling events are eliminated over time with the practice of Gan Puttee Kriya. Eleven minutes for this technique is often adequate; however, 31 minutes is even better, and the maximum time: *Do not go beyond 31 minutes.*

3. Meditation for Balancing the Brain Hemispheres

This meditation will correct and adjust the impulses of the brain hemispheres; it is a very powerful meditation that will greatly benefit the patient with PDD or anyone else. There are no limits on who can benefit from this technique, which was originally taught by Yogi Bhajan in Salem, Oregon, on May 24, 1984 (Shannahoff-Khalsa, 2010). Yogi Bhajan said that this technique will "clean out the karma, and create a very sharp mind, and that it will bring health, wealth, and happiness."

Sit with a straight spine, and if sitting in a chair, keep both feet flat on the ground. The forearms are up in front of the chest and parallel to the ground at the heart-center level, with the elbows pointing out toward the sides and the hands about 4 to 5 inches in front of the chest. The hands do not touch, and the palms are face down.

- The first movement is to touch the respective thumb tips and little fingertips (see Figure 19.1), then release them.
- Next touch the thumb tips to the ring fingertips, and release.
- Then touch the thumb tips to the middle finger tips, and release.
- Then touch the thumb tips to the index finger tips, and release.

The thumb tips and fingertips touch with a light 2–3 pound pressure, not intense. This pressure helps to stimulate a circuit in the brain. The tapping sequence continues at a rate of once per second. Note that the finger tapping pattern is the opposite of that in Gan Puttee Kriya. With each tap, the mantra "Har" is chanted as a whisper. It is not chanted out loud, as is done with Gan Puttee Kriya. When chanting, the mouth is open wide enough so that the upper and lower teeth show, and the lips never touch. The tip of the tongue flicks

Figure 19.1.
Meditation for Balancing the Brain Hemispheres

the upper palate on the sound *Har*, rolling the *r*. The eyes are kept closed and focused at the point where the eyebrows meet with the root of the nose—the third eye point.

To end the meditation, inhale deeply and hold the breath for about 15–20 seconds, then let it go. A good starting time is 11 minutes. It can also be done twice a day for 11 minutes, first in the morning and then in the evening. The patient can progress to practicing the technique once a day for 31 minutes. Once this level is reached, a significant achievement is to practice it for 40 consecutive days—it will have a powerful and transformative effect. It can also be practiced daily for years and years.

4. A Meditation to Balance the Western Hemisphere of the Brain with the Base of the Eastern Hemisphere

This meditation balances the left or western hemisphere of the brain with the base of the right or eastern hemisphere of the brain, which enables the brain to maintain its equilibrium under stress or sudden shock. This technique also helps patients with PDD to further recover from their chronic condition. Yogi Bhajan taught this meditation on October 24, 1978, in Los Angeles.

The patient sits in a chair with both feet flat on the ground or in easy pose on the floor while maintaining a straight spine. The right upper arm is extended straight out to the right, parallel to the ground, with the elbow bent and the forearm drawn in toward the body until the hand is in front of the chest near the level of the throat. Extend the fingers of the right hand without allowing them to spread apart, with the palm facing the ground and the fingers pointing to the left. Draw the thumb back and point it at the body. Relax the left arm

Figure 19.2.
Meditation to Balance the Western Hemisphere of the Brain
with the Base of the Eastern Hemisphere

down with the elbow bent. Draw the left forearm straight up until it is directly in front of the upper arm with the left hand at the same height as the right hand. Extend the fingers, holding them together. Bend the hand back to a 90-degree angle and face the palm upward, with the fingers also pointing to the left. Pull the thumb to the rear and point it back in the direction of the body. Do not move an inch once you are in the position (see Figure 19.2). The eyes are opened and focused on the tip of the nose, the end you cannot see. This employs the eye posture called *ajna band*. The following mantra is chanted out loud in a monotone, repeated three times with one breath as the breath is completely exhaled:

"Sat Nam Sat Nam Sat Nam Sat Nam Sat Nam Sat Nam Whahay Guru."

There are essentially eight parts to this mantra with equal beats and equal efforts for all eight parts. The words *Sat Nam* comprise one part, making six parts all together, and the words *Whahay* and *Guru* also each make one part, totaling eight parts.

Deeply inhale and completely exhale as the mantra is chanted. Upon completion of the meditation, deeply inhale and completely exhale five times. Then deeply inhale and hold the breath while the arms are stretched over the head. Exhale as they are relaxed down. Repeat twice more with the inhalation, hold, and stretch. This meditation is to be practiced for 11–33 minutes. Eleven minutes is a great starting time if the patient has the ability. If not, then start with 3–5 minutes and slowly build up the time.

5. A Meditation to Balance the Two Brain Hemispheres and to Correct Any Spiritual, Mental, and Physical Imbalance

Yogi Bhajan taught this meditation technique on March 20, 1979, in Los Angeles, where he commented: "[This technique] affects the two brain hemispheres to bring you into balance. Breathing through the mouth stimulates meridian points on a ring around the throat, which affects the parasympathetic nervous system. Breathing in strokes affects the pituitary gland."

The patient sits in a chair with both feet flat on the ground or in easy pose on the floor while maintaining a straight spine. Raise the arms with the elbows bent until the hands meet at the level of the heart in front of the chest (see Figure 19.3). The forearms make a straight line parallel to the ground with the fingers kept straight. Press the fingers and thumbs of both hands together from the tip to the first joint. The fingers are spread apart and point away from the body. The thumbs are stretched back and point toward the body.

317

Figure 19.3.
A Meditation to Balance the Two Brain Hemispheres and to
Correct Any Spiritual, Mental, and Physical Imbalance

The fingers are bent back at the knuckles, but the bases of the fingers do not meet because maximum pressure is applied at the fingertips.

The breath pattern is the following: Inhale deeply and completely through the nose, and then exhale in eight parts through the mouth. Continue this pattern. The eyes remain open and are kept focused on the tip of the nose. The pressure on the fingers is the key to this kriya. Be sure it is maintained correctly and strongly. There is no mantra for this meditation. The patient starts by practicing this technique for only 3 minutes, and then can work up to 5, then 11. Eleven minutes is the maximum recommended time.

6. *A Meditation to Correct Language and Communication Disorders: Ad Nad Kriya*

Yogi Bhajan taught this meditation on April 23, 1978, in Los Angeles. There he said:

> This Nad, this secret language or technique, existed with a very powerful sect of yogis, called *Ai Panthis*. Now very few of them exist. It will clear your language. Even if you mumble words, if you practice this for a long time, you will be clearly heard by another person. It is called *Gupt Gian Shakti*, secret power of the knowledge. If you perfect this, you need not speak. You can just send a mental thought, and the other person will totally know about it.

This meditation technique is clearly useful for people who have problems speaking and communicating on any level.

The patient sits in a chair with both feet flat on the ground or in easy pose on the floor while maintaining a straight spine. The arms are relaxed downward, with the elbows bent and the upper arms resting against the ribs. The forearms are pulled up and in toward the chest until the hands meet between the levels of the solar plexus and the heart. The fingers are interlocked, with the right index finger on top of the left index finger and the thumbs joined side by side and stretched back so that they point straight up (see Figure 19.4). The heels of the hands are also joined. The eyes are kept closed and focused on the third eye point. The patient starts the meditation by taking a deep inhalation and chanting the entire mantra as the breath is completely exhaled:

"Ra Ra Ra Ra, Ma Ma Ma Ma, Sa Sa Sa Sat, Haree Har Haree Har."

Each sound receives approximately equal emphasis, time, and effort. The mental focus is on the breath and the sound effects of the mantra. There are no time restrictions on this technique. Starting with 3, 5, or 11 minutes is a great beginning.

Figure 19.4.
A Meditation to Correct Language and
Communication Disorders: Ad Nad Kriya

References

Anahata, C. (2001). Healing Sounds of the Ancients—volume 3 (Ardas Bhaee and Har Har Gobinde Mukande). (Audio recording). Available at http://www.spiritvoyage.com

APA. (2000). *Diagnostic and Statistical Manual of Mental Disorders. 4th ed. (text revision). (DSM-IV-TR)*. Arlington, VA.: American Psychiatric Association.

Bhajan, Y. (1976). *Kundalini Yoga: Sadhana Guidelines*. Espanola, New Mexico: KRI Publications.

Bhajan, Y. (1981). *Kundalini Lectures: Man to Man Part 5, the Real Strength of the Man*. Espanola, NM: Kundalini Research Institute.

Bhajan, Y. (1990). Grief meditation lecture May 17, 1990. Los Angeles, California.

Bhajan, Y. (1995). Meditation to balance the jupiter and saturn energies: A technique useful for treating depression, focusing the mind, and eliminating self-destructive behavior. On *Lecture December 12, 1995*. Los Angeles, California.

Bhajan, Y. (1998). *Self-knowledge: Kundalini Yoga as Taught by Yogi Bhajan*. Espanola, NM: Kundalini Research Institute.

Bhajan, Y. (2000). *Self-experience: Kundalini Yoga as Taught by Yogi Bhajan*. Espanola, NM: Kundalini Research Institute.

Bhajan, Y. (2002). *Reaching Me in Me*. Espanola, NM: Kundalini Research Institute.

Bhajan, Y., & Khalsa, G. (1975). *Kundalini Meditation Manual for Intermediate Students*. Espanola, NM: KRI Publications.

Bhajan, Y., & Khalsa, G. (1998). *The Mind: Its Projections and Multiple Facets* (First ed.). Espanola, New Mexico: Kundalini Research Institute.

CDC. (1994). Chronic fatigue syndrome (cfs). Retrieved November 29, 2010, from http://www
.cdc.gov/cfs/general/case_definition/index.html

Davidson, J. R., Hughes, D. L., George, L. K., & Blazer, D. G. (1993). The epidemiology of social phobia: Findings from the Duke epidemiological catchment area study. *Psychol Med, 23*(3), 709–718.

Kaur, W. G. (2006). Chattra Chakkra Varti. (Audio recording). Available at http://www.a-healing
.com

Kessler, R. C., Stein, M. B., & Berglund, P. (1998). Social phobia subtypes in the national comorbidity
survey. *Am J Psychiatry, 155*(5), 613–619.

Khalsa, H. K. (2006). *Infinity and Me—Kundalini Yoga as Taught by Yogi Bhajan*. Espanola, New
Mexico: Kundalini Research Institute.

Khalsa, S. K. (2000). Tantric Har and Har Haray Haree Wahe Guru. (Audio recording). Available at
http://www.spiritvoyage.com

Shannahoff-Khalsa, D. (2010). *Kundalini Yoga Meditation for Complex Psychiatric Disorders: Techniques Specific for Treating the Psychoses, Personality, and Pervasive Developmental Disorders*. New
York, London: W. W. Norton & Co., Inc.

Shannahoff-Khalsa, D. (2012). Meditation: The Science and the Art. Chapter 228. In V. Ramachan-
dran (Ed.), *Encyclopedia of Human Behavior, 2nd edition*. Amsterdam, New York, London: Elsevier.

Shannahoff-Khalsa, D., & Bhajan, Y. (1988). Sound current therapy and self-healing: The ancient science of nad and mantra yoga. *International Journal of Music, Dance and Art Therapy, 1*(4), 183–
192.

Shannahoff-Khalsa, D., & Bhajan, Y. (1991). The healing power of sound: Techniques from yogic
medicine. In R. Droh & R. Spintge (Eds.), *Musicmedicine* (pp. 179–193). Gilsum, NH: Barcelona
Publishers.

Shannahoff-Khalsa, D., Ray, L., Levine, S., Gallen, C., Schwartz, B., & Sidorowich, J. (1999). Randomized controlled trial of yogic meditation techniques for patients with obsessive compulsive
disorders. *CNS Spectrums: The International Journal of Neuropsychiatric Medicine, 4*(12), 34–46.

Shannahoff-Khalsa, D. S. (1997). Yogic techniques are effective in the treatment of obsessive compulsive disorders. In E. Hollander & D. Stein (Eds.), *Obsessive-Compulsive Disorders: Diagnosis,
Etiology, and Treatment* (pp. 283-329). New York: Marcel Dekker Inc.

Shannahoff-Khalsa, D. S. (2003). Kundalini yoga meditation techniques in the treatment of obsessive
compulsive and oc spectrum disorders. *Brief Treatment and Crisis Intervention, 3*(3), 369–382.

Shannahoff-Khalsa, D. S. (2004). An introduction to Kundalini yoga meditation techniques that are
specific for the treatment of psychiatric disorders. *J Altern Complement Med, 10*(1), 91–101.

Shannahoff-Khalsa, D. S. (2005). Patient perspectives: Kundalini yoga meditation techniques for psycho-oncology and as potential therapies for cancer. *Integr Cancer Ther, 4*(1), 87–100.

Shannahoff-Khalsa, D. S. (2006). *Kundalini Yoga Meditation: Techniques Specific for Psychiatric Disorders, Couples Therapy, and Personal Growth*. New York, London: W. W. Norton & Company.

Shannahoff-Khalsa, D. S., & Beckett, L. R. (1996). Clinical case report: Efficacy of yogic techniques in the treatment of obsessive compulsive disorders. *Int J Neurosci, 85*(1–2), 1–17.

Singh, J. (1996). Sat Nam Wahe Guru # 2 tantric version. Retrieved July 30, 2009, from http://ahw stores.yahoo.net/16317.html

Singh, K. (2006). Chattra Chakra Varti. On *Healing Sounds Vol 1*. (Audio recording). Available at http://www.spiritvoyage.com

WHO. (2007). *International Statistical Classification of Diseases and Related Health Problems 10th revision version for 2007*. Geneva, Switzerland: World Health Organization.

Index

Note: Italicized page locators indicate photos.

Abused and Battered Psyche
  Advanced Meditation Technique for Adolescents and
    Adults, 85–86
  Gan Puttee Kriya Meditation Technique, 92–94
  Jupiter Finger Chakra Meditation, 82–84
  Meditation for Children, Adolescents, and Adults,
    84–85, 85
  Meditation for Eliminating Deep, Long-Lasting Anger,
    88–90, 89
  Meditation for Self-Worth and Achievement for the
    Very Young, 81, 82
  Meditation for Treating Grief, 92
  Meditation for Treating Impulsive Behavior in Youth and
    Others, 90–91, 91
  Meditation Technique for Dyslexia, 86–88, 87
  Sitting Posture to Help Reduce Aggressive Tendencies,
    to be used for "time-outs," 84
  Technique to Induce a Meditative State: "Tuning In,"
    80–81
  ten Kundalini yoga meditation techniques for, 80–94
Acute Stress Disorder (ASD), 5, 57–64
  associated features and disorders, 59
  diagnostic criteria for, 57–58
  diagnostic features of, 58–59
  Ganesha Meditation for Focus and Clarity, 61–62
  Gan Puttee Kriya Meditation Technique, 62–64
  Shoulder-Shrug Technique for Vitality, 61
  Spine-Flexing Technique for Vitality, 61
  Technique to Induce a Meditative State: "Tuning In," 60
  treating, Six-Part Kundalini Yoga Meditation Protocol
    for, 60–64

When You Do Not Know What to Do, 64
ADD. see Attention Deficit Disorder (ADD)
Addictive Disorders, treatment of, Seven-Part Meditation
    Protocol for, 140–49
ADHD. see Attention Deficit/Hyperactivity Disorder
    (ADHD)
Ad Nad Kriya Meditation, to correct language and com-
    munication disorders, 319, 320
affective flattening, Schizophrenia and, 202
Agoraphobia
  diagnostic criteria for, 49–50
  Panic Disorder comorbid with, 52
  see also Panic Disorder With Agoraphobia; Panic Disor-
    der Without Agoraphobia
Agoraphobia Without History of Panic Disorder, 5
Ai Panthis sect, 319
ajna band eye posture, 317
Alcohol Abuse, characteristics of, 130–31
Alcohol Dependence, characteristics of, 129–30
Alcohol Withdrawal, characteristics of, 129–30
alogia, Schizophrenia and, 202
American Psychiatric Association, 5
ancient yogic meditation techniques, historical evolution
    of, 2
Anger
  Childhood, Meditation for Releasing, 186–87, 187
  Deep, Long-lasting, Meditation for Eliminating, 88–90, 89
Angry Mind, Tranquilizing, Technique for, 35, 186, 291
Anorexia Nervosa
  additional diagnostic features of, 134–36
  associated features and disorders, 136

Anorexia Nervosa (*continued*)
  Binge-Eating/Purging Type, 134
  characteristics of, 133
  diagnostic criteria for, 133–34
  Restricting Type, 134
anosognosia, 204
Antisocial Personality Disorder
  associated features and disorders, 243–44
  defined, 235
  diagnostic criteria for, 242
anxiety
  reducing, First Technique for, 29–30
  reducing, Second Technique for, 30, *31*
  reducing, Third Technique for, 30–32
Anxiety Disorder Due to a General Medical Condition, 5
Anxiety Disorder Not Otherwise Specified, 5
  diagnostic criteria for, 6
  Ganesha Meditation for Focus and Clarity, 11–12, *12*
  Gan Puttee Kriya Meditation Technique, 12–14
  Shoulder-Shrug Technique for Vitality, 11
  Spine-Flexing Technique for Vitality, 11
  Technique for Fighting Brain Fatigue, 16–18, *17*
  Technique to Induce a Meditative State: "Tuning In,"
    9–10, *10*
  treating, Seven-Part Kundalini Yoga Protocol for, 9–18
  Vic-tor-y Breath Technique, 18
  When You Do Not Know What to Do, 14–16, *15*
Anxiety Disorders, Panic Disorder comorbid with, 52
arcline
  rebuilding, 52, *55*, 55–56
  weak, 53
Ardas Bhaee mantra, 282–84, *283*
ASD. *see* Acute Stress Disorder (ASD)
Asperger's Disorder, 297
  associated features and disorders, 300–301
  diagnostic criteria for, 299–300
  treating, Dance of the Heart Protocol for, 301–4
Attention-Deficit Disorder (ADD), Meditation for, 88,
    194–95
Attention-Deficit/Hyperactivity Disorder (ADHD), 88
  associated features and disorders, 173–74
  Brain Exercise for Normalizing Frontal Lobes and En-
    hancing Focus, Clarity, and Communication, 185–86
  Brain Exercise for Patience and Temperament, 186
  code based on type, 173
  diagnostic criteria for, 171–73
  11-part Kundalini Yoga Meditation Protocol for, 179–87
  Ganesha Meditation for Focus and Clarity, 181–82

Meditation for Learning Disabilities, ADD, and, 182,
    194–95
Meditation for Releasing Childhood Anger, 186–87, *187*
Meditation to Balance and Synchronize the Cerebral
    Hemispheres, 182–84, *183*
Meditation to Balance the Jupiter and Saturn Energies,
    184–85
Spine-Flexing Technique for Vitality, 180–81
Spine Twists for Reducing Tension, 181
Technique for Tranquilizing an Angry Mind, 186
Technique to Induce a Meditative State: "Tuning In," 180
Autistic Disorder
  associated features and disorders, 298–99
  diagnostic criteria for, 297–98
  treating, Dance of the Heart Protocol for, 301–4
Avoidant Personality Disorder
  associated features and disorders, 248–49
  defined, 235
  diagnostic criteria for, 248
avolition, Schizophrenia and, 202

Baby Pose, 219, *219*, 258
bereavement, 105
binge eating, 137, 138, 139
Bipolar Disorder Not Otherwise Specified, 109, 116
Bipolar Disorders, 109–25
  categories of, 109
  complexity of, 109
  Gan Puttee Kriya Meditation Technique, 118–20
  Phase-Independent Technique for Resolution of Bipolar
    Condition in General, 120–21, *121*, *122*
  Technique for Treating Depressed Phase of the Disorder,
    124, *125*
  Technique for Treating Manic Phase of the Disorder,
    121, 123, *123*
  Technique to Induce a Meditative State: "Tuning In,"
    117–18
  treatment of, Kundalini Yoga Meditation Protocol spe-
    cific for, 116–25
Bipolar I Disorder, 109
  associated features and disorders, 113–14
  diagnostic criteria for, 110
  diagnostic features for, 113
Bipolar II Disorder, 109
  associated features and disorders, 116
  diagnostic criteria for, 114
  diagnostic features for, 115
bird symbol-related Technique, 269–71

BMI. *see* body mass index (BMI)
Body Dysmorphic Disorder
    associated features and disorders for, 25–26
    diagnostic criteria for, 24
    diagnostic features for, 24–25
    treating, 11-part Kundalini Yoga Protocol for, 26–35
body mass index (BMI), 134
Borderline Personality Disorder
    associated features and disorders, 244–45
    defined, 235
    diagnostic criteria for, 244
Brain-Balancing Technique(s)
    for patients with PDD, 309–11
    to Reduce Silliness, Focus the Mind and Control the
        Ego, 287, 310
Brain Fatigue, Technique for Fighting, 16–18, *17*, 101–2
brain hemispheres
    Meditation for Balancing, 314–15, *315*
    Meditation for Balancing, to Correct Spiritual, Mental,
        and Physical Imbalance, 317–18, *318*
    Meditation for Balancing Western Hemisphere of Brain
        with Base of Eastern Hemisphere, 315–17, *316*
Breath of Fire, 219, 221, 258, 260
Brief Psychotic Disorder
    associated features and disorders, 210
    characteristics of, 197
    diagnostic criteria for, 210
Bulimia Nervosa
    additional diagnostic features, 137–39
    associated features and disorders, 139–40
    characteristics of, 133
    diagnostic criteria for, 137
    Nonpurging Type, 137
    Purging Type, 137

Camel Pose, 219, *219*, 258
Camel Ride, 271
Cave Symbol-Related Technique, 257–58
Cerebral Hemispheres, Meditation for Balancing and Syn-
    chronizing, 182–84, *183*, 195, 311–12
CFS. *see* Chronic Fatigue Syndrome (CFS)
Chattra Chakkra Varti, 33, 41, 54
Childhood Anger, Meditation for Releasing, 186–87, *187*
"Children's Meditation," 82
Chronic Fatigue Syndrome (CFS), 162–70
    conditions excluding diagnosis of, 163
    Fifth Exercise for CFS Protocol, *167*, 167–68
    Fourth Exercise for CFS Protocol, 167

rotating the spine while maintaining the hips in a steady
    position, 165
Seventh Exercise for CFS Protocol, 168, *169*
Sixth Exercise for CFS Protocol, 168, *169*
Specific Meditation to follow Exercise Set for CFS Pro-
    tocol, 168–70, *170*
Spine-Flexing Technique in Rock Pose for Vitality,
    165–66
symptoms of, 162
Technique to Induce a Meditative State: "Tuning In,"
    164–65
Third Exercise for CFS Protocol, 166, *166*
Treating, Nine-Part Kundalini Yoga Protocol for, 164–70
claw symbol-related Technique, 266–68
Cluster A personality disorders
    Ardas Bhaee mantra, 282–84, *283*
    differentiating factors and shared characteristics for, 252
    Ganesha Meditation for Focus and Clarity, 273–74
    Gan Puttee Kriya Meditation Technique, 275–77
    grouping of, 235
    Meditation Technique to Help Overcome all Psycho-
        logical Weakness, 284–86
    Meditation to Release Pressure from the Subconscious
        Mind and Overcome Behavior Patterns, *277*, 277–78,
        279
    Meditation with the Magic Mantra, 279–82, *280*
    Ocean Exercise, 273
    Rain Exercise, 278
    Respective Exercise from 10 Symbol-Related Tech-
        niques, 275
    River Exercise, 274
    symbols related to, 253, 257–59
    Technique to Induce a Meditative State: "Tuning In,"
        272–73
Cluster B personality disorders
    Brain-Balancing Technique for Reducing Silliness, Focus-
        ing the Mind, and Controlling the Ego, 287
    differentiating factors and shared characteristics for, 252
    Ganesha Meditation for Focus and Clarity, 286
    Gan Puttee Kriya Meditation Technique, 286
    grouping of, 235
    Homeh Bandana Kriya Meditation, 287–89, *288*
    Meditation for Ego Problems and Mental Disease,
        289–91, *290*
    Meditation for Tranquilizing an Angry Mind, 291
    Meditation to Release Pressure from the Subconscious
        Mind and Overcome Compulsive Behavior Patterns,
        287

Cluster B personality disorders (*continued*)
  Ocean Exercise, 286
  Rain Exercise, 287
  Respective Exercise from 10 Symbol-Related Techniques, 286
  River Exercise, 286
  symbols related to, 253–54, 259–64
  Technique to Induce a Meditative State: "Tuning In," 286
Cluster C personality disorders
  differentiating factors and shared characteristics for, 252
  Ganesha Meditation for Focus and Clarity, 291
  Gan Puttee Kriya Meditation Technique, 292
  grouping of, 235–36
  Meditation for Overcoming Blocks in Subconscious and Conscious Mind and Achieving a Deep Meditative State, 292–94, 293
  Meditation to Block any Negative Approach to Life: Praan Adhaar Kriya, 294–96, 295
  Meditation to Release Pressure from the Subconscious Mind and Overcome Compulsive Behavior Patterns, 292
  Ocean Exercise, 291
  Rain Exercise, 292
  Respective Exercise from the 10 Symbol-Related Techniques, 292
  River Exercise, 292
  symbols related to, 254–55, 264–71
  Technique to Induce a Meditative State: "Tuning In," 291
Cobra Pose, 263, *263*, 264
compulsions
  additional diagnostic features, 21
  defined, 20
Conduct Disorder
  Adolescent-Onset Type, 176
  associated features and disorders, 177–78
  Childhood-Onset Type, 176
  diagnostic criteria for, 175–76
  Unspecified Onset, 176
consciousness
  clarity and stability and higher realms of, 2–3
  Commanding Your Own Consciousness to a Higher Consciousness, Meditation for, 77–79, *78*
  Normal and Supernormal, Tantric Meditation for Creating, *76*, 76–77
Cyclothymia, 109

Dance of the Heart Protocol, to treat Autistic and Asperger's Disorders, 301–4, 309
Delusional Disorder
  associated features and disorders, 209
  characteristics of, 197
  diagnostic criteria for, 208
  seven examples of delusional types (DSM-IV-TR), 208
Delusions, Combating, Meditation for, 227–28, *229*
delusions with schizophrenia
  bizarre delusions, 200
  persecutory delusions, 199
  referential delusions, 200
Dependent Personality Disorder
  associated features and disorders, 250
  defined, 235
  diagnostic criteria for, 249–50
depression, 95
  bereavement *vs.*, 105
  Technique for Fighting Brain Fatigue, 16–18, *17*, 101
  treating, Meditation for Balancing Jupiter and Saturn Energies, 72, 102–4
  see also Major Depressive Disorder
Diagnostic and Statistical Manual of Mental Disorders
  Fourth Edition-Text Revised (DSM IV-TR), anxiety category disorders in, 5
Disruptive Behavior Disorders, Obsessive-Compulsive Disorder and, 22
Dyslexia, Meditation Technique for, 86–88, *87*, 191–93
Dysthymic Disorder, Major Depressive Disorder and, 99

Eating Disorder Not Otherwise Specified, 133
Eating Disorders
  characteristics of, 133
  Ganesha Meditation for Focus and Clarity, 142
  Gan Puttee Kriya Meditation Technique, 142–44
  Medical Meditation for Habituation: A Technique to Cure Any Addiction, 144–46, *145*
  Meditation for Treating Impulsive Behavior, *147*, 147–48
  Shoulder-Shrug Technique for Vitality, 142
  Spine-Flexing Technique for Vitality, 141–42
  Technique to Induce a Meditative State: "Tuning In," 140–41
  treating, Seven-Part Meditation Protocol for, 140–49
Ego Problems, Meditation for Mental Disease and, 289–91, *290*
eight-part broken breath, 306
Eight-Stroke Breath Meditation, 55

emotional anesthesia, Posttraumatic Stress Disorder and, 68

Fears, Managing, Technique for, *32*, 32–33, 54
First Technique for Reducing Anxiety, Stress and Mental Tension: Meditation for Unstable Mind, 29–30
follicle-stimulating hormone (FSH), 135
four-part broken breath, 305–6
Frontal Lobes, Brain Exercise for Normalizing, 185–86, 310
FSH. *see* follicle-stimulating hormone (FSH)

GAD. *see* Generalized Anxiety Disorder (GAD)
Ganesha Meditation for Focus and Clarity, 11–12, *12*, 54, 61–62, 74–75, 101, 142, 181–82, 273–74, 286, 291
Gan Puttee Kriya, eliminating negativity from the past, the present, and the future, 12–14, 62–64, 70–72, 92–94, 118–20, 142–44, 225–27, 275–77, 286, 292, 312–14
Generalized Anxiety Disorder (GAD), 5
  additional diagnostic features for, 8
  diagnostic criteria for, 7
  Ganesha Meditation for Focus and Clarity, 11–12, *12*
  Gan Puttee Kriya Meditation Technique, 12–14
  Panic Disorder comorbid with, 52
  Shoulder-Shrug Technique for Vitality, 11
  Spine-Flexing Technique for Vitality, 11
  Technique for Fighting Brain Fatigue, 16–18, *17*
  Technique to Induce a Meditative State: "Tuning In," 9–10, *10*
  treating, Seven-Part Kundalini Yoga Protocol for, 9–18
  When You Do Not Know What to Do, 14–16, *15*
  Meditation for, 92
Grief, 105-108
  Siddh Shiva and, 106, *107*
  treating, Kundalini Yoga Therapy for, 105–8, *107*
Gupt Gian Shakti, 319
Guru mantra, 308
Guru Prem Singh, 106
Guru Ram Das, 3, 4
Gyan Mudra, Spine Twist Exercise with Hands In, 216, *217*

hallucinations
  Right Nostril Four-Part Breath Using Mantra Sa Ta Na Ma, 231–32
  Silent L-Form Meditation Using Mantra Sa Ta Na Ma, 232–33
  Technique for Meeting Mental Challenges: The Vic-tor-y Breath, 231

Technique to Induce a Meditative State: "Tuning In," 230
  Terminating, Four-Part Mini-Protocol for Help With, 230–33
halo, 52– 53
Hast Kriya Meditation, 269–71, *270*
Haunting Thoughts, Meditation for Removing, 41–42
"Heal Me" (song), 106
heart center, healing, 30, *31*
Histrionic Personality Disorder
  associated features and disorders, 246
  defined, 235
  diagnostic criteria for, 245
Homeh Bandana Kriya, for Self-Pride and Vanity, 287–89, *288*
humanology, 2
"Humee Hum Tumee Tum" (song), 107
hypnagogic hallucinations, 200
hypnopompic hallucinations, 200
Hypochondriasis, Panic Disorder comorbid with, 52
Hypomanic Episode, criteria for, 114–15

Impulse-Control Disorder Not Otherwise Specified, 132
Impulse Control Disorders, 132
  Ganesha Meditation for Focus and Clarity, 142
  Gan Puttee Kriya Meditation Technique, 142–44
  Medical Meditation for Habituation: A Technique to Cure Any Addiction, 144–46, *145*
  Meditation for Treating Impulsive Behavior, *147*, 147–48
  Shoulder-Shrug Technique for Vitality, 142
  Spine-Flexing Technique for Vitality, 141–42
  Technique to Induce a Meditative State: "Tuning In," 140–41
  Treating, Seven-Part Meditation Protocol for, 140–49
Impulsive Behavior, Meditation for, 90–91, *91*
India, 2
Indus-Sarasvati civilization, 2
Intermittent Explosive Disorder, characterization of, 132

Jalandhar Bandh, 269
Jupiter energy, Balancing, Meditation for, 72–74, *73*, 102–4, 184–85, 193–94
Jupiter Finger Chakra Meditation, 82–84
Jupiter mantra, 270

Kapalabhati, 258
Kleptomania, characterization of, 132

Kriya to Make the Impossible Possible (Gan Puttee Kriya), 92, 118, 142, 225, 275, 312
Kundalini yoga
    era of secrecy and, 1
    as taught by Yogi Bhajan, introduction to, 1–4
    as "yoga of awareness," 3

Language and Communication Disorders, Meditation for Correcting, 319, 320
Learning Disabilities, Meditation for ADD, ADHD, and, 182
Learning Disorder Not Otherwise Specified, 190
Learning Disorders
    associated features and disorders, 189–90
    diagnostic features of, 188–89
    Meditation for ADD, ADHD, and, 194–95
    Meditation Technique for Dyslexia, 191–93
    Meditation to Balance and Synchronize the Cerebral Hemispheres, 195
    Meditation to Balance the Jupiter and Saturn energies, 193–94
    Obsessive-Compulsive Disorder and, 22
    Technique to Induce a Meditative State: "Tuning In," 191
    Treating, Five-Part Kundalini Yoga Meditation Protocol for, 190–95
L-form Meditation, Silent, Using Mantra Sa Ta Na Ma, 232–34
LH. see luteinizing hormone (LH)
Livtar Singh, 107
Low Tree Symbol-Related Technique, 258–59
luteinizing hormone (LH), 135

Major Depressive Disorder, 59
    associated features and disorders, 98–99
    criteria for Mixed Episode, 97
    diagnostic criteria for Single Episode, 95–96
    diagnostic features, 98
    Dysthymic Disorder and, 99
    Ganesha Meditation for Focus and Clarity, 101
    Meditation to Balance the Jupiter and Saturn Energies, 102–4
    Panic Disorder comorbid with, 51–52
    Recurrent, diagnostic criteria for, 97–98
    Shoulder-Shrug Technique for Vitality, 101
    Single Episode vs. Recurrent, 98
    Spine-Flexing Technique for Vitality, 100
    Technique for Fighting Brain Fatigue, 101–2

Technique to Induce a Meditative State: "Tuning In," 99–100
    Treating, Six-Part Kundalini Yoga Meditation Protocol for, 99–104
Major Depressive Episode, criteria for, 96–97, 111–12
Manic Episode, criteria for, 110–11
Mantra of Ecstasy, 308
Medical Meditation for Habituation: A Technique to Cure Any Addiction, 144–46, 145
meditation, 1
Meditation with the Magic Mantra, 271–72, 279–82, 280
mental challenges, meeting with Vic-tor-y Breath Technique, 34, 231
Mental Development/Coordination, Brain Exercises for, 310–11
Mental Retardation, 298, 300
mental tension, reducing
    First Technique for, 29–30
    Second Technique for, 30, 31
    Third Technique for, 30–32
Metropolitan Life Insurance tables, 134
Mixed Episode, criteria for, 112
Mood Disorders With Psychotic Features, 209

Narcissistic Personality Disorder
    associated features and disorders, 247–48
    defined, 235
    diagnostic criteria for, 246–47
negative thoughts, turning into positive thoughts, 34–35
Nightmares, Meditation Breath for Prevention of, 159
Nirinjan Kaur, 106
nonrapid eye movement (NREM) sleep, 161

obesity, 133
obsessions
    additional diagnostic features, 21
    associated features and disorders, 22
    defined, 19–20
Obsessive-Compulsive Disorder (OCD), 5, 50
    additional diagnostic features of, 21–22
    associated features and disorders, 22
    diagnostic criteria for, 19–20
    First Technique for Reducing Anxiety, Stress, and Mental Tension: Meditation for Unstable Mind, 29–30
    Second Technique for Reducing Anxiety, Stress, and Mental Tension and Healing Heart Center, 30, 31
    Shoulder-Shrug Technique for Vitality, 29
    Spine-Flexing Technique for Vitality, 28–29

Technique for Managing Fears, *32*, 32–33
Technique for Meeting Mental Challenges: The Vic-tor-y Breath, 34
Technique for Tranquilizing an Angry Mind, 35
Technique for Treating, 33–34
Technique to Induce a Meditative State: "Tuning In," 28
Technique to Turn Negative Thoughts into Positive Thoughts, 34–35
Third Technique for Reducing Anxiety, Stress, and Mental Tension, 30–32
Treating, 11-part Kundalini Yoga Protocol for, 26–35
Obsessive-Compulsive Personality Disorder
   associated features and disorders, 251–52
   defined, 235
   diagnostic criteria for, 250–51
OCD. *see* Obsessive Compulsive Disorder (OCD)
Ocean Exercise, Treatment of Personality Disorders and, 256, 271, 273, 286, 291
Ong Namo Guru Dev Namo Mantra, Technique to Induce a Meditative State: "Tuning In" and, 9–10, 28, 40–41, 53, 60, 69–70, 80–81, 99–100, 118, 140–41, 155–56, 164, 180, 214–15, 272–73, 304–5, 308
Opioid Abuse, characteristics of, 131
Opioid Dependence, characteristics of, 131
Oppositional Defiant Disorder
   associated features and disorders, 179
   diagnostic criteria for, 178

Panic Attacks, 45–48
   additional diagnostic features, 50–51
   associated features and disorders, 51–52
   characteristic types of, 46–47
   determining differential diagnostic significance of, 47–48
   diagnostic criteria for, 45–46
   Specific Phobias and, 36, 37, 38, 39
Panic Disorder
   additional diagnostic features, 50–51
   associated features and disorders, 51–52
Panic Disorder With Agoraphobia
   diagnostic criteria for, 49
   Ganesha Meditation for Focus and Clarity, 54
   rebuilding the arcline, *55*, 55–56
   Technique for Managing Fears, 54
   Technique to Induce a Meditative State: "Tuning In," 53–54
   Treating, Four-Part Kundalini Yoga Protocol for, 52–56
   Vic-tor-y Breath and, 52

Panic Disorder With or Without Agoraphobia, 5
Panic Disorder Without Agoraphobia
   diagnostic criteria for, 48
   Ganesha Meditation for Focus and Clarity, 54
   Rebuilding the Arcline, Meditation for, *55*, 55–56
   Technique for Managing Fears, 54
   Technique to Induce a Meditative State: "Tuning In," 53–54
   Treating, Four-Part Kundalini Yoga Protocol for, 52–56
   Vic-tor-y Breath and, 52
Panj Shabd mantra, 232, 307
Paranoid Personality Disorder
   associated features and disorders, 238–39
   defined, 234
   diagnostic criteria for, 237–38
parasomnias, characteristics of, 151
Pathological Gambling, characterization of, 132
Patience, Brain Exercise for Temperament and, 186
PDDs. *see* Pervasive Developmental Disorders (PDDs)
Personality Disorder Not Otherwise Specified, 235
Personality Disorders
   defined, 234
   in general, diagnostic criteria for, 236
   personality traits *vs.*, 236–37
   treating with Kundalini Yoga Meditation Techniques, 252
   Water Exercises and Treatment of, 256–57, 271–72
   see also Cluster A personality disorders; Cluster B personality disorders; Cluster C personality disorders
personality traits, Personality Disorders *vs.*, 236–37
Pervasive Developmental Disorders (PDDs), 297
   Brain-Balancing Technique for, 310
   Brain Exercise for Normalizing Frontal Lobes and Enhancing Focus, Clarity, and Communication, 310
   Exercise for Mental Development and Mental Coordination, 310–11
   Gan Puttee Kriya Meditation Technique, 312–14
   Meditation for Balancing the Brain Hemispheres, 314–15, *315*
   Meditation to Balance and Synchronize the Cerebral Hemispheres, 311–12
   Meditation to Balance the Two Brain Hemispheres and Correct Spiritual, Mental, and Physical Imbalance, 317–18, *318*
   Meditation to Balance Western Hemisphere of Brain with Base of Eastern Hemisphere, 315–17, *316*
   Meditation to Correct Language and Communication Disorders, 319, *320*

Pervasive Developmental Disorders (PDDs) (*continued*)
  Technique for Brain Balancing and Mental Development, 311
  Technique to Induce a Meditative State: "Tuning In," 304–9
  Treating, Five Techniques for, 229
pineal area, meditation and correcting imbalance in, 146
pituitary gland, meditation and regulation of, 146
Positive Thoughts, Negative Thoughts Turned into, Meditation for, 34–35
Posttraumatic Stress Disorder (PTSD), 5, 50, 59, 65–79
  additional diagnostic features of, 67–68
  associated features and disorders, 68–69
  diagnostic criteria for, 65–66
  Eight-Part Kundalini Yoga Meditation Protocol for, 69–79
  Ganesha Meditation for Focus and Clarity, 74–75
  Gan Puttee Kriya Meditation Technique, 70–72
  Meditation for Deep Relaxation, 75
  Meditation for Patients with, 41–42
  Meditation for Treating Grief, 92
  Meditation for When You want to Command Your Own Consciousness to a Higher Consciousness, *8*, 77–79
  Meditation to Balance the Jupiter and Saturn Energies, 72–74, *73*
  Panic Disorder comorbid with, 52
  Tantric Meditation Technique to Create a Normal and Supernormal State of Consciousness, *76*, 76–77
  Technique to Induce a Meditative State: "Tuning In," 69–70
  When You Do Not Know What to Do, 72–74
Praan Adhaar Kriya Meditation, 294–96, *295*
pre-experience, 75
Primary Insomnia
  additional diagnostic features, 152–53
  associated features and disorders, 153
  diagnostic criteria for, 151–52
  Meditation Breath to Prevent Nightmares, 159
  Meditation Technique to Deepen, Shorten, and Induce Efficient Sleep, 159–61, *160*
  Shabd Kriya for Treatment of, 154, 155, 156–57, *157*
  Technique to Induce a Meditative State: "Tuning In," 155–56
  treating, 153–61
  Yuni Kriya for Treatment of, 154, 155, 156, 157–59, *158*
psychic numbing, Posttraumatic Stress Disorder and, 68
Psychotic Disorder, 209
Psychotic Disorder Due to a General Medical Condition, 197

Psychotic Disorder Not Otherwise Specified, 197
  diagnostic criteria for, 211–12
PTSD. *see* Posttraumatic Stress Disorder (PTSD)
Pushing Palms, 266, 268
Pyromania, characterization of, 132

Rain Exercise, Treatment of Personality Disorders and, 256, 271–72, 278, 287, 292
relaxation
  Deep, Meditation for, 75
  Deep, Yuni Kriya Meditation, 157–59, *158*
Right Nostril Four-Part Breath, using Mantra Sa Ta Na Ma, 231–32
rishis (people of power), 2, 4
River Exercise, Treatment of Personality Disorders and, 256, 271, 274, 286, 292

Sat Kriya, 222–25, *223*
Sat Nam (*bij* mantra), 222
Saturn Energy, Meditation for Balancing, 72–74, *73*, 102–4, 184–85, 193–94
Schizoaffective Disorder
  associated features and disorders, 207
  characteristics of, 197
  diagnostic criteria for, 206
  diagnostic features of, 206–7
Schizoid Personality Disorder
  associated features and disorders, 240–41
  defined, 235
  diagnostic criteria for, 240
Schizophrenia
  Baby Pose, 219, *219*
  Breath of Fire, 219, 221
  Camel Pose, 219, *219*
  catatonic motor behaviors, 201–2
  Catatonic Type, diagnostic criteria for, 203
  characteristics of, 197
  characteristic symptoms of, 199
  delusions with, 199–200
  diagnostic criteria for, 198–202
  disorganized thinking with, 200–201
  Disorganized Type, diagnostic criteria for, 203
  DSM-IV-TR classifications for longitudinal course of, 199
  exercise up on knees with arms over head and with arms extended straight sitting on the heels, 217, *218*
  exercise with arms extended out to sides, 221, *222*
  exercise with arms 6 inches apart in front, 221, *222*

exercise with opposite leg and arm extended, 219, *220*
Gan Puttee Kriya Meditation Technique, 225–27
grossly disorganized behavior with, 201
hallucinations with, 200
leg and arm raise exercise with legs and arms up at 90
   degrees, 217, *218*
Mediation Technique to Help Overcome all Psychologi-
   cal Weakness, 228
Meditation to Help Combat Delusions and to Stabilize
   Healthy Sense of Self-Identity, 227–28, *229*
Multipart Meditation to Release Pressure from Sub-
   conscious Mind and Overcome Compulsive Behavior
   Patterns, 228
negative symptoms of, 202
other associated features and disorders, 204–5
Paranoid Type, diagnostic criteria for, 202
Protocol for Treating Variants of, 212–30
Residual Type, diagnostic criteria for, 203–4
Sat Kriya, 222–25, *223*
Shavasana, 225
side twisting exercise, 219, *220*
Spine-Flexing Exercises in slouch position and with a
   straight spine, 215–16, *216*
spine twist exercise with hands in *gyan* mudra, 216, *217*
Technique to Induce a Meditative State: "Tuning In,"
   214–15
True Glue: Exercise Set to Realign the Spiritual Bodies for Treating and Preventing Psychotic Episodes,
   215–25
Undifferentiated Type, diagnostic criteria for, 203
Schizophreniform Disorder
   associated features and disorders, 206
   characteristics of, 197
   diagnostic criteria for, 205
Schizotypal Personality Disorder
   associated features and disorders, 241–42
   defined, 235
   diagnostic criteria for, 241
Second Technique for Reducing Anxiety, Stress, and Mental Tension and Healing the Heart Center, 30, *31*
Self-Destructive Behavior, Eliminating, Meditation for
   Balancing Jupiter and Saturn Energies, 72, 102–4,
   193–94
Self-Identity, Healthy Sense of, Meditation for, 227–28,
   229
Self-Worth, Meditation for Achievement and, for Very
   Young, 8181
Separation Anxiety Disorder, 5, 50, 52

"Se Saraswati" (song), 106
Sexual Aversion Disorder, 5
Shabd Kriya Meditation, for Treating Insomnia and Regulating Sleep Stages, 154, 155, 156–57, *157*
Shared Psychotic Disorder
   associated features and disorders, 211
   characteristics of, 197
   diagnostic criteria for, 211
Shoulder-Shrug Technique for Vitality, 11, 29, 61, 101, 142
Siddh Shiva, grief and, 106, *107*
Side Twisting Exercise, 219, *220*
situationally bound Panic Attacks, 46, 47
situationally predisposed Panic Attacks, 46–47
sleep
   efficient, Meditation for inducing, 159–61, *160*
   Meditation Technique, to Deepen, Shorten, and Induce
      Efficient Sleep, 159
   regulating stages of, Shabd Kriya Meditation, 156–57,
      157
Sleep Disorders, categories of, 150
Snake Symbol-Related Technique, 263–64
Social Anxiety Disorders, 36
Social Phobia, 5, 50
   Panic Disorder comorbid with, 52
Social Phobias, in general, 36
Specific Phobia, 5, 36–44, 50
   additional diagnostic features, 37–38
   associated features and disorders, 39
   diagnostic criteria for, 36–37
   Meditation for Removing Haunting Thoughts, 41–42
   Technique for Managing Fears, 41
   Technique to Induce a Meditative State: "Tuning In,"
      40–41
   "Tershula Kriya": An Advanced Technique for Overcom-
      ing Phobias, 42–44, *43*
   Treating, Four-Part Kundalini Yoga Protocol for, 39–44
Spine-Flexing Exercise, in a Slouch Position and with a
   Straight Spine, 215, *216*
Spine-Flexing Technique for Vitality, 11, 28–29, 61, 100,
   141–42, 180–81
Spine-Flexing Technique in Rock Pose for Vitality, 165–66
Spiral Shell Symbol-Related Technique, 259–60
Stick or Branch Symbol-Related Technique, 260
Stone Symbol-Related Technique, 264–66
stress reduction
   First Technique for, 29–30
   Second Technique for, 30, *31*
   Third Technique for, 30–32

Substance Abuse, criteria for, 129
Substance Dependence, criteria for, 128
Substance-Induced Anxiety Disorder, 5
Substance-Induced Disorders, 127
Substance-Induced Psychotic Disorder, 197
Substance-Related Disorders, DSM-IV-TR and groups of, 127
Substance Use Disorders, 127
Subtle Body, Developing and Strengthening, Meditation for, 261–63, *262*
suicide
    Bipolar I Disorder and, 113
    Bipolar II Disorder and, 116
    Conduct Disorder and, 177
    Major Depressive Disorder and, 98
    Schizoaffective Disorder and, 207
    Schizophrenia and, 204–5
Symbol-Related Techniques for Personality Disorders
    Bird, 269–71
    Cave, 257–58
    Claw, 266–68
    Low Tree, 258–59
    Snake, 263–64
    Spiral Shell, 259–60
    Stick or Branch, 260
    Stone, 264–66
    Tall Tree, 258
    Waterfall, 260–63

Tall Tree Symbol-Related Technique, 258
Technique for Managing Fears, *32*, 32–33
Technique for Tranquilizing an Angry Mind, 35
Technique to Turn Negative Thoughts into Positive Thoughts, 34–35
Temperament, Brain Exercise for Patience and, 186
Tension, Spine Twists for Reducing, 181
Tershula Kriya Technique, for Overcoming Phobias, 42–44, *43*
Third Technique for Reducing Anxiety, Stress and Mental Tension, 30–32
Tourette's Disorder, 22
Trichotillomania, 126
    associated features and disorders, 23
    diagnostic criteria for, 23
    Treating, 11-part Kundalini Yoga Protocol for, 26–35
True Glue exercise set, 215–25, 257, 258, 259, 260

Tuning In process, 3. *see also* Ong Namo Guru Dev Namo mantra

unexpected Panic Attacks, 46, 47
Unstable Mind, Meditation for, 29–30

Venus Kriyas (Pushing Palms), 266–68, 304
Vic-tor-y Breath, 18, 34, 44, 231
Vitality, Spine-Flexing Techniques for, 11, 28–29, 61, 100, 141–42, 165–66, 180–81

Water Exercises, Treatment of Personality Disorders and, 256–57
Waterfall Symbol-Related Technique, 260–63
When You Do Not Know What to Do Technique, 14–16, *15*, 64, 72

yoga, 1
Yogi Bhajan, 106, 316
    on *Ardas Bhaee*, 283–84
    on dyslexia, 192
    Gan Puttee Kriya taught by, 70, 92, 118, 142
    gifts from "The House of Guru Ram Das" and, 3, 4
    on Homeh Bandana Kriya for self-pride and vanity, 287–88
    "Kundalini yoga as taught by," 1, 304
    on medical Meditation for Habituation, 146
    on Meditation for Overcoming Blocks in Subconscious and Conscious Mind, 292–93
    on Meditations for Balancing the Brain Hemispheres, 314, 317
    Meditation Techniques and Yoga Exercise Sets Transmitted by, 2, 4
    on Meditation to Balance the Jupiter and Saturn Energies, 103–4, 185, 194
    on Meditation to Correct Language and Communication Disorders, 319
    Meditation to Help Combat Delusions Taught by, 227
    on power and knowledge from Jupiter, 270–71
    on Sat Kriya, 223
    Technique for Developing Subtle Body Taught by, 261
    Technique for Fighting Brain Fatigue taught by, 101
    on times for practice, 296
Yuni Kriya Meditation, For Deep Relaxation, 154, 155, 156, 157–59, *158*